A Complete Pattern of Nobility: John, Lord Lumley (c.1534-1609)

Leo Gooch

University of
Sunderland Press

ISBN 978 1 906832 01 8

First published 2009

Cover Image by Permission from the Earl of Scarbrough

Cover Design by Tim Murphy

Published in Great Britain by
The University of Sunderland Press
in association with Business Education Publishers Limited
Rainton Bridge Business Park
Cygnet Way
Rainton Bridge
DH4 5QY
Tel: 0191 3055165
Fax: 0191 3055504

British Cataloguing-in-Publications Data
A catalogue record for this book is available from the British Library

Printed in Great Britain by SS Media

In memoriam
Mary Gooch

Preface

Some time ago I visited a well known National Trust house in Yorkshire. During the guided tour, small portraits of two young English nuns resident in continental convents in the seventeenth century were pointed out with the tart comment that the display of vanity they represented was deplorable in women supposedly governed by strict rules of humility. My attempt to explain that such portraits were ordered by parents who might not see their daughters again was peremptorily dismissed – doubtless because it would have required a change to the guide's longstanding script. At any rate, the incident led me to reflect on the pictorial record of English recusancy. It quickly became evident from a preliminary survey of guide-books to both houses and art-galleries that portraits of English Catholics had been painted since the earliest years of the post-Reformation period. Indeed, likenesses of lay gentlemen and women, children, priests, monks, and nuns had been taken no less frequently than of anyone else in a similar social position. Ecclesiastical allegiance had no bearing on portraiture: rather, it was motivated by a simple and commonly held desire to create a family's painted archive.

At an early stage in my survey of the field, I lighted upon John Lumley, a Catholic Elizabethan nobleman, who had gone so far in his creation of a pictorial pedigree that he had had some fifteen generations of his ancestors painted in what he imagined was authentic contemporary costume. But that plainly eccentric series was in some ways an indulgence, for it was commissioned long after he had proved himself to be an art-collector of major national importance and which placed him in the forefront of art patronage. He had amassed a collection of some two hundred portraits of leading English and foreign statesmen which he displayed in a palace used frequently by Queen Elizabeth, her Privy Council and visiting foreign dignitaries. This was collecting for England, not family pride. Yet, as a Catholic, Lumley was not obviously someone who could aspire to a close relationship with the queen or her ministers, not least, as I was to discover, because he was a strong supporter of Mary, Queen of Scots, and her claim to the English throne.

Lumley, then, was something of a puzzle, apparently adhering to a dissident religion while frequenting the company of the English queen whom he was conspiring to depose. Clearly, all would be made plain in his biography but, to my utter surprise, none had been written. Other than an entry in the old *Dictionary of National Biography*, a book on his library, and one or two pieces about his pictures, scant attention had ever been paid to him despite his substantial rôle in the cultural, political and religious life of the nation. I therefore dropped my general enquiries into recusant portraiture to recover for him the more prominent place in the historiography of Elizabethan England which he undoubtedly deserves. It is a happy coincidence that the book appears in the fourth centenary year of his death.

***

I am most grateful to the Marc Fitch Fund for a subvention towards the costs of publication.

I am particularly grateful to the late Earl of Scarbrough for his hospitality, for allowing me to reproduce family portraits and other images, for encouraging me to write the biography of his ancestor, and for ensuring, to a late stage in his life, that I had not given up on it.

The staff of the National Portrait Gallery, Durham University Library (Palace Green) and the Lumley Castle Hotel management were most helpful.

I should like to thank especially the following to whom I am indebted for help in various ways: Professor Edward Chaney, Professor Thomas A. Birrell, John Davies, David Macfarlane, Michael Hodgetts, Christine Newman, Howard Coutts, Ian Doyle, Mark Weiss, Bendor Grosvenor, Andrea Murphy.

Contents

Introduction

John, Lord Lumley has been described variously as 'a learned eccentric with a wild intensity', a megalomaniac, and a pious reactionary.[1] He could also be characterised as a dangerous conspirator as well as the originator of one of the most important documents in the cultural history of England. Lumley lived for seventy-five years under five English sovereigns (Henry VIII to James I), that is, throughout the flowering of the English Renaissance, and through all the religious upheavals of the late sixteenth century. He was born around the time of the trial and execution of Sir Thomas More and he died a few years after the Gunpowder Plot, punctuation marks in the history of the old religion to which he adhered. Lumley's father and grandfather had been leaders in the Pilgrimage of Grace and he himself became engaged in some of the Catholic intrigues in support of Mary Stewart, Queen of Scots. Her execution ended his participation in public affairs and thereafter he confined himself to cultural pursuits, to which he was, in any case, predisposed and which secure his historical importance. Ever since Horace Walpole coined the phrase, however, Thomas Howard, Earl of Arundel (1585-1646), is generally held to have been the 'father of virtu in England'. John Evelyn who travelled with Howard was similarly impressed and described him as a 'great virtuoso' and 'the great Maecenas of the politer arts'; Rubens described Arundel as 'one of the evangelists of our art' (they met in Brussels in 1612).[2] I beg to differ and intend to show that Lumley, Arundel's great-uncle, was in fact the key figure in the development of connoisseurship in England as demonstrated by his ownership of the largest and most important private art-collection in Elizabethan England. A major feature of this book is the reprinting of the inventory of that collection so as to restore Lumley to his rightful place in the history of collecting and of art-history.

The contemporary source for the concept of *virtu* is Baldassare Castiglione's *Il Cortegiano*. It was written between 1513 and 1524 and parts of the manuscript were in circulation from 1518 before its formal publication in Italy in 1528. This is a compendium of Renaissance thought (based partly on the ancients) on the qualifications required by the ideal courtier. A gentleman should cultivate a love of literature, music and art; where possible he should be a practitioner, that is, he should become proficient in a foreign language, play a musical instrument and learn to draw. The book was intended to be a practical guide for 'the self-contained man of virtu' and its influence on Elizabethan manners can hardly be exaggerated, for its precepts became the accepted standard in English education. Castiglione penetrated English culture by way of Sir Thomas Elyot's *The Boke Named The Governour* (1531), a treatise in seventy-one chapters on politics, education and 'vertue in manners', in which he advocated a balanced education in the study of philosophy, in physical training and in an appreciation of the fine arts. Elyot's sources were the classical authors (especially Plato and Aristotle), Petrarch, Castiglione and *The Education of a Christian Prince* (c. 1515) of Desiderius Erasmus. Lumley would translate Erasmus and he owned a copy of Sir Thomas Hoby's 1561 translation of *Il Cortegiano*.[3] Castiglione continued to exert influence in Protestant England long after Italy fell from favour in the 1560s. In a diatribe against all things Italian at the end of the first book of *The Scholemaster* (1570), Roger Ascham commended Hoby's translation saying that one year's study of it was equivalent to spending three years in Italy which was, in any event, to be avoided at all costs by the young.

The term 'virtuoso' as understood by Castiglione and Elyot refers to a student of the humanities in the widest sense and it applies, necessarily, only to gentlemen. Claims to English gentility derived generally from lineage, the right to bear arms, ownership of a country estate, and an income from rents sufficient to live at leisure. (To be armigerous one needed a minimum rental income of £10.[4]) Henry Peacham in 1634 was the first in England to use the term as a description of a connoisseur and a patron of the arts. Peacham's gentleman does not live at court but on his country estate occupied with 'learned pleasure and delight'. In modern terms, the cult of virtuosity offers 'talented but politically thwarted or indifferent noblemen an alternative for their surplus time, energy and wealth'; a virtuoso's

> main concern in life is with scientific experiment and the collecting of natural or artificial curiosities, with antiquarian research, with aesthetic appreciation and with the purchase of antique sculpture and old masters. He is a gentleman of leisure whose ambition is to deepen his appreciation of the arts and build up a famous collection. He is primarily concerned with himself and no longer seeks to be of service to Prince or Commonweal.[5]

Lumley fits precisely into all the categories of virtuoso as portrayed by Castiglione onwards. He was a studious youth and he cultivated wide-ranging interests in art, geography, literature, cosmography, medicine, music and genealogy. His wife Jane, daughter of Henry, the last of the Fitzalan earls of Arundel, shared many of his artistic and literary interests. The earl, too, was culturally enlightened; he made the completion and decoration of Nonsuch Palace the main work of his later life, a project in which Lumley became his chief partner and successor. Lumley made substantial acquisitions after Arundel's death in 1580, so that the combined Arundel and Lumley collections of pictures and books built up over the sixty years between 1549 and 1609 became the largest in Elizabethan England. Thomas, the first of the Howard earls of Arundel, was, therefore, in the second- or third-generation of English art-collectors, he was not their progenitor.[6]

Of an English population of about four and a half million in 1600 there were perhaps three thousand families of minor gentry rank, five hundred families of higher gentry status and about fifty families in the titular peerage. Taking into account inevitable fluctuations due to minority, vacancy, insanity or extinction, the size of the peerage remained small and stable throughout the Tudor period. The Lords Temporal (lay peers) numbered fifty-two at the end of Mary I's reign and fifty-five at the end of Elizabeth's. Including the twenty-six Lords Spiritual (archbishops and bishops), the total number of members of the House of Lords averaged around eighty in the second half of the sixteenth century. Within the peerage there was a clear divide between the higher ranks of dukes, marquesses and earls, and the lesser ranks of viscounts and barons. The former were at the apex of public life, they enjoyed considerable prestige and exercised the greatest influence; the authority and good offices of the latter, though substantial, were necessarily second-best. To some extent, then, Lumley, as a mere baron, lived in the shadow of his father in law, Henry Fitzalan, Earl of Arundel (1511/12-1580), and that partly explains why he has not been considered a primary candidate for historical investigation.[7]

Acceptance of the Reformation in the peerage was reluctant to say the least. There was a large party of openly Catholic members of the House of Lords in the immediate post-Reformation period and it declined in strength only slowly, though the continuing danger of Catholic proselytism was well recognised. When the twelve-year-old Earl of Cumberland was sent up to university in July 1570 he was warned by his guardian, the Earl of Bedford, to 'avoid the Popish wasps and bees' that would 'be buzzing in his ears to confirm in him a deafness to the true religion' (yet he was sent to Oxford in order to get him away from his Catholic relations, the Montagues, Dacres and Cliffords).[8] In 1567 an observer counted thirty-two Catholic peers and twenty others well-affected which left only fifteen undoubted Protestants. In September 1570 the Pope was told that forty peers were friendly, eighteen were neutral and only six were hostile. In March 1571 the Duke of Norfolk counted thirty-three Catholics, fifteen of doubtful ecclesiastical allegiance, and sixteen heretics. By 1580, however, the Catholic and Catholic-inclined peers ceased to be in the majority: there were then twenty Catholics, ten Puritans, twelve Anglicans and twenty-four with no specific ecclesiastical allegiance. It is not to be supposed, of course, that peers were canvassed for their views and so, because the surveys were made by Catholics for morale-boosting purposes, the numbers were not altogether a precise guide to opinion.[9] In any case, religious preferences could not supersede civil duty entirely, for the governance of the country had to be carried out by the relatively small number in the House of Lords and no peer could reject every administrative task which he might find uncongenial on grounds of conscience. Hence known Catholic peers, including Lumley, were appointed to the Commission which condemned Mary Stewart to death; and the devout Edward, fourth Earl of Worcester, was placed on the Commission for the expulsion of the Jesuits.[10]

The potential for trouble among the Catholic peers could be neutralised, but not eliminated, because they enjoyed certain inalienable privileges. Peers could not be arrested except for treason, felony or breaching the peace; they were not obliged to appear in court or testify under oath. They were tried by their peers, usually for treason; they were free from outlawry and torture and they did not suffer the indignity of dismemberment after execution. Peers were exempt from the oaths of supremacy unless they held office and, although recusants were barred from the House of Commons after 1571, Catholic peers were still summoned to the House of Lords. An English peer, therefore, ran little risk of being executed for religious deviance – loss of office and exclusion from court was more likely, or he would be fined if he was too outspoken.[11] Catholic peers, then, could live undisturbed unless they challenged the new religion, hence many of them chose to bide their time, fully expecting another reversal of the state's religion, for, after all, the reigns of Edward VI and Mary I had been short, and Elizabeth's might be as brief.

Action was also deferred because the ecclesiastical challenge to the old faith in the regions was not entirely successful. It was impossible to appoint a Protestant minister to every one of the thirteen thousand English parishes for some time, and so the majority of people were out of reach for many years. But where reforming clergy did take over and the liturgical changes enacted between 1544 and 1552 were introduced, the process of detaching the people from their old ways accelerated. On the other hand, large numbers of Catholic priests ordained before Elizabeth's reign survived until the 1580s and they practised privately or in noble households where the religion of the family was its own business and was undisturbed if it was practised discreetly.[12] But when incumbent priests died, Catholic practice ceased and the number of people adhering to the old religion began to decline. That situation was exacerbated because little support or guidance came from Rome. It was not until the foundation in 1568 of Douai College and the start of the priestly mission to England in 1575 that the English Counter-Reformation began. It was almost too late.[13]

Although the reformed and unreformed alike profitted from the dissolution of the monasteries, the Reformation divided the upper classes in that most of the old Catholic families came to be concentrated in the north and the Protestants in the south; the geographical divide was mirrored sociologically in the closure of the open marriage market, and religious endogamy became almost universal. And then, while Elizabeth was distrustful of any peer having an independent power-base, she feared most those Catholics in the furthest reaches of the kingdom who enjoyed a feudal following: Arundel in Sussex, Norfolk in East Anglia, Derby in the north-west and Northumberland in the north-east. Throughout her reign she pursued her father's policy of undermining the power of these independent magnates, even though by 1576 only a quarter of the peerage had any military experience. The institutions of regional administration were gradually taken into the hands of the central government, as when the Council of the North was placed under the firm control of the Protestant Earl of Sussex. Elizabeth's desire to avoid establishing new territorial loyalties accounts for the fact that the peerage was no larger at the end of her reign than at the beginning, and that she neither created or revived an English dukedom after the execution of Norfolk in 1572.[14]

Lumley, then, lived in interesting times and he was one of Elizabeth I's most fascinating and multi-faceted subjects. The following account of his life begins with a treatment of his ancestry, education, and his early adult years. By virtue of his birth, Lumley belonged to a highly select, wealthy and influential social group; because of his religion he represented a threat to the English Reformation; and since his ancestral base lay in the far north he was regarded as a potential danger to the Tudor dynasty. Indeed, his marriage into one of the most important courtier families of the kingdom took him into the dangerous arena of royal dynastic controversy between the queens of England and Scotland. The build-up of political tension in the early years of Elizabeth's reign covered in this chapter is followed in the second by a narrative of the plots of 1569 and 1570 which were intended to resolve the question of the royal succession and in which Lumley took a discreet but essential part. The conspiracies failed and he was fortunate to escape the full consequences of his actions but for many years afterwards Elizabeth kept a wary eye on him and he gained only her guarded friendship. Lumley had no option, however, but to withdraw from public life and the remaining chapters of the book deal with the cultural interests he turned to and which fully occupied him in the latter half of his life. Chapter three traces Lumley's bibliographic and antiquarian interests and chapter four is devoted to Lumley's primary interest – the development of his art-collection, which, as indicated earlier, became his greatest achievement. The later dispersal of his collections, told in chapter five, does not detract from Lumley's historic position as the prototype of the wealthy and well-educated gentleman who enjoyed art for its own sake and who became a connoisseur, and to whom we owe the existence of many country-house collections. It was for those aesthetic and scholarly accomplishments that William Camden commended Lumley as 'a complete pattern of nobility'.

Chapter One

The 'Gentlemen of Nonsuch'[1]

The Lumley family claims descent from Liulph, a Saxon noble who held the manor of Great Lumley, County Durham.[2] At the time of Edward the Confessor, Osbert Lumley married a daughter of the Earl of Northumberland and from that point the family carried increasing weight and many of them held senior military and civil appointments in the north. Towards the end of the fourteenth century Sir Ralph de Lumley (a sympathiser of John Wycliffe, the church reformer) was raised to the peerage as Baron Lumley by Richard II, but Lumley was later attainted for his opposition to Henry IV. In 1392 Lumley obtained permission from the king and Walter Skirlaw, Bishop of Durham, 'to build anew his house at Lumley and to embattle and crenellate it with a wall of stone and lime'. (Formal permission was required to crenellate, i.e., to build or strengthen, a fortified dwelling. Brancepeth and Raby, the other great castles of Durham were also granted licenses to crenellate in the second half of the fourteenth century.) In an open and elevated position above a triple bend of the River Wear a mile from Chester le Street, this large, turreted and battlemented rectangular fortress, with projecting towers at each corner and a chapel in the north-east tower, commands the locality. Although altered in the Tudor, Elizabethan and Georgian periods, Lumley Castle remains a characteristically secure mediaeval house, with similarities to Bolton Castle and Sherriff Hutton (all three of which were probably the work of John Lewyn, master-mason to the Bishops of Durham[3]). The first mention of the coal-mining which would come to dominate the economy of the Durham estate occurs in March 1408 and the family's wealth increased in subsequent generations. The barony of Lumley was re-created in 1480 for Sir George de Lumley, whose marriage to Elizabeth, heiress of Roger Thornton, a Newcastle merchant, greatly augmented the family's land-holdings. John, the fourth baron (1493-1544), was said to be a zealous subscriber to the militant crusading ideal of St George. He fought at Flodden in 1513, was present at the Field of the Cloth of Gold in 1520, and he was among those who signed the petition in 1530 asking Pope Clement VII to grant Henry VIII's divorce. His fortunes went into reverse in October 1536, however, with the outbreak of the rising called by its participants 'our pilgrimage of grace for the commonwealth'.[4]

The pilgrimage was an attempt by the common people to check the king's attack on the church and was specifically aimed at the restoration of the socio-economic system destroyed in the dissolution of the monasteries. Like most of the gentry, Lumley and his son George were initially reluctant to take to arms even though they had a grievance against the king. In 1532 Henry, wishing to provide for his bastard son the Duke of Richmond, had required Lumley to surrender five manors in the barony of Westmorland in exchange for an annuity of £50 from the Abbot of Waltham which had been granted to Richmond the year before.[5] In mid-October 1536 Lumley and his son were hare-coursing at The Isle, near Sedgefield in Durham, when they heard of the rising and of Bishop Cuthbert Tunstall's flight to Norham on the border. They, too, packed their valuables and fled. They went first to Maison Dieu, Lumley's house in Newcastle, but they soon left, finding the townspeople 'very unruly and as much disposed to sedition and rebellion as they of the country were and would have risen with them'.[6] Lumley joined Sir Thomas Hilton at Hylton Castle near Sunderland, and George returned to The Isle. The rebels of Durham (led by Henry Coke, a shoemaker) let it be known that if George did not join them his house would be sacked, and he was invited to convey a message to his father that if he too did not join them 'the commons would spoil his house'. The Earl of Westmorland at Brancepeth Castle (a large part of whose family's inheritance had fallen into the hands of the crown in the late mediaeval period) twice declined to take part and received similar warnings, but the rebels agreed that his thirteen-year-old son Lord Neville would be accepted in his stead. Sir Thomas Hilton and Sir Thomas Tempest were coerced in the same way. Reluctantly, then, the Durham gentry accepted captaincies in the rebel force. But the Lumleys and Neville soon developed an enthusiasm for the cause and are said to have ended up on 'the extremist wing' of the pilgrimage's leadership. Indeed, Lumley's aggressive demeanour prompted one observer to call him the 'cock of the north'; he went so far as to propose marching on London so as to physically remove Thomas Cromwell from power. Lumley, under the Banner of the Five Wounds, and Neville, under the Banner of St Cuthbert, led the Durham host to Pontefract and Doncaster. The Durham men wore the black cross of St Cuthbert. The banner of St Cuthbert (which was kept in Durham Cathedral) was magnificent: a five-yards high and one-yard wide embroidered crimson velvet cloth which contained two relics, one of St Cuthbert and a cross held to be miraculous. Attention to the banner was further enhanced by the five sacring bells attached to it. Among the grievances of the Durham rebels was the abolition of one of St Cuthbert's feast-days and governmental interference in the power of sanctuary at the cathedral.[7] Hilton and Lumley were among the negotiators of the truce with the king's representative, the Duke of Norfolk, and in December, having been pardoned, Lumley retired to his estate of Kilton Castle in Cleveland while his son George joined his wife at Thwing. Lumley was confidently expected to take to arms again when the truce broke down early in 1537 but he declined an invitation to lead a second rising and he abruptly left Kilton for Lumley Castle in Durham. George, who had lost none of his militancy, led the pilgrims' assault on Scarborough. At the defeat of the pilgrimage he was placed in the Tower, convicted of high treason and executed at Tyburn on 2 June 1537. He asked for thirty Masses to be said for his soul and he was accounted a martyr by some, though not by the Holy See.[8] Although the pilgrimage was suppressed, it did at least serve to delay the full implementation of the religious changes until the next reign and thus the English reformation was opposed and long-drawn out and not the revolution it was intended to be.[9]

The Lumley barony was attainted and George's estates were forfeited. He had lived principally at Thwing in the East Riding, a property which had been acquired by the family through marriage in the fourteenth century. Although the estate was confiscated, George's widow Jane (née Knightley of Fawsley) was allowed to live there until her death when the crown took possession. Her three children, John, Jane and Barbara, were born there. John was born about 1533/4 and he would have been baptised by Lord John's 'chaplean Syr Thomas Hallyman'. (Pre-

Reformation priests were commonly called 'Sir'.)[10] The infant children were first schooled by their grandfather. Academies in gentry and aristocratic households were not unusual by this time: the earls of Derby, Shrewsbury and Southampton, Sir Thomas More, and many others employed private tutors for their children. Education had ceased to be the preserve of the clergy although many peers and gentlemen still scorned book-learning; in the late 1560s ninety-two of the 146 leading gentlemen of Northumberland (including the M.P. for Berwick) were unable to sign their names. Furthermore, it was becoming increasingly common in these early post-mediaeval days for young ladies of high rank to become 'so nouzled and trained in the study of letters, that they willingly set all other vain pastimes at naught for learning's sake...'[11] Presently, along with a dozen young nobles, John Lumley was sent to court to be tutored with Prince Edward by such humanist luminaries as Roger Ascham, Sir John Cheke, Anthony Cooke and Richard Cox. The Princess Elizabeth, almost the same age as Lumley, may have had a connection with the group; she was certainly tutored by Ascham and Cheke, and she is known to have shared some lessons with her brother Edward.[12]

Lord Lumley died in 1547 having settled the family property on his grandson and in December that year John Lumley was restored in blood in the first parliament called by Edward VI.[13] The barony was revived for him and his male heirs and his father's estates were restored. But neither that conciliatory gesture of the Protestant king, his former fellow-pupil, or the misfortunes of his paternal family persuaded him to abandon his ancestral faith. In any event, Lumley's own Catholic antecedents had been reinforced by his friendship with a classmate, Henry Fitzalan, Lord Maltravers; that relationship would bring him into close association with the powerful Fitzalan and Howard families and would have the determining influence on his life.

Maltravers' father, also named Henry Fitzalan, was born around 1511/12, son of William, eleventh Earl of Arundel, and Lady Anne Percy, daughter of the fourth Earl of Northumberland. At the age of fourteen he was nominated by his father to be a page in the household of Cardinal Wolsey, but he objected strongly and he persuaded his godfather the king to take him into royal service instead. He married, c.1531/2, Katharine Grey, second daughter of the Marquess of Dorset, by whom he had three children: Jane (1537?-77), Henry (1538-56) and Mary (1541-57), and they were given a broad classical education at home.

Fitzalan (senior) attended Henry VIII at Calais in 1532 and he was summoned to the House of Lords in February 1533 as Lord Maltravers. In 1540 he succeeded Arthur Plantagenet, Viscount Lisle, as Deputy Governor of Calais and over the next three years Arundel successfully rebuilt the town's defences and revitalised the garrison. Fitzalan's wife died in 1542 two years before he succeeded as twelfth Earl of Arundel at his father's death in January 1544. Arundel was marshal of the field in command of thirty thousand men at the siege of Boulogne later in 1544 and his military success was rewarded by the king with the Garter and his appointment as Lord Chamberlain. In 1545 he married Mary, daughter of Sir John Arundell of Lanherne and widow of Robert Ratcliffe, first Earl of Sussex. Peace was established in 1546 and henceforth Arundel, of proven expertise in military and civic affairs, became a valued courtier and diplomat. He retained office under Edward VI but his success and his Catholicism brought him many political enemies.[14]

At around this time an ambitious and conscientious peer would acquire a London town-house. Travel was difficult and country life was tedious, so it was preferable to stay in the capital for most of the time to enjoy court, social, and parliamentary life, and by 1560 half the peerage had houses in London. Aldgate, one of the favoured areas, has been called 'the Park Lane of early Elizabethan England'; Mincing Lane, towards Tower Hill, was where the wealthiest foreign merchants lived. A house near Temple Bar known as Bath Place which had first belonged to Lord Chancellor William Fitzwilliam, Earl of Southampton, had been acquired and extensively rebuilt by Sir Thomas Seymour in November 1545 but, following his execution in March 1549, it reverted to crown ownership. Arundel bought it immediately for £41.6s.8d. and renamed it Arundel House.[15] It was probably in this connection that he was loaned thirty pieces of 'Verdors' (French tapestries) from Nonsuch Palace under a warrant signed on 24 August 1549 by Protector Somerset. It seems, however, that this loan, and King Edward's gifts of certain pictures by Holbein gave Arundel's opponents the opening for the trumped up charges laid against him that he had abused his privileged position to enrich himself by stealing from the palace of Westminster, and of having committed various acts of embezzlement such as 'pluking downe of boltes and lokkes at Westmuster, giving of my stuff away, etc.' He was removed from the Privy Council in February 1550, confined to his house and fined £12,000 payable over twelve years but most of the fine was remitted when the injustice of the accusations was established. But then in November 1551 he was implicated in a plot to murder certain royal councillors and was placed in the Tower and fined six thousand marks. He was freed thirteen months later but only on making his 'submission' to the Privy Council which then revoked the fine. He sulked for a while, but he rejoined the Council even though he was out of favour for much of the latter part of Edward's reign. Arundel conspired to prevent the succession to the throne of Lady Jane Grey, the candidate of his enemies, although his wife was her aunt, and his sister had been Jane's father's first wife. Arundel supported Mary Tudor's rights and it was chiefly by his efforts (in alliance with the Earl of Pembroke) that, in 1553, she became the first queen regnant of England and Ireland. Mary made him Lord Steward of the Household and the countess joined her entourage.[16]

At Easter 1549 Lumley, aged about fifteen, matriculated as a fellow-commoner of Queen's College, Cambridge, together with Henry Fitzalan, Lord Maltravers, Arundel's eleven-year-old son. (There was no fixed age for matriculation in the sixteenth century, it varied from ten to eighteen.) A little over a quarter of peers attended a university or an inn of court at this time but, since they were not required to sit examinations, very few took degrees, and neither Lumley or Maltravers graduated. A legal education was necessary for sons who intended to manage their family's estates.[17] Around 1550 Lumley married the fifteen-year-old Jane Fitzalan, Maltravers' older sister. (The age of consent was twelve for girls and fourteen for boys though betrothals could be arranged at any age.)[18] They were both of a scholarly turn of mind; Jane owned at least fifteen books and remarked in one of her letters that she derived *incredibilem voluptatem* from reading the classics. Shortly after their marriage, the Lumleys embarked on an intellectual exercise designed to impress Arundel, her father. John translated Erasmus's *Institutio Principis Christiani* as *The Education of a Christian Prince*[19] and Jane made a free and abridged prose version of Euripides' *Iphigeneia in Aulis.*[20] Their selection of texts was not coincidental. The fundamental assumption of the *Institutio* is that 'the duty of a good Prince is to consider the welfare of his people, even at the cost of his own life, if need be', and Euripides portrays a princess who decides to sacrifice herself for her country. The young couple clearly wanted to show off both their linguistic skills and their appreciation of the attributes of public service and the courage that it might call for. John's work has not been examined in detail but Jane's has attracted attention for being the earliest extant English translation of a Greek play. Expert textual analysis of her work has shown, however, that it is no more than a careless and inaccurate version of a Latin translation and lacks both critical aptitude and poetic vision. A recent claim that it is a major scholarly work and an icon of early feminist achievement cannot be sustained; it is no more than a literary exercise by a young girl undertaken out of filial piety. Little importance has been attached to the writings of her sister Mary, though they were of a similar kind and standard.[21]

While Princess Elizabeth was in the Tower in early 1554 it was thought that she would be less trouble if she were married and Maltravers was one of those proposed as a suitable candidate.[22] The idea came to nothing, of course, and in mid-April 1555 Maltravers married the widow Anne Rich (née Wentworth of Gosfield, Essex). In February of the same year, at about the age of fifteen, Mary Fitzalan had been married to the seventeen-year-old Thomas Howard who had succeeded as fourth Duke of Norfolk the previous year to become England's premier nobleman and the greatest landowner in the country: He could expect an annual income of some £2,500 when he reached his majority.[23] The wedding took place in St Clement Dane's, the parish church of Arundel Place, her father's house, which had been the residence of the bishops of Bath and Wells. Howard was the son of the soldier-poet Henry Howard, Earl of Surrey, who had been executed in 1547 at the age of thirty on a charge of 'treasonable ambition' for using the royal arms. The family was known for its Catholic sympathies; Thomas Howard was tutored firstly by Hadrianus Junius but after his father's execution he was placed with John Foxe and later Bishop John White to be educated as a Protestant, and he would remain as such, though he was no bigot, and he would hold office in the household of Philip II, Mary Tudor's consort. His older sister Jane married Charles Neville, sixth Earl of Westmorland (of Brancepeth and Raby Castles in County Durham), and remained a Catholic despite a similar upbringing. His younger brother, Henry, Earl of Northampton (1540-1614) lived in religious ambiguity and only affirmed his Catholicism on his deathbed.[24] At Mary's accession Thomas was restored as Earl of Surrey and joined the household of Stephen Gardiner, Lord Chancellor and Bishop of Winchester, who was keen to restore the old religion. Thus was formed the nucleus of a young, noble,

Catholic cousinage. The Howards, Fitzalans and Lumleys were prominent figures in the ceremonies associated with Mary's coronation and her marriage to Philip of Spain, and they remained close to the throne throughout the reign.

Lumley had become a man of some substance. The mean income of peers in 1559 is given as £1,780[25] and his estates yielded a rental of £2,000 a year. He owned property in Northumberland, Surrey and Sussex, but his major landholdings were the patrimonial estates in County Durham which comprised:

> 60,000 messuages, 3,000 cottages, 20 water-mills, 20 windmills, 20,000 acres of land, 10,000 acres of meadow, 16,000 acres of pasture, 4,000 acres of waste, 40,000 acres of heath and furze, 6,000 acres of marsh and £100 of rent.[26]

Having attained his majority, Lumley took his seat in the House of Lords on 5 April 1554 in the first session of Queen Mary's first parliament.[27] (It is entirely coincidental that Lumley only became eligible to take his seat after the Protestant Edward's death and the accession of the Catholic Mary.) He was a diligent member of the House and he took part in most of the proceedings; he sat as a judge in state trials and was a member of various committees. Like many other peers, Lumley acquired a London residence. He bought the house of Thomas Wyatt the Younger, who had been executed in 1554, which was valued at £109.6s.8d. It stood at the corner of Hart Street and Woodroffe Lane in the parish of St Olave's on the border of Aldgate and the Tower. It had been part of the priory of the Crutched [or Crossed] Friars which was surrendered to the crown in 1538 and granted to Sir Thomas Wyatt the Elder in 1540; Wyatt had built a house on a plot of ground of the former priory 'where part of their house stood ... and joineth to the Tower Hill'. Maps of London show the rear of the house overlooking the site of the scaffolds and gallows on Tower Hill. Northumberland House, the residence of Henry Percy, Earl of Northumberland, and the Duke of Norfolk's mansion, built on the ruins of Holy Trinity Priory in Cree Church Place, were close by to the north; the fourth duke would also acquire the London Charterhouse in 1564 and rename it Howard House. Arundel House, the parental home of his wife, lay further off to the west in the increasingly fashionable quarter of the Strand.[28]

Arundel, as the premier earl in the realm, Lord High Steward and a member of the Privy Council, was in the most powerful position at the centre of affairs; he led the English delegation to the peace conference with the French in 1558. He was, moreover, at the height of his fortune; his gross annual rental amounted to around £4,000 in 1559[29] and he could well afford to acquire one of the grandest houses in the land – the royal palace of Nonsuch, at Cuddington near Cheam in Surrey at the foot of the North Downs. Henry VIII was the only Tudor monarch with a developed cultural sensibility and he conceived Nonsuch Palace as a rival to the great French palace at Chambord. Building began in April 1538 and England's finest craftsmen were employed on it. Henry also brought in continental experts, including: Nicholas Bellin of Modena, who was paid for 'the guylding and hatching of dyvers peces of the kynges arms badges Roses batons and other devyces cutte and kervyd in slate for the garnyshing of tymber worke';[30] the painter-architect Antonio Toto del Nunziata; the stone-mason Wilhelm Cure, who had been 'sent for hither when the King did byulde Nonesutche';[31] the mouldmaker Giles Gering; and six French clockmakers. The gardens were laid out at the same time; the king's gardener is supposed to have been a French priest named Woolf who was sent abroad to scout around for landscaping ideas and to bring back garden ornaments and specimen plants. The quadrangle was laid with stone brought in from Newcastle.[32] Henry had spent £24,536.7s.7d. on the palace by November 1545 and travellers such as John Leland (d. 1552) were much impressed with it. Though habitable, the palace was incomplete and the decoration unfinished at Henry's death in 1547.

Nonsuch Palace
(detail of an engraving after a drawing by Joris Hoefnagel, 1568)

Largely because of the collapse of the royal finances after Henry's death, neither of his immediate successors, Edward VI and Mary I, were enthusiastic art-patrons and neither had an interest in the palace; the total expenditure on Nonsuch during their reigns amounted to no more than £190, and Mary even thought it 'mete to have beene pulled down and solde by peacemeale than to be perfited at her charges'.[33] In 1556, however, Arundel approached the queen with a proposal to buy the Nonsuch estate with the intention, as he said, of completing the 'buildings, reparations, pavements and gardens, in as ample and perfect sort as by the first intent and meaning of the said king his old master the same should have been performed.' Mary readily agreed and sold the palace to Arundel for £485.13s.4d. and several manors in Norfolk. Thomas Cawarden, custodian of the palace, and leaseholder of the park and other grounds, treated Arundel as an intruder and was so firmly entrenched that Arundel had a great deal of trouble getting him out. Cawarden had been knighted at the siege of Boulogne and was a keen Reformer. He had been suspected of being sympathetic to the Wyatt Rebellion; cartloads of arms had been seized at Nonsuch by the Sheriff of Surrey and he was placed in custody for a time. The Letters Patent recording Arundel's acquisition of the palace were dated 23 November 1556 and Lumley went to Nonsuch on several occasions to carry out estate business for his father in law. It was not until May 1558, however, that all resistance was overcome and Arundel and Lumley gained full and unfettered possession.[34]

In contrast to his public success, however, Arundel was much less fortunate in his private life. Katherine, his first countess, and the mother of his three children, had died in 1542 as had his father two years later. On 30 June 1556 his eighteen-year-old son Henry, Lord Maltravers, succumbed to a fever at Brussels while on a diplomatic mission to the Emperor Maximilian. He was buried in the north aisle of St Agatha's cathedral.[35] On 28 June 1557 Arundel's daughter Mary, Duchess of Norfolk, died in childbirth aged seventeen; and she was followed to the grave in October that year by Arundel's second countess, Mary. The obsequies of both women were conducted at St Clement's by the same clerics. An observer described the countess's funeral:

> my Lady was brought to the church with the Bishop of London [Edmund Bonner] and [St.] Paul's choir and the masters the Clerks of London and then came the corpse

> with 5 paners [?banners] of armes borne; then came 4 heralds in their coats of arms and bare 4 banars of images at the 4 corners and then came the chief mourners, my Lady of Worcester and my Lady Lumley and my Lord North, and Sir Anthony St Leger then came an hundred mourners of men and after as many ladies and gentlemen all in black; besides a great many poor women in black and vails and 24 men poor in black bearing torches and many of her servants in black coats bearing of torches. The 28th day of October was the Mass of Requiem sung and a goodly sermon and after Mass her Grace was buried and all her head officers with white staffs in their hands and all the heralds waiting about her in their coat armours and my lord Abbot of Westminster [...] her a godly sermon and my Lord of London sang the Mass, the Bishop of [blank] sang the Mass of the [blank] then was a [blank] Mass said and aft to [my Lord's] plasse to dinner for there was a great dinner.[36]

Thus within fifteen years Arundel lost two wives, his only son and his youngest daughter; Lady Jane Lumley was left his sole heiress. During the first five years of their married life, the Lumleys had three children, Charles, Thomas and Mary, but they had all died in infancy, and so there was nothing to prevent them joining Arundel at Nonsuch in the summer of 1558. Lady Lumley became chatelaine of the palace and Lord Lumley became Arundel's closest associate and, we may take it, a substitute for the son he had lost.

Together they set about realising King Henry's plans for the palace. The internal arrangements will be discussed later but externally, the gardens, orchard and wilderness, which were all part of the original landscaping and planting scheme, had matured and 'only minor additional work' needed to be done. Little structural work was required and Arundel and Lumley had only to finish off and add various embellishments to the walls of the palace. The exterior of the finished building was 'built entirely of great blocks of white stone on which [we]re represented numerous Roman and other ancient stories', in medallion or relief-bust. With flying turrets and domes, it was an extraordinary sight as can be seen in the wellknown engraving of 1582 by Frans Hogenberg based on a sketch of 1568 by Joris Hoefnagel, a Flemish artist and engraver. (A less flamboyant sketch of the palace appears on John Speed's map of

Surrey). Hogenberg noted that it was adorned 'within and without with magnificent statues, some of which vividly represent the antiquities of Rome, and some surpass them'. Anthony Watson, Rector of Cheam, was lavish in his praise of the palace and he, too, highlighted the carvings on the buildings: 'everywhere there are kings, Caesars, sciences, gods'. William Camden wrote in much the same terms in 1586, as did the Swiss Thomas Platter the following year. In 1598 the German Paul Hentzner remarked that the palace had been built 'with an excess of magnificence and elegance, even to ostentation'. (In 1666, long after it had been abandoned and despite the depredations of the Civil War, John Evelyn was still able to admire the grandiose building.) The finished palace of Nonsuch, then, was a conspicuous, unique and gross building of which Henry would doubtless have been thoroughly proud.[37]

To add to the distress of Arundel's personal bereavements, Queen Mary died in November 1558 and her Catholic court was dissolved. His expectations of being at the centre of English court-life for many years seemed to be dashed and he anticipated being dismissed as Lord High Steward, but Elizabeth kept him on. This was, of course, because he was the premier English earl and his influence as leader of the old Catholic nobility meant that he could not be excluded safely. In January 1559, as a further mark of her favour, Elizabeth elevated Arundel to the place of the recently deceased Reginald, Cardinal Pole as Chancellor of the University of Oxford (but Arundel resigned in June unable to make any headway in 'that Protestant and unregenerated' institution). He had been High Steward of the University since March 1555 and at his elevation to the chancellorship he nominated Lumley as his successor to the stewardship and Lumley would hold that post till his death.[38] Count de Feria, the Spanish Ambassador, reported that Lumley was 'very confidential' with Elizabeth and that Arundel was 'going about in high glee' and was very smart in his appearance. Doubtless that was because it was being rumoured that the queen was considering him as a possible husband notwithstanding his being over twenty years older and a twice-widowed Catholic. The Earl of Westmorland and the son of William Howard were other named candidates but it seems that Arundel was parliament's choice among the English suitors for her hand.[39]

Arundel was in his late forties and his portraits reflect the contemporary description of him as well-proportioned and of middle height, 'stronge of bone, furnished with cleane and firm fleshe, voide of fogines and fatness'. Feria, however, was not impressed with the earl's intellect and considered Arundel 'a flighty man of small ability'. Arundel was old-fashioned; he had an expressive manner and was both blunt and rapid in speech. He knew Latin and French but he was not fluent in either and he positively refused to converse with foreigners except in English, which might have been considered tactless by his interlocutors at the peace negotiations between France and Scotland at which he was Elizabeth's representative.[40] In January 1559 Arundel was reported to be borrowing large sums as well as selling 'all he has' to spend on Christmas banquets and a jewel for the queen's New Year gift. Elizabeth did nothing to scotch the rumours of a possible marriage and Arundel continued to press his suit by showering gifts on her. He was also known to have given jewels worth two thousand crowns to her ladies. He and Lumley entertained the queen with sumptuous banquets, masques and music at Nonsuch over a weeklong visit during her summer progress in August 1559; it cost him around £600, the queen contributed a further £356.[41] By then, however, Arundel had come to realise that the queen was playing games and that Robert Dudley, Earl of Leicester was her true favourite. The Spanish had taken Arundel's prospects seriously until de Feria reported that the queen had joked with him about the earl's pretensions: 'She does not get on with him, nor with Pembroke'[42]. Arundel had nothing to show for his lavish expenditure and he brought his courtship to an end. Indeed, there were even rumours that Elizabeth and Leicester were to be murdered at one of his banquets.[43]

***

Although Elizabeth's accession in 1558 was undisturbed, her hold on power was precarious for some time because of several inter-related personal, political and religious circumstances. She had come to the throne despite being illegitimate under both Catholic and Anglican ecclesiastical law as well as the parliamentary statute (28 Henry VIII) which had annulled the union of her parents Henry and Anne Boleyn and had specifically excluded her from the succession. Next in line was Mary Stewart, great-grand-daughter of Henry VII, Queen of Scotland and the Isles and, briefly in 1560, Queen of France, who was nine years younger than Elizabeth; a *coup d'etat* could be justified on the basis of her legitimacy. Elizabeth could never be brought to admit that Mary was her heir-presumptive for fear of creating an alternative power-base in the kingdom. Mary's claim to the English throne became the consuming interest of her life and the grounds for several conspiracies which would ultimately bring her to the block. Then there was the question of religion: Elizabeth Protestant and Mary Catholic. Mary had no intention of abandoning her faith in order to gain the English throne though she was not averse to marrying a non-Catholic, and at various times Elizabeth suggested, though without confirming Mary's claim, that she might do well to marry a reliable English Protestant.[44] All the while, Elizabeth dissembled about her own marriage intentions by encouraging a series of suitors even though she had privately decided to remain unmarried so as to keep the question of the English succession open and to avoid any dilution of her personal power. Hence a dynastic impasse arose between them and the political nation became increasingly concerned. There had been three changes of sovereign and religion in less than twelve years; Henry VIII had married six times; his successor had died aged sixteen; he was followed by a woman who had taken a Spanish husband and who had died childless. Now they had a queen who was reluctant to marry at all.

Inevitably, the matter complicated England's foreign relations, for France, Spain and the Holy See all had an interest in furthering Mary's prospects as a Catholic sovereign as the means of bringing England back into the Church. Elizabeth therefore encouraged the European Protestants whenever possible so as to preoccupy their Catholic rulers with internal security. She also supported the Scottish Protestants so as to keep England's northern border less vulnerable to French expansionist ambitions. In 1561, Mary Stewart, a nineteen-year-old widow, returned from France to a Scotland which lay firmly under Elizabeth's political hegemony and exposed to John Knox's Protestantising ambitions. As a way of uniting both the Scottish and the English Catholic claims to the English throne, Margaret, Countess of Lennox, grand-daughter of Henry VII and second in line after Mary, immediately but secretly proposed a marriage between her son Henry, Lord Darnley, and the Scottish queen (notwithstanding the impediment of his being her first cousin and the lack of a papal dispensation). Temple Newsam, the Lennox mansion near Leeds, was a known meeting-place for northern Catholics and Elizabeth had it watched. On discovering the marriage-plan, the furious Elizabeth had the Lennoxes detained and they were not readmitted to her presence until the autumn of 1563. Arthur and Geoffrey Pole, nephews of the cardinal, sought support for Mary Stewart from the French and were put in the Tower. Arthur was married to a Percy and was a protégé of the Catholic Lord Hastings.[45]

Domestically, Elizabeth secured her position in several ways. In May 1559, within six months of her accession, she sanctioned the passage of the Acts of Supremacy and Uniformity thereby reviving the Henrician and Edwardine Reformation legislation but now it would be enforced by oaths of allegiance. The oath in the Act of Supremacy was compulsory for the clergy, judges, justices, mayors, royal officials and university graduands; in 1563 the oath was extended to members of parliament, schoolmasters, lawyers, sheriffs and all officeholders. Crucially, however, peers and landed gentry were not included and they were able to hinder the process of enforced loyalty to the Anglican establishment in their own rural fiefdoms. Recusancy put down its roots at once, especially in the ultra-conservative northern parts. Elizabeth reduced the size of the Privy Council and replaced the majority of her predecessor's staunchly Catholic advisers with Protestants though she retained a handful of Catholics (Arundel, Derby and Pembroke) because of their wide-ranging influence and potential for trouble if slighted. In all, of around thirty councillors fewer than a third kept their places.[46] Elizabeth also dismissed the Catholic noblewomen who had served as Mary Tudor's ladies in waiting. She purged the Council of the North (Richard Norton would prove one of the more dangerous casualties) and removed potential troublemakers from the wardenries and other positions of influence on the Scottish borders. The Earl of Northumberland was especially aggrieved at his dismissal.[47] Elizabeth further alienated the old peerage by looking outside their ranks for her new councillors; the promotion of commoners, chief among them William Cecil, was much resented. Thus Elizabeth progressively entrenched Protestantism and gained mastery over her kingdom by curtailing the powers of the old nobility and ousting Catholic peers from the governance of the realm, by surrounding herself with new advisers, by procrastinating about her marriage intentions, and by avoiding direct confrontation with Catholic Europe while discreetly supporting the French Huguenots and Dutch Calvinists.

The Catholic rump on the Privy Council was increasingly distrusted and the queen's councillors began to warn that they were losing patience with her refusal to acknowledge Mary Stewart as her heir.[48] As strong advocates of the Scottish queen's rights, both Arundel and Lumley were becoming more deeply involved in political and dynastic intrigue on her behalf. Arundel had maintained communications with the Spanish after Mary Tudor's death and he expressed his affection for King Philip to the new ambassador, Don Diego Guzman de Silva, who had been appointed in 1564 in succession to Don Alvaro de Quadra, Bishop of Aquila who had died in the plague of 1563.[49] Arundel came to blows with Admiral Clinton at a Privy Council meeting when discussing anti-Catholic legislation and he held a meeting at his house, attended by Norfolk, to discuss the succession for which he earned the queen's displeasure. He resigned the Stewardship in July 1564 'with sundry speeches of offence towards the Queen's Majesty'.[50] The affronted queen ordered that he be confined to Arundel House 'for a season' and forbidden visitors, the court being

> suspicious that some plot may have been brewing, as the Earl's house has been much frequented by the principal nobles and gentlemen of the reign, many of whom must be concerned with him.

Arundel was freed at the New Year, and, a reconciliation with the queen having been patched up, 'all ended in merrymakings'.[51]

Elizabeth's lack of interest in Arundel as a suitor was made plain when, in an attempt to sideline Darnley, she suggested him or Leicester or Norfolk as a possible husband for the Scottish queen. On the grounds that he no longer held office, Arundel declined to add his signature to a letter from the Privy Council inviting Mary to marry Leicester rather than Darnley.[52] But Darnley had become Mary's preferred candidate and she married him in 1565. Later that year Lumley and the earl of Sussex were appointed ambassadors to visit Scotland in an attempt 'to restore the amity' between Mary and Elizabeth and to obtain Mary's agreement that she would not press her claim to the English throne during the life of Elizabeth or change the religion of her own country.[53] But Mary knew that she had many friends in England who acknowledged her right to succeed, 'especially among those of the old religion'. She was also told that the papists were 'ready to rise in England when she will have them'.[54] The Earl of Bedford, Warden of the East March, feared that, as a zealous Catholic, Lumley would only encourage Mary's ambitions and foment conspiracy, and indeed that was precisely why she would accept his embassy. Lumley could be expected to interpret events to Mary's advantage. On reconsideration, therefore, the Privy Council agreed that Lumley could not be trusted and the mission was suspended before he set out.[55]

On 16 March 1566, with the queen's consent, Arundel went abroad, to recover his health (he was suffering from gout) though the general opinion was that 'as a Catholic he wished to be out of the country to enjoy greater liberty'.[56] He made over all his possessions to Lumley shortly before he left. Arundel was accompanied by Humphrey Lloyd, an Oxford don whom Arundel had earlier engaged as his physician and who had married Lumley's younger sister Barbara. Lloyd's academic background was obviously of wider scholarly value and he was appointed additionally as librarian at Nonsuch. Lloyd left Arundel's service in 1563 and died in his native Denbighshire five years later, bequeathing his books to Lumley. Arundel visited Antwerp, Brussels, Venice (where Lloyd bought books) and Milan, and he was treated with the utmost deference wherever he went. He spent much of the time in Padua. The University of Padua was the most popular foreign university among the English and many Catholics pursued academic careers there, particularly in its medical faculty. Arundel, however, went to take advantage of the mud-baths at Abano Terme, the Roman *aquae patavinae*, a few miles south-west of the city which were thought to have medicinal value (Lloyd found those at Bath more efficacious).[57]

A year later Arundel received a letter from Elizabeth congratulating him on his restored health, adding that she had visited Nonsuch in January (while he was in Milan) and 'did so well air every part of your house, as at your coming we think you shall find it seasonable for you. And so we wish you to find it'.[58] Arundel prudently construed this as an invitation, or summons, to return home. (Sir Francis Englefield ignored a similar letter and suffered the confiscation of his estates.[59]) Lumley thought she wished to re-employ Arundel but she knew only too well that a lengthy stay in Italy made for easier contact with papal and Spanish representatives.[60] At any rate on 21 April 1567, restored to perfect health, Arundel arrived in London to an extraordinary welcome: church-bells were rung and some two thousand mounted gentlemen escorted him through the capital to court. One Robert Owen composed some Greek and Latin verses congratulating Arundel on his return. Among 'such Lords and Ladies as were of his own family and near allied unto him' who greeted him at Arundel House was the Spanish Ambassador.[61] This was yet another indication of the continuing involvement of Arundel and his circle in the Catholic political intrigues which had rumbled along *sotto voce* since the beginning of Elizabeth's reign. The birth of a Scottish prince in the summer of 1566 had opened the prospect of a new Catholic dynasty and the English Catholics became even keener to see Mary Stewart inherit the English crown.[62]

By 1568 Elizabeth's balancing-act was becoming increasingly precarious as diplomatic relations with the continental powers worsened and a political crisis arose in Scotland. The Holy See was dismayed by Elizabeth's increasing anti-Catholicism and was seeking to exploit every opportunity to recover Britain for the Church. The progressive hispanicisation of the Netherlands under the Duke of Alva and the consequent threat to English interests in the Low Countries led to a deterioration in Anglo-Spanish relations, which were ruptured by a successful Spanish attack in the Caribbean on an English squadron commanded by John Hawkins. Matters came to a head in December 1568 when a number of Spanish ships carrying bullion worth £85,000 to Alva put in at Plymouth Sound to evade pirates in the Channel but Elizabeth detained the squadron. Alva immediately placed an embargo on all English property in the Netherlands and Elizabeth retaliated with a like measure in England. At about the same time the French distrained English arms and money at Rouen destined for the Huguenots. In Scotland, Darnley had proved to be dissolute and incompetent and was excluded from power. His murder at Kirk o'Field in February 1567 and Mary's marriage in May to the chief suspect, James Hepburn, Earl of Bothwell, a Protestant, caused an outcry. In July she was imprisoned at Lochleven and forced to abdicate in favour of her infant son James. She escaped in May 1568 and revoked her abdication but, unable to reassert her authority in Scotland, she fled to England to obtain Elizabeth's protection and in hopes of gaining assistance in the recovery of her throne. Elizabeth had steadfastly declined permission for Mary to enter England, let alone meet her, for fear of appearing to endorse her claims, and so she was not best pleased with this turn of events, even though Mary was her cousin, her neighbour, an anointed ruler like herself and her presumed successor.

Thus in the early months of 1569 the most critical period in Elizabeth's reign opened. War was possible because her ministers had pursued an interventionist anti-Catholic foreign policy which had driven the Papacy, Spain and France into an aggressive coalition against her, and Scotland had been destabilised. Elizabeth continued to refuse to acknowledge Mary's rights to the succession. Mary had moreover now set foot in the kingdom to which she laid claim, and her marriage to the most senior English peer was being actively pursued. Elizabeth increasingly disregarded the old nobility and her policy of eliminating the old faith was proceeding apace. There was, therefore, a degree of discontent, popular and elitist, which represented an opposition which could cohere and lead to civil disorder and, ultimately, insurrection.[63] The Catholic peers (Arundel, Derby, Lumley, Montague, Northumberland, Pembroke, and Westmorland) certainly thought so and were prepared to seek a restoration of Catholicism under a Catholic sovereign and to repair relations with Catholic Europe, even if this meant taking to arms in open rebellion.

Chapter Two

'Popish Wasps and Bees'[1]

Mary Stewart took ship at Dundrennan in south-west Scotland, crossed the Solway Firth and landed at Workington. After a brief confinement at Cockermouth she was removed to Carlisle Castle on 18 May and placed in the charge of Richard Lowther, the Deputy Governor. Numbers of Mary's English adherents hastened from all parts of the north to greet her. The Earl and Countess of Northumberland were the first to pay court and, in accordance with Border custom, the earl demanded that Lowther release Mary into his care, she having landed within his liberties, but Lowther declined. Leonard Dacre and Christopher Norton and 'many gentlemen of diverse shires' followed hard on their heels. The local people were heard to 'rejoice at the liberty of the Queen of Scots, and many utter their good minds to her' and that 'her behaviour wins the affection of many'; they 'would laugh in their sleeves' at the government if she managed to abscond. Elizabeth had been warned for long enough that there was a strong Marian party in the north and she should not have been taken unawares, but she now hurriedly ordered that Mary be kept more privately. Northumberland was told 'not to meddle any further', Christopher Lascelles and Francis Dacre were turned away, and the Council of the North was rebuked for sending Mary a welcoming message.[2]

Despite the crown's assiduous efforts over many years to erode the powers of regional magnates, northern England remained highly independent and politically unreliable. Feudalism had yet to wane, for the great families of Dacre, Neville and Percy held sway from Yorkshire to the border: as Lord Hunsdon would famously remark, Northumbrians 'knew no other prince but a Percy'.[3] Although Catholicism was no longer the religion of the establishment, it remained the religion of the people and adherence to it involved 'no Tridentine fervour or Jesuitical subversiveness, but simply [a capacity] to discern cheese from chalk...'[4] The Pilgrimage of Grace was still fresh in the minds of many of those whose fathers and grandfathers had marched behind the banners of the Five Wounds and St Cuthbert little more than thirty years before. The despoliation of the churches had been resisted and Protestant evangelism had proved difficult. In 1560 it was found that Newcastle and the neighbourhood were 'far out of order in matters of religion and the altars standing still in the churches contrary to the Queen's Majesty's proceedings'. In 1568 it was admitted that 'in many churches there [had] been no sermons for years past' and even twenty years later there were 'not passing three or four preachers in the whole shire ... most of the gentlemen there being papists'. Scottish Catholic priests fleeing Knox's intolerance had simply moved their ministries across the border.[5] The Archbishop of York remarked that the justices could not be relied upon and a survey in 1564 showed that barely of them half were sound in religion. The Captain of Berwick feared that trouble was bound to break out unless loyal magistrates could be found because popery was so deeply rooted among the gentry. The oath of supremacy was generally brushed aside, if it was administered at all.[6] Bishop James Pilkington, the first Protestant Bishop of Durham, likened himself to St Paul having to fight the beasts at Ephesus. In 1569 Catholicism was still so much the 'natural' religion that Sir Ralph Sadler could observe. 'The ancient faith still lay like lees at the bottom of men's hearts and if the vessel was ever so little stirred came to the top'. The series of changes in religion in recent years had been confusing and some clergy had kept their mouths shut only to reveal their true Catholic loyalties in the rising of 1569. Thomas Swalwell, appointed curate of Brancepeth by the Earl of Westmorland that year, was said to have been 'a notorious favourer of popery' in the north of County Durham for twenty years; Cuthbert Ward, however, said he had known Swalwell for forty years 'but what religion he is of [I] cannot depose.'[7].

Hence Mary Stewart had natural allies throughout the region. Thomas ('Simple Tom') Percy, seventh Earl of Northumberland, aged forty in 1569, whose father had suffered for his participation in the Pilgrimage of Grace, had prospered under Mary Tudor. The earldom was revived for him in 1557 and the lands forfeited by his father were restored. He was appointed Warden of the East and Middle Marches and Governor of Redesdale, Tynedale and Berwick. But his fortunes went into decline from the accession of Elizabeth; he was forced to resign his northern offices in 1560 and the award of the Garter three years later did nothing to mollify him. In 1565 Elizabeth was advised that Northumberland, being 'obstinate in religion', ought to be detained in London. He and his countess, Anne, daughter of Henry Somerset, second Earl of Worcester, had exchanged letters and tokens of affection with Mary.[8] Leonard Dacre, head of a powerful and staunchly Catholic family in Westmorland, also had grievances against the government and had corresponded with Mary from around 1566.[9] The Catholics of the North Riding were led by the eighty-one-year-old Richard Norton of Norton Conyers, who had accompanied his father in the Pilgrimage of Grace. Norton had been dismissed from the Council of the North, his wife was a Neville, one of his sons married Jane, a relative of Dr Nicholas Morton, and a daughter had married Thomas Markenfield. Norton, Markenfield and Morton were all active in Mary's cause. Lords Pembroke and Darcy ('with the crooked back') and Sir Thomas Stanley, brother of the Earl of Derby, also sent Mary 'friendly letters' from Lancashire.[10] The most influential Catholic nobleman in County Durham was Charles Neville, sixth Earl of Westmorland. He had succeeded his father late in 1563 aged twenty and was married to Jane, daughter of Henry Howard, Earl of Surrey and sister of the Duke of Norfolk; Alva thought him 'a man of very little substance as far as his judgement and manner of life, for there is no rule or order in his affairs', and Archduke Albert would find him 'of little use, for nothing of great moment can be entrusted to him'. But that was later, for now what mattered was that Westmorland and his uncles Christopher and Cuthbert Neville, were among Mary's more ardent supporters.[11]

Then there was Lumley; he was mostly resident in London with his father in law and hence his influence in Durham was not great, except among his tenants, but he had an important rôle as the link between the northern Catholics and those in the south, and then there was his diplomatic contact with the main continental Catholic power. He had dealt routinely with the Spanish during the reign of Mary and Philip and he maintained communications with the Spanish Ambassador after

Elizabeth's accession (he showed Don Guzman de Silva over Nonsuch in July 1565). Philip was told that he and Arundel had spent such large sums in promoting Mary's claims that they had fallen into debt. In 1561 the manors of Stranton and Seaton Carew were sold to the financier Sir Thomas Gresham and James Rawe, a Newcastle merchant bought High Friarside. In July that year Lumley Park and other properties in Durham were leased for eight years 'in consideration of settlement by lessees of certain debts' of Arundel amounting to £2,000. Other manors belonging to Lumley worth £4,000 were let to Sir Walter Mildmay in 1564. In 1566 Christopher Chaytor bought the manor of Butterby; Ludworth went to Richard Bellasis; and Murton was bought by Lumley's tenants. Lumley borrowed £1,900 in the city of London in 1567 but he forfeited certain lands for the non-payment of the debt when the creditor died in 1571. Their increasingly precarious finances led Arundel and Lumley to apply for a Spanish subsidy. Lumley's credentials as a devout and zealous Catholic and a worthy gentleman were conveyed to Philip in November 1565 and again in February 1566 by Don Guzman. Lumley was also reported to be 'a devoted adherent of your Majesty...'[12]

Norfolk and Arundel attended the meeting of the Privy Council which discussed Mary's future. Elizabeth was advised to keep Mary in custody, though not in Carlisle which was too deep in the fractious borderland for comfort. And so, on 15 July 1568, she was moved further south and further inland to Bolton Castle in Wensleydale, some forty miles west of York. But still she could not be isolated from her supporters, for Christopher Norton visited her and was thought to be plotting her escape with Northumberland. At the same time, Roberto di Pagnozzo Ridolfi, head of the Guild of Florentine Traders of London and a banker with an informal papal status who had been in England since 1560 and was intimate with most of the leading English Catholics (Arundel and Lumley in particular,) wrote to the Pope urging him to support their endeavours on Mary's behalf, which would include military action.[13] Don Guerau de Spes, the new Spanish Ambassador, arrived in London in July 1568 and immediately made contact with Mary's English supporters and found that Arundel, Lumley and a small group of nobles had been engaged for some time in serious conversations about Mary's future.[14] From the English Catholic point of view a marriage between Norfolk and Mary would solve some major political problems. Norfolk had been widowed in September 1567 and, still in his early thirties, he was highly eligible. Although he was not a Catholic, his deceased wife, a Dacre, had been strongly so, and he was said to have promised to embrace Catholicism openly when it was expedient to do so. The French and the Spanish endorsed the marriage, as did Arundel and Lumley, though other northern peers were less enthusiastic, at least initially. Northumberland disapproved because Norfolk was not a Catholic; he wanted Mary to marry Philip, at which proposal the Spanish Ambassador merely 'wagged his head'. Westmorland did not disapprove but feared for Norfolk's life; Derby was opposed. Mary, however, assented to exploratory talks and Norfolk allowed himself to be drawn into the plan.[15]

In October 1568 a commission of enquiry was convened at York to determine Mary's guilt or innocence of Darnley's murder. The commission was headed by Norfolk and Arundel was a member. When it became clear within the month that the enquiry would be inconclusive Elizabeth transferred the commission to Westminster but the matter remained unresolved and the commission was dissolved in January 1569. During a Privy Council meeting at which Elizabeth was present, Arundel courageously averred that Mary was innocent and that he would object to any measures being taken against her. But Mary's release was never taken into consideration and in February the increasingly nervous Elizabeth took the precaution of moving her 'with all haste' to Tutbury, a crumbling mediaeval castle southwest of Derby belonging to George Talbot, Earl of Shrewsbury and his wife Elizabeth ('Bess of Hardwick').[16]

Whatever differences they may have had about the proposed marriage, the Catholic peers were unanimous about the main thrust of their strategy. They argued that Mary's forced abdication by Protestants and her confinement by the heretic Elizabeth was intolerable. There was little prospect of Elizabeth making a suitable marriage whereas Mary had agreed to enter negotiations with their nominee. In January 1569 Mary told Philip that with his assistance she could be mistress of the realm and lead it back to Catholicism within three months.[17] In February de Spes notified the king that he had been approached by Ridolfi in the name of Norfolk and Arundel who had disclosed that they were gathering strength to force a military resolution of the situation. The Pope had provided Dr Morton with twelve thousand crowns to foster the Catholic resistance; Francis Norton would later say that Morton and Markenfield were 'the most earnest movers' of a rebellion. Don Guerau was therefore urged to advise both Philip and Alva to seize this heaven-sent opportunity to bring Elizabeth and her ministers down. If Spanish troops were sent to assist, Northumberland, Westmorland and Dacre stood ready to raise an army and march south to free Mary and depose Elizabeth. The Tower of London would be seized by Arundel and Lumley operating out of the latter's house on Tower Hill. Hence, Philip was told, a determined effort would instal a new Catholic dynasty, England's governance by heretic upstarts would be ended, the *ancien regime* would be reinstated, and a reversal of religious and foreign policy would be effected, resulting in peace with Catholic Europe. In short, Philip could hardly pass up the chance to get English affairs of state back to what they had been in the previous reign. In February Don Guerau delightedly informed the leading conspirators that his master was persuaded that the time was indeed ripe for action and in March Ridolfi reached an understanding with the Catholic peers about their intentions.[18]

Alva, however, told Philip that he did not have the resources to mount an invasion of England. Moreover, he was not convinced that the English Catholics were not deceiving de Spes and that they should prove themselves first. De Spes worked hard to convince his masters of the conspirators' *bona fides*. He reported that Arundel genuinely wanted to change the government and restore Catholicism 'whilst benefitting himself somewhat, as he is very needy' and he recommended a loan of six thousand crowns, for which Lumley's involvement was sufficient guarantee. He also said that Lumley was highly security-conscious; they had exchanged messages but each had returned their copies for safety. Philip had come to doubt Norfolk's intentions and had to be reassured that the duke's conversion to Catholicism would take place in due course. De Spes reported that Norfolk and Arundel had 'very little courage' and were acting 'in the usual cautious English fashion with one another'; they would 'not declare themselves frankly and the affair drags more slowly than it would elsewhere'. He also remarked that since Norfolk and Arundel were 'English and not entirely Catholic' made him 'always suspicious of them'. By June, however, Philip and his Council of State had come round to the view that war was undesirable and Alva was instructed to seek a diplomatic solution to the Anglo-Spanish dispute.[19]

In the absence of Spanish military support, the malcontents abandoned their plan to depose Elizabeth and remove Cecil but they persevered with the scheme to liberate Mary, marry her to Norfolk and have her title to the succession proclaimed. The new plan, concocted in the gallery of Arundel House between Lumley, John Leslie, Bishop of Ross, Ridolfi and one Lyggons (representing the Earl of Westmorland), was for the northern earls to muster an army to sweep quickly south to free Mary and get her to Arundel Castle, presumably because it was convenient for the capital if Elizabeth was deposed, or for the south coast if she was not. Early in August the Spanish Ambassador reported that he believed there would be 'some great event soon ... these gentlemen of Nonsuch have some new imaginings'. De Spes, apparently without authorisation, assured Northumberland that Alva would supply arms, troops and sufficient money to maintain twelve thousand Englishmen and 'arrive at Hartlepool within eight days of the rising' breaking out.[20]

Although Hartlepool was the only active port in County Durham, commissions appointed by Elizabeth in 1559 and 1565 to enquire into the state of the harbours of north-east England had found that it was much decayed and that the pier was in need of repair. The religious changes of the early decades of the century had been resisted by the inhabitants and the resumption of reform under Elizabeth had been no more acceptable. Hartlepool had become known to Catholics as a suitably discreet and friendly place for priests and agents to enter and leave the country. The French, moreover, were known to have a map of the port in 1560 'where they mind to set men a land, and to fortify the place ...' When Mary Queen of Scots left France for Scotland in 1561 the English government ordered that a watch be kept and that any foreign ship entering the port be searched. Now in 1569 the Spanish Ambassador advised the northern earls to secure Hartlepool as a landing-place for Alva and his army. Elizabeth and Cecil both anticipated its use for that purpose but they were reassured that Hartlepool could not be held by a rebel force for more than three days. In any case, the haven would 'not receive any great ship at full sea, and at low water all vessels lie upon dry ground; so as hardly can it serve for foreign power'.[21]

Some six months had passed since the plans for a rising were first aired. Inevitably, the delay led to leaks and both Elizabeth and Cecil independently got wind of Norfolk's intended marriage. Though Cecil was dubious about it rather than hostile, he was quite certain (as, indeed, was everyone else) that Elizabeth's prior approval had to be sought. But Norfolk was too frightened to broach the matter with her and he passed up several opportunities of doing so during the summer. All the while, the conspirators kept in touch with him in an endeavour to bolster his courage; Lumley and Leslie called on him at Howard House on 22 September (the latter bringing Norfolk a ring as a token from Mary[22]) but to little effect, for the next night he fled to his country house at Kenninghall in a funk. His fellow-conspirators, however, took his precipitate departure from London as the signal for their plans to be put into effect. Elizabeth, too, interpreted his move in the same way. She peremptorily forbade the marriage, recalled Norfolk to court, and ordered immediate military dispositions to repel an invasion. The fleet put to sea, coastal defences were strengthened and the county musters were authorised. Having realised the peril he was in, Norfolk craved the royal pardon on 24 September and sent a frantic message to prevent the northern earls taking to arms. A wave of arrests took place the following day and several Italians and Spaniards were taken up; Ridolfi was given into Walsingham's custody. Norfolk was recalled to court and was committed to the Tower on 11 October. Arundel, Lumley, Pembroke, Leslie, Sir Nicholas Throckmorton and Matthew Arundell were also summoned to Windsor and placed under guard to await interrogation. Arundel was confined firstly in Arundel House and then at Nonsuch with Lumley 'so none could have access to them for conference touching their affairs'.[23]

Philip thought that Lumley and the others would break under questioning but they did not. Arundel flatly denied having anything to do with the conspiracy or that he had discussed the marriage with Lumley.[24] Lumley was brought to London and interrogated three times. On 29 September and 11 October he denied assenting to the marriage between Mary and Norfolk despite having discussed it with many people because he knew that Elizabeth would have had to be consulted first. He had seen letters from Mary to Arundel but he did not know what they contained. He had received two letters of 'commendations and acknowledgements of good will' from her. He had not advised Norfolk to leave court. His only contact with the Spanish Ambassador was the courtesy call he had made when 'coming one evening from Greenwich with his wife and Lady Dacres'. He knew nothing of a plan to take the Tower. Elizabeth was dissatisfied with his answers and on 21 October further questions were put to him about the marriage and the debt but his replies are not recorded. On 30 October Lumley assured the queen of his good behaviour and asked to be allowed to return to his wife at Nonsuch.[25]

With the principal conspirators in the south safely neutralised, attention shifted to those in the north, particularly to the earls of Northumberland and Westmorland. On 9 October they assured the Earl of Sussex (President of the Council of the North) that not only had they no intention of rising but that they would suppress any disorder should it break out. They declined, however, to attend on the queen at Windsor because they feared for their lives. Sussex submitted that they harboured no evil intent and would keep their word. Yet the earls regularly conferred with their friends and relations, all known to be dissidents. They prepared their tenants and servants for action, they bought up all the weapons they could, and they rode menacingly about the county in armour. A month would pass before Sussex accepted that there was more to their belligerence than the preservation of civil order or self-defence. On Thursday 10 November intelligence was gained that on or about the following Sunday the earls would make a public appeal to gauge the support for a return to the old religion so as to

> prove if this will move the multitude to follow them, and if it will not, they have a ship ready to pass away; but this is a report delivered upon great uncertainty. Another is that without doing of evil they will [go] into Northumberland and lie at Alnwick or, as some say, at [Holy] Island and this is much spoken.[26]

Sussex now had no doubt that rebellion was intended and the queen's officers throughout the north were instructed to quell any disturbance and to take appropriate defensive measures.

The rising broke out at four o'clock on Monday afternoon 14 November when the earls, the Nortons, Nevilles and Markenfield, led sixty armed men into Durham Cathedral and 'defaced, rent and broke into pieces' the communion-table and books, and forbade the performance of any religious service. The Council of the North told the queen 'it appears directly they intend to make religion their ground'. Indeed the earls had said that 'their purposes and meanings are to reduce all the said causes in religion to the ancient customs and usages before used'.[27] They did not mention their intention to liberate Mary Stewart on which mission they presently set forth. On the evening of 16 November the rebel army (wearing red crosses) began their southward advance, proceeding from Richmond to Ripon, Wetherby,

Knaresborough, Tadcaster, Cawood and on to Selby where they halted on 24 November. Tutbury lay some seventy miles further to the south-west but Mary was moved to greater safety in Coventry the following day. The queen's army, already large but still gathering strength (ultimately it would number fourteen thousand men) was rapidly moving northward and it already stood between Mary and the earls.

The principal aim of the rising had been thwarted and there was nothing for it but to retire, but the earls did not give up. The main body of rebels laid siege to Barnard Castle. Then, on 29 November, to the great dismay of the authorities, Christopher Neville managed to garrison Hartlepool just before a small government detachment reached the town. It was reported that Neville intended to fortify it, expecting aid from King Philip, and that the rebels had 'ships there to make away by if they be strained by land'.[28] Northumberland, Cuthbert Neville and several priests went up to Durham to ensure that the religious element of the rising was not forgotten. For some two weeks from St Andrew's Day Catholic rites were practised; the priests said or (at 'Mr Neville's pleasure') sang Mass in the cathedral and conducted other services in Latin. The churchwardens of the city churches and other parish churches in the county were instructed to re-erect the old stone altars and to destroy the Protestant service-books.[29]

Although the earls had support in the north, it was dispersed and, it was soon noticed, the rebel force was 'confused, without order, armour or weapon'. Government forces, on the other hand, were concentrated, disciplined, and well able to deal with the rebels and were racing north 'to give them the overthrow'. The siege of Barnard Castle, the taking of the undefended port of Hartlepool, and the restoration of Catholicism in Durham were all very well, but a direct engagement between the rebels and the queen's forces could have only one outcome – defeat for the earls. It was clear that the aims of the rising could not be realised. The siege of Barnard Castle was lifted; Neville abandoned Hartlepool on 18 December; and the earls fled into Scotland with government troops in hot pursuit.[30]

Retribution followed immediately. Northumberland was betrayed and repatriated; he was tried and beheaded at York, but Anne, his countess, was protected by the Scottish Catholics until she got away to Flanders at the end of August 1570. She spent the remainder of her life subsisting on a small allowance from the Spanish king trying to engage the Catholic princes in Mary Stewart's cause but to no avail. She died at Namur in 1596. Her daughter Lady Mary Percy accompanied her into exile and founded a Benedictine convent in Brussels in 1598. Westmorland escaped to Flanders in the autumn of 1570 leaving his countess behind. As a Protestant she was exonerated by Elizabeth and allowed to retire to Kenninghall where she lived on an annuity of £300 from the queen. But, while she unceasingly sought her husband's rehabilitation, he countered her efforts by traipsing about the continent promoting the cause of the English Catholics. She died in 1593 in Norfolk; he died still in exile in 1601. His daughters were all convicted recusants. Leonard Dacre escaped abroad and he died in poverty at Brussels in 1579. The capture of the Nortons was eagerly sought by Elizabeth but Richard got away to Flanders with his sons Francis and Sampson. Of his remaining sons: five of the younger were not involved in the rising and were left at liberty; Christopher was hanged at Tyburn with his uncle Thomas; William, George and Marmaduke were imprisoned in the Tower but later released. Richard's seven daughters mostly married rebels and/or recusants.[31]

On 5 December Arundel wrote to the queen from Nonsuch as 'her Majesty's faithful subject and true prisoner' but neither he or Lumley was freed or permitted to return to court until the spring of 1570. Arundel was restored to the Council as a sop to the traditionalists though he counted for little. He even contemplated continuing the fight from France. In July, Norfolk was transferred from the Tower to house-arrest at the Charterhouse. Ridolfi, too, was released, nothing incriminating having been found in his house and having been able to persuade Walsingham that his dealings with Arundel, Lumley *et al* were all 'in the ordinary way of banking'.[32]

Despite having a wide-ranging set of religious and secular motives calculated to attract most sections of society, both elite and plebeian, the Northern Rising failed for a number of reasons. Poor leadership and indecisiveness were major shortcomings and, considering it had been so long in the minds of the leaders, the execution of the rising was irresolute: Norfolk's pusillanimity was particularly unfortunate. The absence of certain northern Catholic or Catholic-inclined peers was also important: Cumberland, Darcy, Derby, Shrewsbury and Wharton held aloof and the impression was given that the high command of the rebel army 'did not represent the whole party, or get effectively into touch with it'. The number of insurgents, which ultimately numbered four thousand foot and seventeen hundred horse, was therefore much smaller than expected. No support was evident in Lancashire. Of the Percy tenantry in Northumberland, only eighty to one hundred men joined, and they were mostly from Tynedale; the sixty men who turned out from Bywell were Neville tenants. The Yorkshire participants were mostly Norton and Percy tenants, and in Durham only the Salvins, Claxtons and Tempests came out in support. The Countess of Westmorland said that disagreements among themselves were also instrumental in their defeat. [33]There was the additional complication of personal enmity between Norfolk and Leonard Dacre. The duke's third duchess had died leaving him guardian of George, Lord Dacre, her son by her first marriage. When George died in May 1569 the duke laid claim to the vast Dacre estates, inherited by Dacre's three sisters, and, to the fury of their uncle, Leonard Dacre, Cecil, as Master of the Wards, adjudicated in Norfolk's favour. The duke went further by marrying the girls to his three sons and so the estates passed into the Howard family's inheritance.[34]

The conspiracy in London was thwarted at an early stage and, although Norfolk's tenants at Kenninghall declared themselves adherents, that was as far as it went. Then there was Alva's distrust of the English Catholics and his scepticism that they could actually see the rising through. The lack of international coordination was also disastrous, especially the delay of three months between the request for and the issue in February 1570 of a papal bull excommunicating Elizabeth.[35] The main significance of the failure of the rising was that it showed that the north was not so insubordinate as had been feared. The nobility and gentry found that the secular allegiances which had been called for in the Pilgrimage of 1536 had lost force and were waning steadily. Religious change had also ceased to be a major motivating factor for the majority of ordinary people – anyone aged under thirty-five years had never known politico-religious continuity and older people simply hedged their bets yet again.[36]

***

While strengthening the anti-Catholic penal laws, Elizabeth invited the Catholics to keep well clear of plots for the future and enjoy a quiet life, but neither their leaders, or Mary, abandoned their political ambitions. An inveterate plotter, Ridolfi took it for granted that many of the participants involved in the rising of the previous year would remain intransigent, and he presumably anticipated that the publication of the papal bull *Regnans in Excelsis* excommunicating the queen would reinvigorate them.[37] Certainly, both Arundel and Lumley maintained communications with him, and with de Spes, and the Bishop of Ross. At any rate, undaunted by recent setbacks, Ridolfi outlined a new scheme in a long, encyphered, letter to the Pope dated 1 September 1570 in which he envisaged a general uprising in Lancashire, Shropshire, Derbyshire and other counties. He was certain that the Catholic peers could raise an army of some 50,000 men: 12,000 in the north west, a similar figure in the south west, 6,000 in the midlands, and 15,000 elsewhere; the duke's contribution from eastern England was given only as 'many'.[38] Ridolfi was also confident that Arundel, Lumley and Montagu, the three peers whom he trusted most, 'would rise on the landing of the troops from abroad' and he proposed that an invasion force of ten thousand men under Alva's command, should land at Yarmouth, Leith or Harwich. Other Spanish forces should be sent in to divide and pin down Elizabeth's forces: 1,000 men to Scotland, 2,000 to Lancashire, and 3,000 through a port on the south coast.[39] The scale of these operations was wildly optimistic given that the collapse of the rising of the previous year had exposed the shortcomings of the English Catholic leaders, most of whom had proved wholly incompetent. In any case, the number of peers he expected to appear in arms was entirely conjectural. As well as that, Ridolfi had loaned a mere six thousand crowns (£1,800) to Arundel and Lumley, which was quite inadequate to finance such an ambitious military campaign. Norfolk's steward, Sir John Blennerhasset, remarked of Arundel and Lumley in July 1570 that 'There wanteth nothing but money, whereof they be greediest...'[40] In the event, the discovery of the plot meant that Ridolfi's absurd plans were never put to the test.

On 13 May 1571, encyphered letters being carried to Ross were seized by the English authorities and yielded the first intelligence of Ridolfi's plans. Confessions extracted from Mary's followers soon revealed further details and confirmed that the aims of the conspirators were essentially those which had motivated the rising in 1569. Arundel, Lumley and some others were taken up for questioning. Arundel was confined at Nonsuch and Lumley was put in the Tower.[41] Two of Ridolfi's letters addressed to 'Trenta' and 'Quaranta' were for Norfolk and Lumley.[42] But, as he had done the previous year, Lumley flatly denied everything. He had no knowledge of Mary's letters and was unaware that his servant was privy to her affairs. He had had no dealings with Ridolfi and knew nothing of any codes. He had been passed a letter, partly in Italian and partly in cypher which he did not understand and burned. He had, moreover, rebuked a servant for bringing it to him since it was not addressed to him and he had told the man not to do it again. He had not been involved in any plan for Mary's liberation. His only communications with Norfolk were on personal business. This all flew in the face of the evidence. Even Norfolk admitted that he had made Arundel privy to the marriage plan and 'my brother Lumley from time to time how we proceeded'. Ross too would shortly confirm everything: the planned invasion, the papal subventions, the contents of Ridolfi's letter to Lumley and his discussions with Norfolk.[43]

Furthermore, Lumley was clearly involved in one of the plans formulated for Mary's escape should she be freed, though he denied all knowledge of it. It was intended to convey Mary 'to a castle of Lord Lumley's in Yorkshire, and thence as might be determined'.[44] This was Kilton Castle, between Saltburn and Loftus on the coast of the North Riding, which had belonged to the Lumley family since the fourteenth century. This mid-twelfth century castle stood on a high, narrow promontory projecting into a ravine formed by the Kilton Beck which drained into the North Sea at the secluded inlet of Skinningrove a mile and a half away. Hartlepool lay a few sea-miles to the north. The castle was approachable only from the west along a thin neck of land defended by a series of ditches and palisades. On all other sides the ground fell away steeply into the valley gorge and the far side of the ravine facing the castle was outside the then effective range of artillery. Though small, this well-nigh impregnable castle was at one time 'the most powerful baronial fortress in Cleveland'. It would certainly have been a secure refuge and, since it was located so close to the coast, Mary would be well placed there to embark in a Spanish ship for her return to Scotland or for her evacuation to the Spanish Netherlands if that became necessary. Its proximity to Hartlepool needs no emphasis.[45] As it was, of course, the Ridolfi Plot was nullified before any escape plan could be activated.

In May 1571 Pope Pius V expressed his gratification for the zeal shown by Arundel, Derby, Lumley, Montagu and Windsor in the cause of the Catholic faith, but its prospects, like Mary's, were not auspicious. Throughout the Elizabethan period the nobility and gentry would protect and harbour priests coming in from the continent armed with all the accoutrements of Catholic devotion but neither side fully recognised that adherence to the old faith and feudal loyalties were in irreversible decline. The discovery of the Ridolfi plot put paid to the marital ambitions of the Queen of Scots, and the execution of Norfolk for high treason in June 1572 at Tower Hill brought to an end the political crisis which had begun in 1568. The external threat to Elizabeth had been defied and the internal opposition effectively eliminated.[46]

***

Arundel was released just before Christmas 1572 and was brought back onto the Council. It was even thought he would be restored to the Stewardship but he was not; and both he and Lumley were removed from the lieutenancy of Surrey and Sussex.[47] If Arundel ever thought of himself as the leader of the English Catholics, he must have relinquished the idea at this point and Lumley was neither inclined or influential enough to take his place. Arundel and Lumley made their peace with Elizabeth but she never again admitted them into her full confidence though they came into close regular contact. Nonsuch was one of the queen's favourite palaces; she first went there in 1559 and she visited it almost every year up to 1567 and again after 1573. It has been suggested that the Grove of Diana in the gardens of the palace was created for her by Lumley in the mid-1570s as an expression of remorse for his disloyalty. The concept derived from the story of Diana and Actaeon in Ovid and Italian examples were used for the layout of the grove of shrubs and trees, and for the statuary which illustrated the myth. A small stone temple and an arch were inscribed with cautionary Latin verses and a representation of a pelican. The whole was intended to signify both Lumley's repentance and his gratitude for being spared the fate of Actaeon by the Huntress-Goddess Diana-Elizabeth.[48] Arundel is not mentioned as a participant in this undertaking although he owned the palace and was, presumably, equally contrite. The project may not have had his unstinting support, of course, for it was an expensive business and he already had many debts and by this point he had wearied of court life and, insofar as he could, he wanted to live out his days in seclusion.

Arundel went to his grave on 24 February 1580 and was buried in the Fitzalan Chapel of Arundel Castle. In 1596 Lumley erected memorials to him and to the two previous earls (Thomas, d. 1524 and William, d. 1544) in the style of a mediaeval chantry. Lumley also composed the long biographical notice inscribed on the monument. The memorial is incomplete, however, for the inscription concludes with the statement that, as his last funerary duty, he had erected 'this equestrian statue'. The memorial at Cheam to Lumley's first wife, Jane Fitzalan (who died in 1577) was surmounted with a mural tablet depicting the 'Arundel Horse' – a prancing white steed. It was probably Lumley's intention to have the tablet reproduced at Arundel Castle, but it was never made.[49] The earldom passed to Philip Howard, son of the fourth Duke of Norfolk, Arundel's son in law and Lumley (who had been Arundel's sole executor and residuary legatee by the will of 30 December 1579) conveyed the castle and honour of Arundel to him on the payment of an annuity of some £275.[50]

Since Ridolfi's plot was discovered before anyone could take to arms, Lumley could not be accused of treason but there were firm grounds for him to be 'endyted of misprision of treason, and ... tryed by his peirs'. In June 1572 he was convicted and fined £1,000. Lumley had to suffer other consequences of his actions before he could recover his rightful place in society. He had been summoned to attend the House of Lords at the opening of parliament in 1571 (the first to be called since 1567) but he did not attend after 21 April. Following his arrest in October and incarceration in the Marshalsea he was omitted from the *Journals of the House* as an eligible peer. He was not rehabilitated until his release from custody in February 1573.[51] It has been remarked that

> disenchantment with honour, fame and nobility belong to a period in his life when, after a decade of futile involvement in the aristocratic oppositionism of the fourth duke of Norfolk and the northern earls, he turned to conformity and obedience, becoming a prop of the regnum Cecilianum.[52]

That is largely true; the *Journals of the House of Lords* show that he was summoned to attend every session of parliament for the rest of his life and he attended from 1575 to 1607. But there was no place for him in Elizabeth's councils. His duties in the House were routine and he was never again as close to political power as he had been in earlier days. He was now aged forty and he fully appreciated that times had changed. His erstwhile colleagues Pembroke, Northampton, Winchester, Derby and Cumberland had all died in the early 1570s, and the rate of attrition would continue. The new Protestant peerage was rapidly displacing the old Catholic nobility.

In some quarters, however, Lumley was still thought of as a likely participant in Catholic political intrigue but he took no part in the Throckmorton Plot of 1583 or in the Babington Plot three years later. In December 1585 Thomas Morgan told Mary, Queen of Scots, that he had approached Lumley on her behalf but to no avail. He suggested that if the honourable and courageous Lumley made 'an intelligence with you, I doute not but you will so entertayne him by letters, as he shall be incoraged by your letters to serve you'. In the following Spring Morgan sent Lumley 'an alphabet' (a cypher) and reminded Mary that Lumley 'may do some good offices towards Scotland'. In September Thomas Phelippes wrote a memorandum for Walsingham about the 'Plot against England' of 1585 in which he remarked that Lords Howard and Lumley had been suspect because they were Mary's 'old servants that have endured for her'. But there was nothing to fear because Lumley continued to ignore Morgan's approaches. In October 1586 Morgan again reported that he had written to 'my Lord Lumley verye earnestlye' but had not 'receaved answer from him and others to whome I wrote...'[53] Morgan was completely out of touch for by that point Lumley was in a wholly different position.

He was sixth in the list of barons on the Commission of October 1586 which came to a unanimous verdict at Fotheringhay on the guilt of Mary Stewart (though he was probably included involuntarily). He was also one of the judges in the trial of William Davison who issued Elizabeth's warrant for Mary's execution in 1587. Lumley said that Davison's breach of the royal trust was 'the most heinous offence against the Prince he [had] heard of for many years'.[54] In 1580 and 1584 Lumley was a Commissioner for the Muster in Chichester together with his fellow-Catholics Arundel and Viscount Montague and he nominated one of the M.P.s for Chichester in 1593.[55] Mary's demise provoked the Spanish but Lumley was not moved to break his truce with Elizabeth. In June 1588 all peers were summoned to attend on the queen and to state what military support they would provide to defend her person during the Armada crisis. Lumley furnished ten lances, thirty light horse, ten petronels and twenty footmen, which was about usual for one in his station. In August 1599 Lumley was included in the Privy Council's order to provide a troop of horse to attend on the queen.[56] In September that year Lumley was reported to be in the faction of the Earl of Essex but he was one of those who tried the earl in February 1601 and found him guilty.[57] After 1573, then, Lumley carried out the public duties which went with his peerage, some of which may have been distasteful to him, but he was really much more concerned about his personal affairs, particularly his financial problems and his social rehabilitation.

As Arundel's residuary legatee Lumley had inherited Nonsuch Palace and its contents (which were, of course, already his by the gift of 1566) and estates in Sussex as a reward for the 'great travaile and paines' taken on his behalf. Apart from Arundel Castle the principal property was Stansted Park near Rowlands Castle in Sussex. This early mediaeval castellated and turreted brick building of substantial proportions was rebuilt in 1480 for Thomas, Lord Maltravers. Stansted was used by subsequent lords Maltravers and as the dower house of their widows, and it would have been furnished and decorated as befitted a peer's residence. Stansted was included in the queen's progress at least twice, in 1587 and 1591.[58] Lumley, however, was left to discharge Arundel's debts and they both had longstanding and considerable liabilities. This was largely due to their taking on of two 'Florentine' debts with a combined value of £26,250 owed to Henry VIII in 1525 and 1546 by a consortium of Italian merchants. It is not known why they took this debt over but they must soon have regretted doing so, for, as might have been expected, the payment of interest, made through the London agent Leonardo Frescobaldi, was frequently in arrears and Arundel and Lumley had had to cede property to the value of £800 a year to the Lord Treasurer to ensure that the crown always got its annual payments: £11,000 was still owing at Arundel's death.

There was also the expenditure on the purchase, decoration and upkeep of Nonsuch, Arundel's year long visit to Italy, his courtship of Elizabeth and his expenses on the Scottish queen's behalf. But the situation was manageable so long as Arundel lived: in 1574 his expenditure exceeded his income of £3,819 by about £80; in 1577 the debit balance was a mere £17. Settlements were required at his death, however, and capital had to be repaid. Hence some lands were sold, although the remark that Lumley's inheritance 'was sold up to pay off the enormous debts of his father in law' is wrong. Lumley estimated that the value of Arundel's residual estate was reduced to no more than £1,900 a year and that he would have only £400 a year to live on, and even that depended on the queen not calling in the Florentine debt but allowing it to continue for thirteen years. In any case, she had to be asked to forego the next instalment of interest payments until his more pressing commitments were discharged.[59]

A cynic might connect Lumley's search for a new wife (Jane, his first wife, died in 1577) to his parlous financial condition. In 1578 Sir Richard Cholmoley arranged for his daughter Mary to marry Lumley and paid £1,000 as part of her portion. On her wedding day she begged her father to cancel the marriage saying that she would rather die than marry someone she could never love and he agreed (though it is unclear whether the dowry was recovered). Lumley had to sell his estate at Thwing to Sir Thomas Heneage in 1579. At last, in 1582, Lumley married Elizabeth, sister of Thomas, Lord Darcy of Chiche (1565-1640) and he immediately settled the Nonsuch estate on her.[60] Lumley's financial position was transformed. In 1582 he paid £5,350 for the northern estates of the impoverished third earl of Cumberland which included the manors of Hart and Hartlepool in County Durham which soon began to yield substantial revenue. In 1585 a report circulated that Lumley's state was 'repayred sithence the death of his father in law' and, in the circumstances, this was a highly satisfactory outcome. Notwithstanding the improvement in his fortunes, however, Lumley had one other financial problem.[61]

The Florentine debt to the queen was still outstanding in 1590 and Lumley was in arrears.[62] Unlike many peers of the period he did not have to build a new mansion but he had four substantial houses to maintain: Nonsuch Palace, Lumley Castle, Stansted Park and the house on Tower Hill (and there were other smaller properties, including a house at Greenwich which was used when the court moved to Greenwich Palace). Lumley therefore ordered an inventory to be taken of the contents of his residences. It immediately became obvious that the value of his possessions was insufficient for his needs and he concluded that he would be unable to maintain all his properties while at the same time keeping up the annual debt repayment of £600 to the queen. The largest drain on his resources was Nonsuch Palace. The queen continued to visit it almost every year and it was also used from time to time by the Privy Council and for diplomatic purposes. His house on Tower Hill was used for an Anglo-Dutch diplomatic conference on the status of Flushing in July 1585 and the resulting Treaty of Nonsuch was signed at the palace the following month.[63] Lumley could hardly call the palace home, and he therefore offered to surrender it to Elizabeth in lieu of his debts to her, which, he emphasised, at the way things were going would take a further nineteen years to clear. Negotiations were successfully concluded in January 1592 and he ceded the palace to the crown though he remained Keeper for which he received a yearly allowance of £300. Stansted became Lady Lumley's dower in lieu of Nonsuch.[64] He was his own master at last and he could now devote himself to those cultural pursuits he had long enjoyed but from which he had so often been distracted in the past.

Chapter Three

'A Complete Pattern of Nobility'

Catholics out of favour at court generally kept to their estates and developed private interests. Sir Thomas Tresham turned to architecture, and the Kytsons to music.[1] At his withdrawal from active politics in 1573 Lumley rejoined Arundel at Nonsuch and became fully absorbed in the library and picture collection which had been growing apace since Arundel acquired the palace almost twenty years earlier. Those pursuits continued to engage Lumley after Arundel's death in 1580 and he would devote himself to them for the rest of his life. As well as his principal interests in art and bibliography Lumley cultivated an interest in many other scholarly subjects: genealogy, history, geography, cosmography, music and medicine. In 1586 William Camden described Lumley as 'a person of entire virtue, integrity and innocence, and now in his old age a complete pattern of nobility'.[2] In those terms, Camden, himself an erudite antiquary and historian, commended Lumley as a practitioner of true nobility as defined by Castiglione and Elyot (and later by Peacham) – the gentleman occupied in 'learned pleasure and delight'. Lumley's cultural and religious life will therefore occupy the remaining pages of this study.

Lumley was the sole surviving peer and the leading lay magnate in County Durham after 1569 and although he had to spend much of his time in the south he began to restore and refurbish Lumley Castle, a project which was expedited after his second marriage in 1582. There were several reasons for doing so. He wanted to create a comfortable, dry and draught-free residence (the principal rooms were on the first floor) now that the castle had no military function. But Lumley had a more immediate purpose. He had been devoting greater attention to his distinguished ancestry, and the renovation of his patrimonial home gave him the opportunity to display it more conspicuously than had been done hitherto. Pride of ancestry and a related interest in genealogy, heraldry and antiquarianism was a particularly marked feature of the period. It has been dismissed as something of 'a quasi-intellectual hobby for the idle rich'[3] but there was much more to it than that. The dissolution of the monasteries and the wanton destruction of monastic libraries engendered in the post-Reformation generations an acute sense of historical loss and uncertainty which they now sought to recover. One aspect of this was the highly pertinent debate between Catholic and Protestant divines about whether the English church had Saxon origins and hence whether papal supremacy or the royal prerogative properly held sway. The argument was paralleled among the old nobility and gentry who were determined to trace their pedigrees to the pre-Conquest age and thus prove an enduring connection with their native localities and their ancestral burial sites. As a result, many of the surviving mediaeval parish churches and Elizabethan mansions of England have extensive displays of armorial stone-carving and glass. The Great Chamber of Gilling Castle is a veritable monument to genealogy and heraldry. In addition to a painted frieze displaying the armorials of Yorkshire, the windows boldly proclaim the heraldic history of the Fairfax, Stapleton and Constable families in forty-five separate fine stained-glass panels, begun in 1585 by Baernard Dininckhoff, a glass-painter of York. The sixteenth-century east window of St Michael's church in Baddesley Clinton represents Sir Edward Ferrers, his wife and sons, and one of the achievements has thirty-two quarterings; the windows in Baddesley Clinton Hall were similarly designed.[4] These would have left no-one in any doubt as to the social and territorial importance of the local gentry. Catholic gentlemen derived the additional satisfaction of demonstrating that however marginalised or persecuted they were at present, their claims to antiquity could not be taken from them and that they might well come into their own again. The old families also wanted to distinguish themselves from the *nouveaux riches* who had profited under the new order and who were contriving to establish a respectable lineage. Inevitably, however, in many of the latter cases, the compilation of family trees was more creative than accurate. William Cecil, later Lord Burghley, took great pains to establish a long pedigree but could get no further back than his grandfather; he nonetheless converted his modest Monmouth family of *Sitsilt* into a branch of the Roman *Caecilii*, to the great merriment of many according to Aubrey. Henry Ferrers remarked in 1590 that since the reign of Henry VII, aided and abetted by 'heralds who have been without skill', coats of arms 'have corruptly been used by gentlemen that have risen since that time being very near the one half of the gentlemen of England at this day'. But, Ferrers was pleased to say, 'ill coats borne at this day which being discovered upon better skill are every day amended'. [5] This was due largely to the reconstitution of the College of Arms in 1555 which encouraged families to base their family histories and arms on firmly-based evidence.

The courtyard, Lumley Castle (from a Victorian print)

Genealogical discipline was further enhanced by the publication in 1586 of the first printed historical description of Britain (as distinct from a chronicle): *Britannia* by William Camden who later became Clarenciux King of Arms. Lumley has been derided for his obsession with his lineage, but he was not exceptional, and he was probably not even the most brash of the large number of contemporary peers and gentlemen who were deeply interested in their ancestry.

The family's pedigree was proclaimed immediately to everyone arriving at Lumley Castle. On the east wall above the main gateway were, and still are, six 'auncient scutchions with their crests ... cutt in hard stone'. In the centre and above the others are the arms of Richard II, quartering those of France and England. Below on each side are the arms of Percy (with a crest of a lion passant), Neville (a bull's head), Cowley (a ram's head), and Hilton (a head of Moses), and at the bottom centre are the arms of Lumley adapted from the old Thweng arms. (A comparable display could be seen at Hylton Castle, home of the Hilton family, a few miles east of Lumley.) Passing into the courtyard the visitor would see on the opposite wall eighteen 'great scutchions of whyte marble, having the Armes ingraven of my Lords Auncestors inhabiting there since the Conquest' which showed how the family's arms had quartered over the generations in matrimonial alliances, culminating in Fitzalan and Darcy. Lumley remodelled the courtyard elevations of the castle and several dates are carved into the walls of the castle; a stone in the tower is inscribed *I L 1570.*[6] The *nouveaux riches* were not unique in their heraldic invention, however, for the earliest of these armorials were devised conjecturally and pre-dated by a century the first known use of heraldic arms in the tournaments of the twelfth century. (Liulph died in 1080.) William Segar, who painted Lumley's ancestors, may well have supervised the carving of these coats of arms.

In the centre of the courtyard there stood

> a Condeth [conduit] of 17 foote high with two bolls of whyte marble, standing upon foure great pillers of whyte marble contayining my Lords's Armes and my Ladie Elsabeths, his second wife.

After 1592, the visitor would see the garden ornaments, columns, fountains and an obelisk decorated with the Lumley armorial popinjays, which were removed from Nonsuch. (They presumably date from the 1580s after he inherited the palace.)

In addition to the display of his lineage in the external fabric of the castle, Lumley continued the theme in its internal decoration, as we shall see, but he also felt the need for a more accessible setting in which the past glories of his family might be displayed for the edification of the wider public. Conveniently, Elizabeth's settlement of religion in the late 1550s, which brought the iconoclasm of the immediate post-reformation years to an end, created the need for a new iconography in tomb-sculpture to replace the pious monuments of earlier times which were regarded as idolatrous and were no longer made. Aware that sepulchral memorials can be powerful statements of pedigree and social prestige, Lumley appropriated large parts of the two parish churches with which he was associated to imprint his lineage on the local communities but in the new, approved secularised fashion. Fourteen recumbent effigies purporting to be Lumley's ancestors, 'carved in stone, resting on as many altar-tombs, like the Sultans in Caliph Vathek', occupy the whole length of the north aisle in St. Mary and St. Cuthbert, the parish church of Chester le Street. (Liulph is at the west end and John, fourth baron, is nearest the chancel; Lumley added a long inscription giving their history). To get them all in Lumley had to cut them off at the knee and place some in double file. Perhaps only the Crusader is a genuine Lumley for the others, as Camden observed, were 'either gotten together out of monasteries that were subverted or caused to be made anew'. Bishop Tobie Matthew allowed Lumley to remove from the precincts of Durham Cathedral in 1594 two effigies in barrel helms (Ralph and John) of the early fourteenth century, carved from the local Frosterley marble, because their shields depicted what he thought were three popinjays. They are actually memorials to Sir John and Sir Richard Fitzmarmaduke of Hordern Hall who included three parakeets in their arms (a mistake made by later genealogists). A monument to Sir Thomas, which lay

> broken and wasted nere the ruynes of the chappell in the first ward within the castel called Barnard's castel, was at the honourable means and motion of John baron Lumley, sent by Sir William Bowes, knight, into this church at Chester ... April 1594.

The Lumley 'warriors', St Mary & Cuthbert, Chester le Street

The rest were made to order by Lumley but the reproduction of the dress and armour of earlier ages is unconvincing. George Lumley (executed in 1536) is represented only by a wall-plaque yet he was an undoubted warrior. The incumbent of St Cuthbert's was paid 6/8d. and the clerk 13/4d. a year 'to sweep and rubb' the monuments to keep them 'fair and beautiful'. Pevsner interpreted the project as 'an extremely interesting case of early, self-conscious medievalism' whereas it was an extension of Lumley's ancestor-worship under the Elizabethan dispensation, which is not quite the same thing.[7]

The family's ancestral parish church was in Chester le Street. Until the Reformation it had two chantries, one dedicated to St Mary, the other to St George who was a patron saint of the Lumley family. There is no evidence that Lumley had any particular devotion to St Cuthbert, the most famous and best-loved of the northern saints, whose body was enshrined in the church for a century after 883AD before it was moved to Durham. Lumley chose instead to use St Dunstan, Cheam, for the burial of himself and his immediate family, doubtless because of its close proximity to Nonsuch Palace which he had every reason to expect would continue as a royal residence into perpetuity. The rector, Anthony Watson, Durham-born and a Cambridge graduate, was a protégé of Lumley's by whom he was presented to his two parochial living: the rectorships of Cheam (1581) and Storrington (1592). Watson also became Dean of Bristol (1590) and Chancellor of Wells (1592). Again enjoying

Lumley's recommendation, he became Bishop of Chichester in 1596, in which capacity he died, unmarried, in 1605. He was buried at Cheam, the rectory he had held for twenty-four years. In 1582 Lumley began the conversion of the chancel of the twelfth-century church at Cheam into a sepulchral chapel. The church was demolished in 1864, leaving this chapel (measuring twenty-seven by twenty feet) to stand alone in the churchyard about fifteen feet from the new church.[8]

Lumley replaced the old wooden ceiling with a 'delightful' barrel-vaulted plaster ceiling and frieze (one of the pendentives incorporates the date 1592) and installed a larger east window, of late Perpendicular style, which was removed from some other church. The chief features of the chancel were memorials, commissioned by Lumley, to his wives, children and himself.[9] The designs for the memorials appear in the 1590 inventory, and the finished monuments (thought to be the work of an Italian craftsman) follow them closely, but not exactly; and they comply with approved post-Reformation secularised iconography that no image could be taken as idolatrous. The first, on the south wall, commemorates Lady Jane Lumley who died in March 1577 and her three children who 'hardly indeed saw the light'. According to one authority, 'the bodies of Jane and her three children are not interred in the massive table tomb to which the 'Nonsuch' panels are affixed'. Another suggests that their bodies were first buried elsewhere, perhaps in the churchyard, and moved into the chancel after the vault was constructed. [10] The memorial takes the form of a table-tomb, measuring some eight and a half by four and a quarter feet, with classical architectural features. The slab is of black marble and the front lower section consists of alabaster bas-relief panels showing the figures of the infant children kneeling in a room which, if it represents Nonsuch Palace, is its only known interior view. The panels at each end have the arms of Lumley impaled with those of Arundel. Fixed to the wall and resting on the table is a bas-relief alabaster effigy of Lady Jane; she is shown in side-view kneeling on a cushion with cap, ruff and a pomander.

Above the effigy occur the frets of Maltravers and, between two popinjays, an oval onyx marble picturing St. George and the dragon. Surmounting the whole is a plaque with a bas-relief 'Arundel Horse' with a sprig of oak in its mouth. The carved figures of this beautiful monument are finely executed and the memorial has been described as one of the most noteworthy historical artefacts in Surrey. Other than that the figures are portrayed kneeling, however, nothing else in the monument has a Catholic, let alone a Christian reference.

Monument to Jane, Lady Lumley, in the Lumley chapel of St Dunstan's, Cheam

The other two memorials, though impressive and well-executed, are more restrained. Lumley's own memorial on the north wall, which he designed and which may well have been erected in advance of his demise, is a large rectangular wall-monument with marble columns, pilasters and a pediment of classical design. At the centre is a large panel of red-veined marble on which there is a long Latin inscription, of his own composition, tracing his pedigree back through the generations to Liulph. On each side of the inscription there are eight shields of the Lumley arms impaling those of the wives of his respective predecessors.

Monuments to Lord Lumley and Elizabeth, his second wife, in the Lumley Chapel, St Dunstan's, Cheam

Below the inscription are the arms of Lumley himself, and those of his wives and two popinjays. The memorial is surmounted with yet another shield of the Lumley arms. Elizabeth, Lumley's second wife died in 1616; she had asked 'to be buried near the bodye of my late deare husband in the Tombe there prepared already for me ...' Her memorial is alongside Lumley's and directly opposite Lady Jane's. Two short, thick marble columns support the horizontal slab of the deeply recessed tomb on which is placed her life-sized recumbent marble effigy which resembles that of Mary, Queen of Scots in Westminster Abbey and was possibly carved by the same hands, Cornelius and William Cure. (William Cure was working at Nonsuch in the 1540s and his son was there in 1616.)[11] The Lumley arms are displayed at one end of the recess and the arms of Darcy are at the other. A panel above the tomb bears the Lumley motto *Murus aeneus conscientia sana* (An easy conscience is a wall of brass). The soffit in marble is decorated with popinjays and cinquefoils. The memorial is bounded by two classical columns supporting a pediment on which stand two obelisks and an oval shield with the Lumley coat of arms impaled with the arms of Darcy. These monuments are undoubtedly impressive, but they are certainly not Christian; they are entirely secular objects and commemorative only of genealogical status; their classical elements reinforce their non-religious, humanist, programme – they neither excite grief or compel prayer.

***

Lumley succeeded Arundel as High Steward of the University of Oxford in 1555 and he would hold that post for the unprecedented period of fifty years. His house on Tower Hill became known as a meeting-place for men of letters; Edmund Spenser who is thought to have been related in some way to the Lumleys is said to have been familiar with the house and its contents.[12] Lady Lumley was in the circle of Sir Nicholas Bacon and, 'at her desire' he sent her an elegant, illuminated vellum manuscript of a collection of classical sententiae (wise and witty maxims, mostly from Seneca's *Epistolae Morales*, edited by Erasmus in 1515 and 1529) which she had seen painted on the walls of the long gallery at Gorhambury, built between 1563-8.[13] Carved and painted texts on walls was central to the visual culture of the Elizabethans. Lumley's retirement from politics in 1572 may well have prompted his having verses painted on the walls at Lumley celebrating the transience of the world: 'Christ does not pass away; worship not that which passes away'.

Lumley and his brother-in-law Humphrey Lloyd became members of the Elizabethan Society of Antiquaries, which was founded in London around 1572. Members included most of the leading scholars and antiquaries of the day and they dined each Friday during the law terms to discuss a wide range of previously chosen topics. The Society flourished until around 1608, coincidentally the year in which Lumley ceased to attend both the House of Lords and the Society's meetings. In 1617 Henry Ferrers and others were included in a list of suitable members for an Academy Royal; James I showed some interest but it faded after his death in 1625. These are examples of the practice found throughout the recusant period of the toleration of well-connected and intellectual Catholics going along with a deeply-held suspicion of Catholicism and a hatred of Italy for its popery but admired as the birthplace of the Renaissance.[14]

Lumley was related to and in contact with a number of noble antiquaries including Henry Howard, Earl of Northampton (1539/40-1614) (younger brother of the fourth duke of Norfolk). Northampton was the most learned nobleman of his time and has been described as a brilliant scholar and 'a sinister bachelor don'. He was sympathetic to Catholicism and was suspected of conspiracy on behalf of Mary Queen of Scots and he remained under a cloud for many years.[15] Then there was Philip Howard, Earl of Arundel (father of Thomas, Earl of Arundel, the connoisseur), and his brother Lord William ('Belted Will') Howard of Naworth Castle (1563-1640) who married Elizabeth Dacre. Philip and William had been prisoners in the Tower along with Nicholas Roscarrock, a Cornish recusant and antiquary. At his release, Roscarrock went north to Naworth, which William had restored, where he could enjoy 'the security and peace for what was, next religion, nearest his heart: his antiquarian studies' in Howard's library, and there he passed the rest of his days. William excavated Roman sites in Cumberland and he rescued important mediaeval carved and painted ceilings from Kirkoswald Castle.[16] Like the Howards, many other Catholic gentlemen were antiquaries (the possession of old books and manuscripts was sometimes taken as evidence of popish tendencies) including Sampson Erdeswicke in Staffordshire, Henry Ferrers in Warwickshire, Thomas Habington in Worcestershire, Sir Thomas Shirley in Leicestershire and William Claxton of Wynyard in Durham, an erstwhile follower of the Earl of Westmorland. Claxton, one of the earliest Durham antiquaries, collected materials for a history of Durham in the 1570s; he gave assistance and hospitality to the heralds when they made their visitation of the county in 1575.[17]

***

> If Ptolemy could come back to life, he would die again of envy when he saw this library, with its books on the arts, philosophy, jurisprudence, medicine, mathematics, theology, history, and spheres, globes, bronze and paper instruments of all kinds.[18]

Thus did Anthony Watson marvel at the contents of the library at Nonsuch in 1582. The nucleus of the library was Arundel's collection of some four hundred volumes. He seems to have had a possessive rather than an intellectual taste for books; he liked fine bindings, some of which he stamped with his arms, but he had little scholarly use for around fifty manuscripts which he acquired after the dissolution of the monasteries when 'manuscripts flew about like butterflies'. His favourite volumes were those on military topics, reflecting his soldiering days under Henry VIII, and historical works, reflecting the antiquarianism he shared with Lumley. As might be expected of any gentleman, he also had a large number of the classics, but they were unread by him and used only by the tutor to educate the children.

In 1553 Archbishop Cranmer was attainted and deprived, and his property was confiscated by the crown. Much of the furniture and furnishings were sold (the Arundels and Lumleys were prominent among the purchasers) but the books were kept for incorporation into the royal library and Queen Mary had them moved from Cranmer's archiepiscopal residence at Croydon in Surrey to Nonsuch, the most conveniently located royal residence. When Arundel bought the palace from the queen three years later he accepted Cranmer's books with it.[19] Cranmer had owned some five hundred printed works, which he had collected himself, and around one hundred manuscripts which he had acquired at the dissolution. It was a working library comprising mostly of heavily annotated and worn volumes on theology and religious controversy in English, Latin, Greek or Hebrew. It can have had little interest for the Catholic Arundel but Lumley probably encouraged him to retain it, pointing out that it had considerable intrinsic and historical significance and that it would be appropriate to keep Cranmer's books together. Moreover, it would complement and, indeed, double the number of volumes in his own collection. Arundel took the advice but he marked only ten of Cranmer's more desirable and finely bound items as his personal property, allowing Lumley to have most of the rest; a few volumes were given to his librarian Humphrey Lloyd.

By the time of Arundel's death in 1579 the library at Nonsuch numbered close to one thousand printed books and one hundred and fifty manuscripts, and was second only in size to that of Sir Robert Cotton. Already widely known as 'right worthye of remembrance', it would grow further and become increasingly important in later years. Lumley had the library catalogued in 1596 at Nonsuch by Anthony Alcock, a member of the household of Anthony Watson, Bishop of

Chichester.[20] An endorsement of the catalogue indicates that some books, mainly duplicates, had been 'dysparsed sundery ways'. Some went to individual friends and acquaintances (including five which were given to Prince Henry) but most were donated to the universities.[21] It is said that there was 'a struggle' between the two universities over the library around 1585, and certainly both could make a cogent appeal to Lumley's benevolence: he had matriculated at Cambridge, and he was High Steward at Oxford. On 24 August 1587 in response to a request from the Vice-Chancellor and the heads of colleges in Cambridge, delivered in person by the Archbishop of Canterbury, Lumley wrote:

> My purpose is to confer the cataloge of your bookes with myne, and the Authors which I find duble and be wantynge in your Librarye, I promise shalbe yours.

In the event, he donated eighty-nine of his Greek and Latin books to Cambridge in 1598, many of which had been Cranmer's. The following year he gave thirty-four volumes to Oxford University. There is some circumstantial evidence that he also gave twenty-five books to the newly-founded (1584) Emmanuel College at Cambridge.[22]

At his death in 1609 'there was no library in England better equipped than Lumley's for the study of any of the sciences'. It comprised some four hundred manuscripts and three thousand printed works (in 2,800 volumes) divided into seven classes: arts and philosophy, theology, history and genealogy, medicine, cosmography and geography, canon and civil law, and music. Since some of the catalogue entries refer to volumes containing two or more printed works or manuscripts bound together (especially in the music section), the size of the library *by title* was considerably larger and it has been calculated that Lumley's collection comprised 3,600 books and manuscripts.[23] That compared with 2,600 items belonging to Dr John Dee, the celebrated Elizabethan magus, 6,000 shared by Archbishops Whitgift and Bancroft and 1,800 owned by Dr John Rainolds of Oxford. Only 12% of the library was in any vernacular language, including English; the rest was mostly in Latin though there were volumes in Greek or Hebrew. This reflected the general scholarly attitude of the day that Latin was the principal cultural medium. Lumley was well known for his 'incredible' love of books but it is somewhat surprising that so few were dedicated to him.[24] An almanack of 1567, Edward Fenton's *Certaine Secret Wonders of Nature* of 1569 and

Thomas Hood's two volumes of 1590: *The use of the celestial globe* and *The use of two mathematicall instruments* are the only ones listed, which does not seem very many for so well-known a bibliophile.

In order to explain the acquisition of the library by Prince Henry (1594-1612), it has been claimed that Lumley was a tutor to Prince Henry and that he either sold or bequeathed the library to King James I for the prince, but no substantiating evidence has been cited. There is no record of a sale and Nonsuch had been ceded to the crown many years before either of the two versions of Lumley's will were written early in 1606.[25] It is known that Henry was vehemently anti-Catholic and it is highly unlikely that a sixty-five-year-old Catholic with a history of rebellion would be engaged as a tutor to the heir-apparent. (The presence in the prince's household of Lumley's great-nephew Thomas Howard, fourteenth Earl of Arundel (1585-1646) is irrelevant; although Arundel came from within the old Catholic cousinage, his religious affiliations were deliberately kept unclear in these years. The ambiguity was not cleared up during Prince Henry's lifetime because Arundel was not received into the Church of England until 1615.) In any case, until his father's accession to the English crown in 1603 Henry lived in Stirling Castle where his education had begun under Adam Newton. Although a 'courtly college' was then established at Nonsuch for the young prince and the sons of peers, that was a temporary arrangement, for the prince's household was established in the palace of Oatlands, near Weybridge, where his education continued under Newton.[26]

The actual circumstances arise from the shared interest of Lumley and Prince Henry in Nonsuch. As Keeper of the Palace and lessee of the Great Park (succeeding in 1599 to have the rent remitted for the remaining fourteen years of the lease) Lumley was responsible for preparing the house and grounds for royal and official visits. King James first visited in 1603 and he went there frequently in the following years with his sons Henry and Charles (born in 1600) to hunt and to escape the formalities of the capital; the king spent some £5,600 on the palace during his reign. Lumley considered the library to be an integral feature of the house and he left it there when the palace was surrendered in 1592. He took it for granted that the books would be kept together and *in situ* and this would have been clearly understood by Queen Elizabeth and later by King James. Prince Henry would certainly have used the library when visiting the palace even though he was not a particularly bookish youth. In 1607 the Venetian Ambassador wrote that, 'He studies, not with much delight and chiefly after his father's spur, not of his own desire...'[27] Presently, however, the king settled the estate on the queen, Anne of Denmark; she wanted to eject Lumley from the Great Park and in September 1605 he surrendered his leases in lieu of an annuity. (Privately, Salisbury accused Anne of 'loving no body but dead pictores in a paltry gallery'.[28]) It is highly probable that Lumley gave the library to Henry at the same time. In October 1609, six months after Lumley's death, an entry in Prince Henry's Privy Purse Account showed: 'To Mr Holcock for wreating a Catalogue of the Library whiche his highnes hade of my Lord Lumley, £8.13s.4d.'[29] The term 'hade of' is ambiguous and may, or may not, indicate that the library was a gift rather than a bequest, but it certainly makes clear that the library went directly to Henry and not through the king or queen for the prince. 'Holcock' is undoubtedly Anthony Alcock who compiled Lumley's earlier catalogue.

Prince Henry prized his acquisition and had a large number of Lumley's folios lavishly rebound during the years 1610-11 and it was at this point that he merged the library with that at St. James's Palace. The Venetian Antonio Correr remarked in a dispatch of 1611 that Henry was 'collecting books for a library he has built'.[30] Regrettably, however, not only was one of the greatest libraries of the Elizabethan age moved from what was intended to be its permanent home, it was almost immediately pruned and whole sections removed, especially from the legal and medical classes. It was cut back further when the Old Royal Library was moved to St. James's following Henry's death in 1612, and yet another weeding-out took place two years later. It has been estimated that as a result of the mergers and disposals by sale, gift or destruction of duplicates, the Lumley library was reduced to around two thousand volumes. The library to which Lumley had devoted himself for over fifty years ceased to be a distinct collection. Fortunately, however, a number of volumes survive in the Royal Library which was given by George III to the British Museum.[31]

***

Medicine was one of Lumley's interests, and his contribution to the subject endures. On 3 July 1582 the queen licensed Lumley and Dr Richard Caldwell to grant an annuity of £20 each to the College of

Physicians to endow an annual lecture on surgery. The recipient

> for his further and better knowledge in Surgerye shall travell into the partes of beyonde the Seas (that is to saye) into Frannce, Jermany and Italy and there shall remayne duringe the space of Twoe whole yeeres to thintent that he may there heare the best and most learned and experte Surgeons, reede and see theire practises, whereby he maye be the better able to execute the saide place of readinge in the saide Colledge of Phisicons in London at his retorne into Englande.

The first payment, made on 29 September 1584, was to Richard Forster. William Harvey expounded his theory of the circulation of the blood as the Lumleian lecturer in 1616.[32]

***

Lumley was greatly fond of music and his activity in the field was of some significance, not least because he lived during an important period of musical development. Since Arundel was Lord Chamberlain and responsible for entertainment at court he provided recreational and ceremonial music at Nonsuch and in London. The music at Nonsuch also had a therapeutic rôle, as Anthony Watson rather fancifully noted, though referring primarily to the large number of books on medicine and doctors:

> If you should fall into a fever, and are afflicted by hardships or made desperate by ill health, there is at hand either a throng of physicians ... or a chorus of musicians, who will alleviate grief and mitigate the frenzies of sickness.[33]

Such was the importance of musical life at the palace that the establishment for its provision was appropriately large. The choir came to rival that of the Chapel Royal and Arundel assembled one of the most impressive collections of musical instruments of the day. There were eight organs, five pairs of virginals, two royals, two Irish harps, eight lutes, ten howboyes, two bombards, four crumhorns, fifteen recorders, thirteen violins, forty-one viols, four sackbutts, and twelve cornets – a total of 126 musical instruments for use in many varied combinations. It does not seem, however, that either Arundel or Lumley themselves played an instrument. The catalogue of the music library at Nonsuch lists forty-five items but that figure conceals the actual size of the collection because scores were frequently bound together (as many as fourteen or fifteen in some instances) and the true total is over a hundred printed editions and at least nineteen manuscripts. Lumley would inherit and add to the library and make it the largest private music-library in England. These holdings were not just important for contemporary performance, they became fundamentally significant in later British music historiography for no other British library could have provided Charles Burney (1726-1814) with the primary source material he needed for his pioneering history of Renaissance music.[34]

Most scores were of European origin and most of the major continental printing-houses were represented. Arundel collected printed music and texts during his foreign travels. He was in Flanders during Mary's reign and the Netherlander Derick Gerarde gave him an autograph collection of motets, chansons and madrigals, and Gerarde may have joined the earl's household for a time. When Arundel was in Italy in 1566 he met Innocenzo Alberti at Ferrara and commissioned a set of five-part madrigals from him; the completed manuscript was despatched to England in 1568. Other items with Italian bindings of a slightly later date were probably sent to Nonsuch from Italy as presents for the earl. The collection included music in all genres: sacred and secular, solo and ensemble, song and dance, native and continental. The greatest contemporary composers were represented: the Italians, Palestrina, Donato and Gabrieli; the Flemings, Josquin, Willaert and Rore. The library had the first collection of chansons and motets by Orlando de Lassus to be printed in England (1570) which was dedicated to Arundel by the printer, the Huguenot refugee Thomas Vautrollier, whose printing-shop in the Blackfriars district had been established with Arundel's help in 1562. The earliest item was a Mass composed in 1503 and printed in Italy by Petrucci in 1516. Arundel, and Lumley after him, then, were central figures in the national musical life of the period. Nonsuch was an outpost of the Renaissance and a showcase of continental musical taste.[35]

It is striking, however, that fewer than twenty items in the music library at Nonsuch contain English compositions or have English connections, although the listing in the catalogue of 'A songe of fortie parts, made by Mr Tallys' could be the earliest reference to the motet

Spem in Alium by Thomas Tallis. Similarly, the presence of the first (1605) volume of William Byrd's *Gradualia* indicates that Lumley was fully aware of contemporary developments. Indeed, Lumley's connection with Byrd (1539/40-1623), the most prodigious musical talent of the age, was particularly important. Byrd's attachment to Catholicism became increasingly evident from the early 1570s and he had come to know Arundel and Lumley and gain access to the music library at Nonsuch, but he had also begun to associate with other musical recusant families. In February 1579 the Earl of Northumberland justified writing to Burghley on Byrd's behalf because 'he is my frend and cheffly that he is scolle master to my daughter in his artte…'[36] An inventory of Northumberland's house at Topcliffe in Yorkshire taken after the Rising of 1569 included

> one black chest with five vyolandes, one other with three vyolandes, one other with four vialles, one other with five vyalles, one other chest with a bandora, a pair of double virgynalles, a pair of single virgynalles, one sett of great recorders and one sett of cornettes.[37]

In 1580 Byrd's house was a known resort of Catholics; he was indicted as a recusant in 1584 and two years later he was moving in Jesuit circles. Sir John Arundell and his wife often appear with Byrd as recusants in the Middlesex gaol delivery rolls of the 1580s; they lived in Clerkenwell where Jesuits were discovered later in the decade. Byrd was often a guest of Sir John Petre at Ingatestone. In 1589 Byrd dedicated his *Liber primus sacrarum cantionum* (for five voices) to Edward, fourth earl of Worcester, whom the queen admired for having reconciled the irreconcilable: being 'a stiff papist' but a good subject.[38]

In 1591 Byrd dedicated his *Liber secundus sacrarum cantionum* to Lumley. In the dedication Byrd praised Lumley for his willingness to share his library, his 'most intense' love of the arts and sciences, and for his advice which was 'hardly mediocre in matters concerning music'.[39] The *cantiones* are of a somewhat sombre tone, the texts pleading for divine help in time of sorrow and trouble, and bewailing the fate of Jerusalem, the chosen city. It is widely accepted that these pieces refer obliquely to the condition of the English Catholic recusants and were intended for use by those who would understand the intended message, among whom, clearly, Lumley was counted. In 1594 Byrd moved to Essex and became increasingly intimate with the Catholic gentry families of the county. Byrd's two books of *Gradualia* (1605/7), intended for liturgical use, were dedicated to his friends Sir John Petre and Henry Howard, Earl of Northampton. Byrd is also heavily represented in the 'Fitzwilliam Virginal Book' which constitutes the largest and most valuable treasury of English keyboard music of the second half of the sixteenth century and was compiled by the Cornish recusant Francis Tregian, another of Lumley's intimates. Among the compositions are: 'Pavana and Galliarda of my Lord Lumley' by John Bull and 'Tower Hill' by Giles Farnaby.[40]

***

The remark that after the Ridolfi Plot was thwarted, Lumley 'was left more or less in peace at Nonsuch to practise his faith with all the pomp of the tridentine liturgy, even down to such details as six candles on the altar of his private chapel and with a choir to sing Masses specially written by Byrd...' is grossly exaggerated. [41] Lumley was not so indiscreet and, in any case, Byrd composed just three Masses, one each for three, four and five unaccompanied voices. It is, therefore, appropriate to deal with what little is known of his religious life. Most Catholic peers had chaplains in their households but before the arrival of the seminary priests in 1574 they would have been ordained in the Marian period and were usually left undisturbed by the authorities. Moreover, since they often undertook the secretarial work of their patron or tutored his children, their presence would have gone unremarked.

Apart from his Catholic political and social associations, however, no specific evidence of Lumley's religious practice is known in the first half of his life. The Catholics in Durham got along quite well without aristocratic leadership or support, for it was the gentry families who sustained the old faith. Bishop Matthew complained in the 1590s that the magistrates would take no action against the recusants for harbouring priests or saying Mass if they were chaplains to the gentry: 'I cannot reach to the height to enquire effectively into persons of that quality; only three laymen were put to death and none of them a gentleman'.[42] Lumley was well out of Matthew's reach. Whether Lumley financed a priest in the Chester le Street locality is not known. In the south he would have benefitted from the ministrations of Arundel's chaplain at Nonsuch as well as those of the 'old priest named Mr Leaver' who was living in Tower Street and who would have been known to Lumley and the other Catholics nearby. That Lumley sheltered under Arundel's wing in this, as in other ways, is clear from the fact that evidence of his religious activities only emerges after Arundel's death in 1580.[43]

Lumley owned an extensive collection of Catholic ecclesiastical artefacts, though whether they were kept as historical mementoes or for liturgical purposes (or both) is not clear, but they figured in an incident in which he was involved somewhat discreditably. William Carter (1550-84), a recusant stationer, lived in Hart Street, Tower Hill, near Lumley. He acted as amanuensis to Dr Nicholas Harpsfield and was imprisoned in 1578 and from December 1579 to May 1581 for printing 'pamphlets, Popish and others, against the Government', including Gregory Martin's *A Treatise of Schism* (1580) which was boldly dedicated to the queen.[44] On 19 July 1582 a spy informed Walsingham that Carter's wife had told him that she wished she had never known Lumley. Her husband had been arrested for being so stupid as to take in 'all the books, copes, vestments, crosses, chalices, & all the rest' belonging to Lumley 'by the means and entreaty of Mr Smyth and Mr Caynes or Caymes, two of my lord's gentlemen' (though the circumstances are not explained). The spy recommended that both gentlemen be taken up, together with Mrs Carter

> who knows as much as her husband, not only in this but in all other affairs and causes concerning the dealing of the Papists. And of this I am most assured, that there is neither Jesuit, priest, nor papist of any account within England but he knoweth them. I have known him myself these 20 years, and he married his wife from the Lady Carew's, who was so often in prison for religion. But to be short, if this be ripped to the bottom, there will be such matter revealed as long hath been full secret...

Carter was arrested that day and taken to the Tower. In November it was reported that he had been 'racked nearly to death' in an attempt to wring from him details of the Catholic literary network, but he had given nothing away. He was tried on 10 January 1584, was found guilty and was executed at Tyburn the following day. Lumley did nothing to help the Carters.[45]

Scraps of information about Lumley's religious affiliations appear in later years. In 1586 he had five Catholic household servants: 'Smith thelder, Smith the younger, Kanys, Saunders, Ingleby'.[46] In 1594 the informant Benjamin Beard in the Fleet prison told Lord Keeper Puckering that Lumley had harboured priests: 'Stamp, lately released out of Wisbeach, and another seminary [priest] lay in my Lord Lum.'s house. Penwerne a Cornish man verified this...' The seminarist, Penwarne, served in Lumley's household.[47] Thomas Stamp had ministered for some years in London and was closely associated with the Vaux and Tresham families before his imprisonment in London and then at Wisbech.[48] Lumley's Fitzalan relations were also important Catholic and Jesuit connections; Anne Arundel sheltered Robert Southwell S.J. in Arundel House and she supported him when he was imprisoned in 1592. The Arundels and Howards were also associated with the Jesuit Richard Blount, and in his final years Lumley was a member of the congregation of Thomas Abercrombie, S.J.[49]

In 1601/2 a Protestant traveller reported that at the English College in St Omer he had 'fortunately [i.e., fortuitously] found a priest named Keynes who had been sometime secretary to the Lord Lumley'. He was the 'Kanys' or 'Caynes' mentioned earlier whose real name was George Keynes, a Somerset man who became a Jesuit novice in 1594 and was at the college from 1595.[50] In June 1602 Burghley wrote to Cecil from York that he was much troubled by the seminary priest Trollop, 'an obstinate and perilous fellow', who was to be sent to London to be questioned by the authorities and thereby, to the dismay of Burghley, 'to save his life, at [the] suit of Lord Lumley, whose servant is Trollop's brother'. Trollop appears to have been banished for he signs a document in Paris in 1603, but he was back on the mission in County Durham in 1610. (In 1593 a servant named Thomas Trollop, 'a base born desperate and dangerous fellow', acted as a guide for seminary priests landing in the north-east from the continent.)[51] In 1608 Lumley wrote as one of 'so manie beggars of Recusants' asking Lord Salisbury to allow George Smith, his servant of many years, to make a reasonable composition for his recusancy rather than have him imprisoned because Smith was so important to Lumley in his old age. Smith's father had been out in '69 for which he was attainted and, though pardoned, his lands had not been restored and Lumley was petitioning on his behalf.[52] Lumley died at his house in London on 11 April 1609, aged seventy-five. His corpse was laid in a wooden coffin which was placed in a lead coffin and that was put into an outer wooden coffin covered with brass-studded red leather. On the following day his remains were conveyed to the parish church at Cheam for burial by night, a sure sign of his Catholicism.[53]

It is clear from what has been covered in this chapter that Lumley occupied a position of some importance in the cultural life of England in the last quarter of the sixteenth century. His full participation in the political life of the nation had been dispensed with and he was not a prominent figure at court. For someone who had a natural disposition towards a studious life, the intellectual milieu into which he was compelled to withdraw was both congenial and fulfilling. Even so, as an increasingly senior baron, he cannot have been entirely content merely to carry out some minor administrative tasks that came his way in the House of Lords from time to time, all the while descending into amiable and harmless old age and post mortem obscurity. There was, however, one activity which he could pursue and which would give him personal satisfaction as well as provide him with a political rôle, though at one remove. That was the development of the art-collection in Nonsuch Palace which had been started by his father-in-law with a small group of portraits of family and friends. Arundel, and Lumley after him, so expanded and diversified the collection that by the end of century it had become the largest and widest ranging in the country. Moreover, the gallery of portraits of contemporary and historical figures, both English and European, came to have a diplomatic importance. It is clear that Lumley's art-collecting became as much of an enthusiasm as his genealogical researches, to which, in his case at any rate, it was partly related. A close inspection of this remarkable art-collection is therefore essential.

Chapter Four

An International Portrait Gallery: The Arundel–Lumley Collection

The Arundel–Lumley Collection, the largest and most important private art-collection in Elizabethan England, was built up over sixty years. Its formation around 1547-50 and its early development can be ascribed with confidence to Henry Fitzalan, twelfth Earl of Arundel but from about 1557, when his daughter Jane and son-in-law John, Lord Lumley, joined him in the completion and embellishment of Nonsuch Palace, it becomes difficult to ascertain whether pictures were acquired by Arundel or Lumley individually or collaboratively. The enlargement of the collection after Arundel's death in 1580 was due entirely to Lumley who continued to collect pictures until his death some thirty years later. Before examining the collection in detail, it is appropriate to place it in the contexts of the history of collecting and of art-history.

In 1981 a study was made of English collections of works of art in the sixteenth century. Over six hundred inventories of property compiled for probate purposes between 1417 and 1603, but falling mostly within the period 1480 to 1580, were examined. The owners were prosperous members of society in southern England below the rank of peer. Although the majority of them owned tapestries and other painted room-hangings, only sixty-seven (about ten percent) of them possessed pictures or sculptures. That group comprised a bishop, four clergymen, seven knights, and fifty-five wealthy land-owners (two were women) and merchants. The average number of pictures in a collection was one or two, but collections of up to half a dozen items were not uncommon in the earlier part of the period, though the very large collections of Robert Amadas and Alexander Plymley in 1533 of seventeen and sixteen items respectively are exceptional, and collections of such a size were rare even in the second half of the sixteenth century; both were extremely wealthy men. In the latter half of the century the largest collections were those of Sir Ralph Waren in 1554, with twenty-three items, largely unspecified, and William Lovelace in 1577, who had thirty pictures.

Most of these inventories listed religious art, indicating that its production did not come to an end during the iconoclastic reign of Edward VI, but two areas of change in taste were detected. Religious sculpture declined markedly over the period, which is explicable given that most pieces would be objects of Catholic devotion: representations of Christ (crucifixes and statues), the Virgin and the saints. Religious painting did not decline but biblical narratives and moralistic subjects superseded devotional imagery. Secular art became increasingly popular: battle scenes, genre and allegorical subjects. Portraits became more common in the second half of the sixteenth century but 'the number of Englishmen in the Elizabethan period who commissioned portraits of themselves seems to have been very small' and they did not always give pride of place to their commissions. There is some evidence for series of portraits in the earlier period, especially of the English monarchy. It was concluded that: 'the collecting interests of the English in the sixteenth century were much less narrow than has hitherto been supposed'. The Arundel-Lumley collection, even though it was so much larger than any other and intended for a palace, may be examined in relation to the socio-political and religious background illustrated by these inventories to ascertain whether any common principles applied regardless of social rank or other considerations.[1]

In art-historical terms the creation and expansion of the Arundel–Lumley collection was largely uncritical, particularly in the earlier years. Portraiture was by far the largest category in the collection and indeed most of the pictures which have survived from Tudor England are portraits. But it would be inappropriate to suppose that these collectors had anything in mind other than the acquisition of likenesses of those personages who interested them and, in many cases, with whom they had some association. This was a practical, often political or diplomatic, objective rather than an aesthetic project based on scholarly principles or standards; the desire to have an image of a sitter in the collection was independent of the work's quality or, indeed, of the artist. In any case, inventive techniques such as the free expression allowed to artists in Italy were generally denied to those in the north where the style of portrait-painting set by the Flemish school in the fifteenth century was still dominant. There was no *avant garde* in native Tudor portraiture; the archaic or neo-mediaeval style held its ground until the end of the century at least. This is not to say that Arundel and Lumley had no appreciation of good work, for they and their wives were highly cultured and would, in due course, acquire the work of accomplished artists and employ leading painters for their own portraits, but they were bound to have to accept portraits in the traditional manner if they wanted a comprehensive collection, which was in fact their aim. Moreover, works of doubtful quality were not discarded as their tastes became more sophisticated. It would be anachronistic, then, to impute to the collectors any formal or erudite thinking to their collecting practice or to compare them unfavourably with, say, the contemporary Italian school. At any rate, what follows is an account of the formation and growth of the collection, and the treatment is deliberately innocent of art-theory, corresponding to the approach of the collectors themselves.

In 1590, in financial circumstances already described, Lumley ordered an inventory to be taken of the contents of his various residences. The premises were not specified but included Nonsuch Palace, Lumley Castle, Stansted Park, and his houses on Tower Hill and at Greenwich. This was the first and only time the collections were documented and it is fortunate that Lumley's steward John Lampton (or Lambton) did the work intelligently and comprehensively for, despite some few shortcomings in his identification of some artists and sitters (which even Lumley may have had difficulty in remembering), the inventory is a uniquely important document for the study of the cultural history of the period.[2] It is bound together with other documents in what is known as the 'Red Velvet Book', because of its binding, and it is appropriate to describe briefly the other contents of the volume before discussing the register of the pictures.

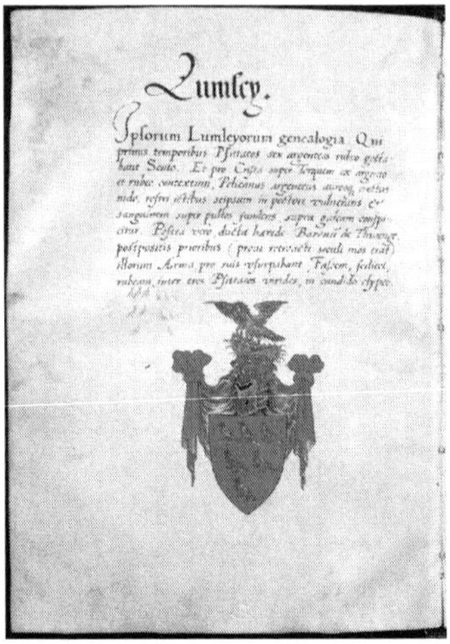

A page depicting the Lumley genealogy (The Red Book)

The book comprises nineteen pages of watercolours depicting sculpture, furniture, fountains, columns, an obelisk and designs, which have been dated to 1597, for the funerary monuments which would be erected in the parish church at Cheam for Lumley himself and his two wives.[3]

Architectural features at Lumley castle (The Red Book)

The majority of the garden ornaments as well as the fountain of Venus, based on an Italian example of c.1556, had been made for the Privy Garden at Nonsuch in the early years of Elizabeth's reign. The drawings for the fountains 'suggest a timid and clumsy adaptation of Flemish Mannerist art, and are likely to have been made by Netherlandish craftsmen'.[4] It is unclear, however, whether the objects bearing the Lumley arms were procured before he inherited the palace in 1580, although it seems unlikely that Arundel would have objected since his own device, a prancing horse, already featured prominently. A marble column stood by the south-east tower of the palace at the top of which the Arundel Horse was placed, and a fountain in the inner courtyard was topped by a similar figure.

There is a brief treatment of some of the external features of Lumley Castle and a description, with sketches, of the great hall.

The Great Hall, Lumley Castle, early 20th Century

Two marble bas-relief figures of Plato and Aristotle in carved marble frames (the original, or perhaps similar, plaques are in the Prado Museum, Madrid) flanking a cross which has the shield of the Lumley arms superimposed at its centre were mounted in the hall initially, but they are now to be seen externally in the courtyard on the inner wall above the eastern gateway. The wall at the lower end of the great hall supported 'a Riche Lavatorie of touch and whyte marble contayning in height 20 foote'. That has survived and is at Sandbeck Park, but the 'sixe most rare heads of beasts' have not. Thirteen 'Emperors heades of mouldworke' were 'garnishing the hall about'; six are lost but the surviving seven were used in the redecoration of the ballroom during the renovations of the eighteenth century and are still to be seen.[5] There was also a 'faire table wherein is written in letters of golde', a melancholy Latin poem *Theatrum Mundus, Spectator Deus* reminding the household, at great length, of the brevity of life and the rewards of virtue. The author is not known but it is more than likely that it was written by Lumley himself since he was given to composing long memorial inscriptions.[6]

Those items were incidental to the main purpose of the great hall which was to exhibit the Lumley lineage (in continuation of its external display on the castle walls) and place it firmly in national history to show how it paralleled that of the royal line. On the west wall stood a prominent stone fireplace classically-styled with carved columns, lintel and pediment surmounted by the Lumley arms. A large oval tablet bordered with arms, inscribed with a long Latin painted pedigree from Liulph to John and his deceased infant children was also on display. That complemented sixteen full-length portraits of the Lumley ancestors from Liulph to the present. Drawings show that on the east wall above a dais there stood 'a great statuarie on horsback, as bigg as the life, within an arch of stone, in memorie of King Edward the 3 in whose tyme the most of this Castle was built ...'[7]

The Lumley Horseman

This polychrome wooden figure (now known as the 'Lumley Horseman') was the first equestrian statue to be made in England and is based on antique or recent Italian examples. At the feet of the horseman were

> six small pictures, in whyte marble in memorie of his six sonnes, viz: Edward Prince of Wales, Willm of Hatfield who died yung, Lyonell Duke of Clarence, John of Gaunt, Duke of Lancaster, Edmond of Langley, duke of Yorke, Thomas of Woodstock, Duke of Glocester.

Immediately to the right of the horseman there were

> foure livelie statues all wrought in white marble in memorie of K Henry the 8, King Edward 6, Quene Marie and Q. Elizabeth, in whose raignes his Lop lived.

They are shoulder-length busts, almost life-size, and are unique for there are no comparable free-standing busts of the Tudor monarchs. They 'have individuality but it is not easy to suggest the nationality of the sculptor, and by Continental standards he was not an artist of great distinction'. As the varied quality of the details indicate, they are based on portrait-medals, and, though undoubtedly carved from Italian marble, they are probably of English manufacture, conceivably by Cornelius Cure, with a date of no earlier than 1565 but more probably of the 1580's when Lumley was designing the layout of the hall. The busts of Henry and Elizabeth are related to medals made in 1562 by the Dutch artist Steven van Herwijk (1562-7); that of Edward VI is closely related to a unique lead medal of 1547; and that of Mary relates to medals of 1555.[8]

Surprisingly, the group of busts was not extended to include James I, son of Mary Queen of Scots, the proclamation of whose accession Lumley signed and in the sixth year of whose reign he died. Lumley had told the Earl of Salisbury that he hoped to remain on the right side in the new reign and James had continued him in office as Keeper at Nonsuch where they met frequently. It hardly seems likely that Lumley would have harboured a grudge over a disparaging remark made by James when visiting Lumley Castle on his way south to London in 1603. Having been subjected to an exhaustive and exhausting treatment of Lumley's ancestry, the king wearily said: 'Oh mon, gang nae further. I maun digest the knowledge I hae gained this day, for I didna ken Adam's other name was Lumley'. James cannot have helped but notice that pictures of Adam and Eve, as well as Father Time, were hanging in the house. [9]

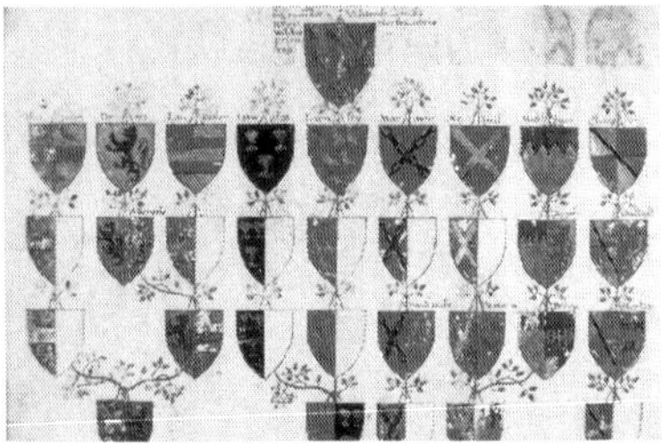

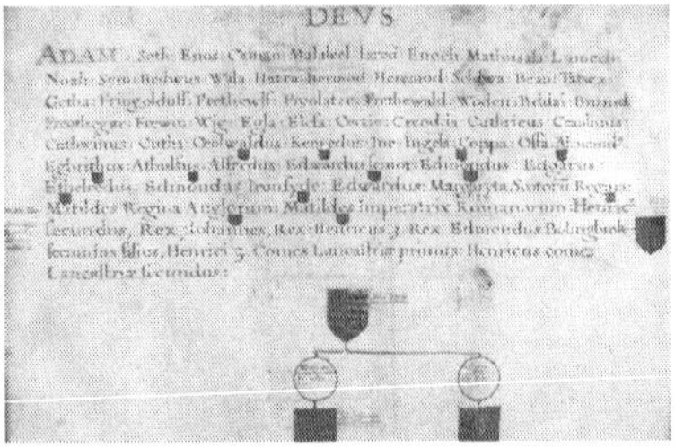

Pages from the Lumley genealogy (The Red Book)

The Red Velvet Book contains several pages of pedigrees. One of them traces the English sovereigns back to Adam, a lineage not usually claimed by royal dynasties; it is, moreover, headed DEUS which is a further step not normally taken, except by the most fervent of genealogists. A beautifully emblazoned coat of arms precedes a lavishly illuminated Lumley pedigree in the form of a tree extending over ten pages. No-one wishing to make his way in the College of Arms can have done so without being an accomplished heraldic artist, and Lumley had connections with two members of the college, William Segar and Robert Glover. William Segar trained as a scrivener and entered the college by favour of Sir Thomas Heneage. He became Portcullis Pursuivant in 1585, Somerset Herald in 1589, Norroy King at Arms in 1593 and Garter King of Arms in 1603. That is the period which corresponds roughly with what we know of his dealings with Lumley. They encountered each other around 1580 when Lumley was engrossed in proving his lineage to the most distant past and it was Segar's facility for heraldic art which first secured Lumley's patronage. Segar produced the detailed ten-page genealogical tree and he would go on to paint fifteen portraits of the Lumley ancestors and one of Lumley himself to hang in the hall of the castle, the chief characteristic of which is the display of heraldic achievements. There is also a roll of thirty-two emblazoned shields of Lumley ancestors on a single page but it is in a very much plainer style and is clearly from a different hand, probably that of Robert Glover, Segar's predecessor as Somerset Herald from 1571. Glover accompanied his father-in-law William Flower, Norroy King of Arms (whose province was all England north of the Trent) on a heraldic visitation in 1575 and enjoyed the hospitality of William Claxton at Wynyard in County Durham from July to September. Glover's 'zeal, skill and unwearying diligence' were generally prized in the college, as well they might, given that he emblazoned some 752 shields during that single visitation; nearly a third of them were done at Wynyard.[10]

The inventory proper follows and it is headed:

> A Certyficate from Mr John Lampton Stewarde of Howseholde to John Lord Lumley, of all his Lo: monumentes of Marbles, Pictures and tables in Paynture, with other his Lordshippes howseholde Stuffe and Regester of Bookes. Anno 1590.These sorted together for the memorye of yr Lo: house.

In a Lumley estate register of 1592, John Lambton is described as Bailiff and Constable of Lumley and Seneschal of Lord's Hospital and he also rendered the accounts of the Tower Hill house. The precise date on which the inventory was compiled is not known. The second part is dated 22 May and it might be that the first part was compiled at the same time. As will be explained later, however, Lumley acquired a number of pictures from Leicester House when the contents were sold in June 1590 and they are in Lampton's original inventory listing (i.e., not added or interpolated subsequently like other later acquisitions). This suggests that the inventory (or the fair copy) was written up in the latter half of the year.[11] The first part lists the collection of pictures, a book of Holbein sketches and sixty-six engravings. None of these were priced individually but the total value was given as £623. The second part comprises

> A Sumarye of certayne stuffe within your Lo: houses the xxiith of May Anno 1590 the Inventoryes of the partyculers remaynyng in bookes subscribed by John Lambton, gentleman, steward of household to yor Lo: and under the handes of the severall wardropers there.

The 'stuffe' was assessed as being worth £5,380 and comprised a substantial collection of musical instruments, over a hundred Turkey carpets, a large quantity of furniture and fifty-seven tapestries. Although portraits make up the largest surviving category of domestic art from the sixteenth century, tapestries or cheaper wall-hangings were more common and often more highly valued. The 1609 inventory of Lumley Castle listed seventy tapestries, twelve pieces of buskin hangings and four hangings of gilt leather, the total value of which was given as £833; the same appraisers put a value of £88 on the 233 pictures in the house. The armour was not itemised but was given an overall value of £480.17.8d. As Lampton indicated, it was intended that a catalogue of the library would form the third part of the inventory but it was made separately, as was explained in a footnote to the inventory written by Lumley in or after 1596:

> The Library Registred in a boke wryten by Alcocke, my L: of Chechester his L: servant, A 1596 with all the rest of my bokes myselfe have dyspersed sundery ways.

The first part of the inventory is of greatest interest for present purposes and the following discussion deals exclusively with it. Inventories often list pictures by artist with the dates of composition or by the order in which they are hung in a room. Occasionally an inventory gives only the total number of pictures in a house or a room, especially when the interest is entirely financial. At Lumley's death in 1609 the inventory of paintings in the saloon of Lumley Castle was given simply as '76 little pictures £12, 15 great pictures £5'. In 1590, however, Lampton had been given a very precise brief, which was to compile a single combined and 'sorted' list, hence the inventory does not specify which item was in which of Lumley's houses. The paintings were divided into three sections; the first two of portraits. They were sorted, firstly, according to the size of the image and then, within that category, by the social status of the sitter. Thus the first section was headed 'Pyctures caryinge the fowrme of the whole Statuary', that is, full-length portraits, of which there were forty-two. The second section listed 'Pictures of a Smaller Scantlinge', that is, portraits depicting sitters at less than full-length, of which there were 165.

Clearly, Adam and Eve, Lumley's ancestors and Father Time were to be regarded as pre-eminent for they were given pride of place in the list of the full-lengths, but strict attention was paid to the more conventional social hierarchy thereafter. English royalty came first, followed by European royalty or heads of state. Then came English peers and one or two foreign aristocrats. The larger number of portraits in the second section emphasised Lumley's scheme. English kings, then queens (at a later date four foreign royals were inserted incorrectly at this point) were followed by the higher ranking English male peers in order. The Pope, three cardinals and two bishops were sandwiched between the English earls and barons who were followed in their turn by English knights and gentlemen. Then came European royalty and aristocracy and a small group of clerics, artists and literary figures. The inventory then turned to English royal ladies and one or two foreign female consorts; English peeresses were followed by a miscellany of historical and anonymous contemporary women (Mary Magdalen, Cleopatra, A Bride of Constantinople, *et al*). Evidently, then, Lumley had the highly developed nationalistic, hieratic and gender-conscious frame of mind common in his day.

The third section: 'Other Pictures and Tables', lists forty-eight miscellaneous paintings of genre, classical and religious subjects in no discernible order. (A 'table' could have been a portable panel painting, a painted or unpainted sculpture, glass or a hanging.) The section includes marbles, hangings, the Holbein sketchbook, one or two portraits and sixty-six 'Pictures in small of Christ, our Ladie and his Saints, wrought upon brass, and adorned with marbles and marble Pillars' by which, presumably, is meant line-engravings on copper-plate subsequently embellished (the engraving of Mary Magdalen is attributed to Titian). It is probable that these engravings were of Flemish origin, conceivably by a member of the Wierix family of Antwerp who specialised in portraits and Catholic religious subjects.[12] It is not clear how and where these were displayed.

The inventory gives a total of 255 pictures (not including the engravings or the contents of Holbein's sketchbook), but the implication of a number of contemporary interpolations, though clearly signalled when it was published, does not appear to have been fully considered subsequently. Of the total, forty-one pictures were added after the inventory was compiled (including a portrait of Lumley himself dated 1591, and at least three other dated English portraits). In 1590, then, the collection can have numbered no more than 214 pictures. Since the inventory was drawn up by Lampton and thirty of the post-1590 acquisitions were written into it by him, they must have entered the collection before his death in Lumley's house on Tower Hill on 5 April 1605. Eleven further acquisitions were made between 1605 and Lumley's death four years later on 11 April 1609. Therefore the picture-collection only rose to its ultimate total of 255 in the twenty years after the inventory was compiled. Even allowing for that correction, however, the collection was still the largest in the country.

The Earl of Leicester had 180 pictures in three houses in 1588 which included a number of Italian works, particularly Venetian; Lord Cobham had seventy-seven hanging in his two houses at the turn of the century; and the Earl of Northampton had 100 pictures in his London house in 1614.[13] But the premier English peer, the Duke of Norfolk, had a mere twenty-eight 'vysenamies [likenesses] of divers noble persons' and twenty tapestries at Kenninghall in Norfolk in the middle of the sixteenth century.[14] Moreover, the total number of pictures owned by Arundel may be somewhat higher than is presently assumed because the pictures hanging in Arundel Castle and in Arundel House in London (which was stripped by royal agents in 1589 following Philip Howard's imprisonment) would not have been included in the inventory. Known portraits of Arundel and his son Lord Maltravers attributed to John Bettes I (fl. 1545-59), 1558 and c.1555, and one of his mother may well have been in the house or castle.[15]

The Arundel-Lumley collection of paintings can be classified as shown in the following table. Less than a fifth of the collection comprised decorative or sacred art. Most pictures in those categories are listed in the inventory by title only, without a date or an artist's name or any indication of when they were acquired. Moreover, the genre subjects were not uncommon (*A young man fancying the riche old woman, The Ficleness of Fortune*, and a painting in 'the manner of banquetting in Flanders') hence little can be said about them except that they were painted by Flemings and were the kind of thing which graced many noble households.

General Classification of the Pictures in the Lumley Inventory, 1590

	Full-length	Other than Full-length
Portraits (207)		
Family & patrimonial ancestry (26)	20	6
English royalty (25)	4	21
European royalty (18)	5	13
English peerage (61)	9	52
Foreign aristocracy (20)	4	16
English knights and gentry (27)		27
Literati, artists, &c. (10)		10
Churchmen (9)		9
Anonymous and miscellaneous (11)		11
[Holbein's book of portrait-drawings 85]*		
Others (48)		
Allegorical subjects (3)	1	2
Classical or mythological subjects (6)		6
Old Testament subjects (7)	1	6
Christian subjects (15)		15
Genre scenes (8)		8
The Nine Worthies (9)		9
[Engravings of Christ & the Saints 66]*		

*not included in the overall total of 255

The sacred art in the collection also depicted constantly repeated subjects, but it is of greater significance. After the change in religion in England, say from around 1536, it became impossible to draw a distinction between the pietistic and aesthetic purpose of religious painting for it fell victim to Protestant suspicion of the visual arts as somehow idolatrous and likely to lead back to popery. It was no longer possible to give a picture an artistic value independent of its religious function. Henceforth a picture was to be wholly didactic, beauty was irrelevant, if not a positive distraction. On the whole, contact with Italy was terminated, religious sculpture (statues) was virtually discontinued, and devotional paintings were no longer essayed. In order to eliminate nostalgia for the old faith, a large part of the great artistic inheritance of the middle ages was indiscriminately destroyed in a programme of officially sanctioned iconoclasm which reached a peak in Edward's reign. The image-breakers were not always able to get into the private houses of the gentry which were to some extent outside official reach, and so the fact that any paintings survived at all is due almost entirely to the private patronage of a few English aristocrats, chief among them Arundel and Lumley. They declined to abandon their humanist education about the suitability of all the visual arts for a gentleman's edification and delight, and who, together with Lords Cumberland, Morley, Northampton, Stafford and Vaux, can be counted as the most cultivated of the mid-Tudor peerage. But even they could do little more than preserve a tiny proportion of pre-Reformation art-objects.[16]

It was only with the Elizabethan Anglican settlement of 1559 and a proclamation in 1560 against further destruction, that the campaign came to an end. Nonetheless, for a long time prudent patrons and artists concentrated on narrative biblical themes rather than those of the middle ages which had stressed the devotional aspects of religious practice. Ironically, England's break with Rome laid the foundation for a gradual replacement of the religious icon with the secular image of the sovereign – many of Elizabeth's portraits reproduce attitudes traditionally adopted by religious figures. But the old ways were difficult to eliminate. In his primary diocesan visitation of 1578 the Bishop of Durham ordered that all popish articles be removed from the churches and popish paintings be 'perjetted' over with lime, thus indicating that in the north-east, at least, remnants of the old church-art were still to be seen.[17]

In such a climate it would not have been surprising if Arundel and Lumley had made some attempt at discretion when hanging their religious paintings, but they did not. Paintings of biblical subjects from both the Old and New Testaments (*Joseph and His Brethren, The Building of Babel,* and *The Conversion of St Paul*) were hung alongside others capable of a more popish interpretation (a *Nativity*, a *Madonna and Child, Our Lady with the Infant Jesus and Saints*, and *The Temptations of St Anthony*). Lumley's large collection of engravings and his 'cunning perspective of

Death and a woman' by Hilliard (the *memento mori* was a genre congenial to the Elizabethans) were not particularly obtrusive, and presumably representations of the *Passion of Christ,* were not thought altogether objectionable. In 1609 a depiction of the Crucifixion hung in the Great Chamber of the castle behind 'a sarcanet curtain'; of course, that might just as well have been to protect the picture from the elements and careless servants as to hide it. But an ostentatious parade of the Madonna and saints would have been less discreet, even in the small chapel at Lumley into which the religious art could have been placed. Of particular interest among Lumley's later acquisitions are portraits of the recently-deceased Ignatius Loyola (d. 1556), founder of the Jesuits, and Francis Xavier (d. 1552) the famous Jesuit missionary. Their inclusion in this collection indicates how quickly and widely their *cultus* spread, for they were not beatified until 1609, the year of Lumley's death, and not canonised until 1622. To have had these portraits on display at a time when the term Jesuit was synonymous with treachery, was imprudent even for a peer, let alone one who was known in earlier days for militant Catholicism and who described himself as a recusant to the end of his days.[18]

International politics in the Tudor age was largely a matter of personal relations between rulers, and portraiture was the servant of diplomacy. Sovereigns obtained portraits of fellow heads of state and statesmen and soldiers displayed those of their opposite numbers and enemies. Institutions might have a set of their founders, and bishops' palaces one of the Protestant reformers. Religious paintings were collected by the devout, and those interested in the antique would obtain representations of classical figures. By serving as introductions to potential suitors, portraits could also play a crucial role in marriage negotiations for good or ill. On seeing her portrait, Henry VIII proposed marriage to Christina of Denmark but she turned him down. Henry then fell for Anne of Cleves through her portrait by Holbein but immediately regretted his choice when seeing Anne in person, comparing her to a horse (a 'Flanders mare'). In 1553 Mary of Hungary sent Mary Tudor a portrait of Philip of Spain by Titian and advised that the English queen should not look for the precision of Holbein and that she would best see Philip's likeness by looking at the picture in daylight and from a distance. Such a hazard was much in Elizabeth's mind when a match between Archduke Charles von Habsburg and herself was under discussion. The queen insisted on seeing him in the flesh saying she would rather become a nun than put her trust in portrait-painters.[19]

Many of the English gentry, however, simply wanted formalised representations of themselves and their families for conspicuous display at home in a form of social oneupmanship and for the ancestral record: portraits complemented written pedigrees.[20] To get around the post-Reformation nervousness that the representation of human beings might be construed as a form of idolatry, early portraits often had a flat, iconic style and included prominent details which effectively proclaimed them as commemorations of major secular events in the sitters' lives: marriage, pregnancy in a woman, appointment, achievement or promotion for a man; victory in war. To prevent any confusion about identity they were often (but not so often as the art-historian would wish) inscribed with the sitter's name and attributes of rank, coats of arms, staffs of office, and insignia of various kinds. In the Tudor period few subjects sat more than once in a lifetime but a sitter might order duplicates for relatives or for his university, say, or a professional institution. Borrowing portraits to be copied was routine by the end of the century, and though copies could be numerous, they conformed to a small number of types or patterns altered to reflect age, additional honours or changed circumstances. Although royal and court portraiture was of a high quality (due largely to Holbein who was in constant demand) in general portraits were utilitarian documents of record, not exercises in psychological penetration and likenesses were stereotypical and superficial, often executed by hacks. It was partly because few native artists were comparable with the likes of Holbein that Arundel and Lumley gave their patronage to a number of foreign painters coming into England and they also supported artists in other fields, such as Petruccio Ubaldini, the Florentine illuminator who gave manuscripts to Maltravers and Jane Lumley in 1550; he later produced a calligraphic and illuminated manuscript of a psalter and ten canticles for Arundel.[21]

At this point it is appropriate to consider whether foreign travel was a stimulant to the development of the collection. Arundel is known to have been employed on diplomatic missions, though he can only have been chosen because of his rank not his tact, of which he had none, nor for his comunications skills, because he declined to speak foreign languages. Though he might have done, there is no evidence that he brought back any portraits from his travels (except in one minor case) yet he did bring back musical scores. It has been said that Lumley was appointed Ambassador to Florence in 1566 charged with the recovery of a debt owed by the Medici to Henry VIII, and that when he saw the gallery of portraits of *uomini illustri* assembled by Cosimo de Medici, Duke of Florence, he was inspired to form his own collection. Lumley is also said to have brought back to England a number of marble tables, as well as ideas for the re-design of the gardens at Nonsuch.[22] But these suggestions are untenable for a number of reasons. In the first place, Arundel had laid the foundations of the collection a decade previously and it had grown substantially by the mid-sixties with Lumley's collaboration. Secondly, there is no direct evidence for Lumley's visit; indeed, it is possible to track him in England throughout the sixties. He was at the centre of affairs in the reign of Mary I, and he would have kept close to London and Nonsuch during the first years of the next reign when his father in law had high hopes of maintaining his influence at court and even of marrying Elizabeth. Documents relating to property transactions which required Lumley's immediate signature are recorded in the Patent Rolls at intervals between 1561 and 1568.[23] *Ad vivum* portraits of Lumley and his wife are dated 8 May 1563 and others are datable to around 1565.

Thirdly, the assumption that Lumley went abroad to attend a memorial service for Emperor Ferdinand I who died in Ratisbon in July 1564 is a misreading of the contemporary evidence. The queen certainly intended to send someone to commiserate with and offer her compliments to Maximilian II, the new emperor, but 'more was meant than condolence or congratulation. It was an intention for marriage'. She prevaricated so long about whom she could trust with such an important mission that it became too late for her to be represented at the service at all (she had to pretend that she had been awaiting the return of the old emperor's insignia of the Garter as was customary). On 23 September it was resolved that the emperor's

> funerals should be *here* [i.e., London, emphasis added] honourably celebrated within six or seven days hence. And so they were, the solemnities beginning October 1 and ending the 3d. The mourners were, the lord treasorer, the earls of Sussex & Huntingdon; the lords Strange, Darnley, Herbert,

> Lumley and Hunsdon; Mr Solicitor, Mr Vice-Chamberlain, secretary Cecil, Mr Sackvile, and Mr Throgmorton. And the bishop of London preached...[24]

Finally, Lumley did not accompany Arundel on his year-long stay in Italy but stayed behind to look after the earl's interests. Moreover, in March 1566, prior to his departure, Arundel conveyed his estates to Lumley, in trust, so as to avoid their confiscation should the queen take it into her head that the earl was engaged in conspiratorial business with the Pope. A document relating to a property-sale signed by Lumley confirms his presence in Sussex on 1 October 1566. Arundel returned to England in April 1567 just as the affairs of Mary Queen of Scots were building to a crisis. She fled into northern England in June 1568 and Lumley became increasingly involved in the discussions and plans which culminated in the Rising of the Northern Earls and the Ridolfi Plot in 1569-70, and he was kept in custody for some time afterwards. A proposal to visit Italy in the years following 1572 would not have been entertained by Elizabeth. Anyway, Lumley was always pleading poverty and continental travel was difficult and expensive; while an ordinary mortal might get by on around £200 a year, Edward de Vere, Earl of Oxford spent £4,561 over fourteen months in 1575-6.[25]

Although Lumley's failure to visit Italy was an exception to the rule, it is notable that there was comparatively little Italian art in the collection or literature in the library. A large part of Roger Ascham's *The Scholemaster* (1570) comprised a general warning against Italy and the Italians for fear that the plain Englishman might fall into popery and filthy living. Translations of Italian books were to be avoided: 'Mo[re] Papists be made by your merry bookes of Italie than by your earnest bookes of Lovain'. Lumley was a papist, of course, but, after the excommunication of Elizabeth in 1570 he had no intention of running the risk of being dubbed an *Inglese Italianato* (or, for that matter, being thought 'Spaniolized', which was probably a term of greater abuse after 1588).[26] At any rate, his only book on Italian history was Francesco Guicciardini's *History of Italy* (1561, translated into English in 1579). There was a 1535 edition of Vitruvius *De Architectura*; Leon-Battista Alberti *De Pictura* (Venice 1547); Pomponio Gauricus *De Sculptura* (Florence 1504; Antwerp 1528); and Hoby's 1561 translation of Baldassare Castiglione's *The Courtier* , but there was no copy of any edition of Giorgio Vasari's

Lives of the Artists (1550). Nor were there any guide-books to Italy, not even a copy of the volume published at the end of the century specifically for armchair travellers: Samuel Lewkenor's *A Discourse not altogether unprofitable, nor unpleasant for such as are desirous to know the situation and customes of forraine Cities without travelling to see them* (1600).[27]

There are only five portraits of named dead Italians in the collection: (Pope Julius II, Andreas Doria, Sebastian Cabot, Raphael Sanzio (perhaps a self-portrait) and Lucrezia Borgia; one of 'thre[e] Italian Ladyes', and another of 'an Italian Gentlewoman in great reputacon wth her husband for her beawty'. (The four portraits of Italian mediaeval *literati* which were acquired almost at the end of Lumley's life are irrelevant in this context.) Some of the devotional and mythological pictures were of Italian origin, such as 'A Speciall picture of Christ cast in mould by Raphael de Urbino, brought into England from Rome by Cardynall Poole', that is, before 1558, but only one Italian picture is stated to have been acquired by Arundel during his visit of 1566: 'an Italian gentlewoman drawen by her selfe and presented to the olde Earle of Arundell in Italy'. It is possible that some of the others were brought back by him, too, though they would have been specified in the inventory (the Raphael portrait was singled out). The Lumley Horseman was probably copied from the engraved record (in the library at Nonsuch) of ancient classical or contemporary Renaissance models. The most obvious and accessible images were the antique *Marcus Aurelius* in Rome to which Donatello's century-old monument *Gattamelata* (c. 1450) owed much. Arundel would have seen the latter for himself in Padua and might even have drawn it (or had it drawn), it being so similar to the 'Arundel Horse' – a prancing white steed.

The paucity of Italian art in the collection need not be regretted, for it simply reflected the main interest of the collectors: they wanted portraits of North Europeans and those, of course, were almost always painted by artists in the north. It is highly likely, then, that the few Italian pictures in the collection were acquired in England. Similarly, 'ten marble tablets with their frames' valued at £30 in the 1609 inventory could easily have been bought in London. The classical designs of the Lumley tombs at Cheam are early examples of the secular post-Reformation sculptural style which was partly intended to evade iconcolastic attention. In short, Arundel did not like going abroad and he only went to Italy in a fit of pique; Lumley had neither the inclination or the opportunity to visit Italy, and did not do so. Indeed, if Lumley had come to know more of the high quality of contemporary Italian portraiture, he might well have engaged more Italian painters and the collection might have taken a different course.

An analysis of this inventory is complicated because the scope of the collection so widened, as time went by, that questions of attribution and dating arise more frequently. Although a high proportion of the portraits in the collection are by named artists, or from their studios, some ninety-five portraits (46%) are by unknown artists and many are of inferior quality. It must be borne in mind, however, that signed portraits were not common in the sixteenth century. Only a handful of painters enjoyed a substantial income and a personal reputation entitling them to sign their portraits and they were usually foreigners. William Scrots's salary of £62.10s. a year was about twice that earned by Holbein, whereas unknown workshop artists of low status might be paid £4 a year. In comparison, around 1563 a carpenter might get £5 a year and a goldsmith £8. Prices for individual pictures varied enormously. Pictures in inventories from the first half of the century were rarely valued at more than a pound and many were put at much less. Of course, salaries and prices increased as time went by. In 1573 George Gower got 10s. for a half length male portrait and £3 for a full length; Ketel and Peake commanded £5 for a full length. The portrait of Archbishop Warham by Holbein was valued at £5 in 1575.[28]

Inevitably, many of Lumley's pictures are by unknown artists. Some are patently manufactured images which could have been painted and acquired at any time during the sixty-year collecting period. The depictions of mythical figures (Venus and Adonis, Juno and Jupiter) and of classical Romans (Cleopatra and Pompeia) are impossible to date, and some portraits of sitters who died in the first half of the sixteenth century may have been painted or copied later (Brandon, the early Norfolks, Emperor Maximilian I, Jane Shore). Among others, those of Margaret Beauchamp, Countess of Shrewsbury, who died in 1473 and Sir Anthony Browne, who died in 1548, were not acquired until after 1590, and images of the fourteenth-century Italian writers (Ariosto, Boccaccio, Dante and Petrarch) were the last to enter the collection.

Although a little over half (54%) of the portraits in the inventory can be attributed to a named artist or can be said to have derived from an artist's prototype, or for which some indication of the dates of composition or of acquisition can be obtained, in many cases their full provenance remains difficult to establish. The portrait of Sir Christopher Hatton (b.1540) is said by Lampton to depict him 'as he was being vice-chamberlayne to Q. Elizabeth'. That dates the portrait to 1578-87. A search of the catalogues reveals that two portraits of him were painted around 1585. Hence the portrait (or a copy) must have been acquired by Lumley (Arundel was dead) between 1585 and 1590. But Lampton is rarely so helpful and the time-span is more often too wide for even an approximate refinement. The portrait of Edward Fiennes de Clinton (1512-85) is inventoried as: 'Lo: Clinton, afterwards created Earle of Lincolne, Lo: Admirall'. He was Lord High Admiral twice, 1550-4 and 1558-85; he was created earl in 1572. He was drawn by Holbein and a large number of portraits in oils executed between 1560 and the year of his death are known. It is impossible to say which one was in this collection.

Mary I *(1516-58) with the Lumley* cartellino. *Copy by Gerlach Flicke in 1555 of the 1554 portrait by Antonis Mor.* (Courtesy of Durham Cathedral)

Lumley may have anticipated such problems, for in a number of cases he followed Holbein's practice of having a *cartellino* or label painted in to identify the sitter with a brief biographical note and the date of the portrait. The label takes the form of a *trompe-l'oeil* representation of a folded or crumpled white slip of parchment or paper apparently opened out and stuck on to the picture with blobs of red sealing-wax. Lumley probably adopted the convention during the period of his sole ownership of the collection, that is, after 1580. But then, few of his labels include all the information required to give a complete provenance.

Lumley's Wives: Jane Fitzalan (above), Elizabeth Darcy (right)

Moreover, only thirty *cartellini* are known, some of which have been painted over or removed (Wentworth and Christina of Denmark are examples) but others may yet be revealed. Lumley did not need to label all his pictures since in many cases the painter had already painted in the sitter's name at a convenient blank space on the portrait, or included a coat of arms, a motto or some other specific identifying feature. It would seem to have been unnecessary to label the portraits of Mary I and Edward VI, but it was, presumably, an attempt to ensure that there could be no ambiguity in the future. It was also an indication that he was not collecting just for his own satisfaction but that he intended the collection to have an interest for future generations. Lumley was not the only collector to add a label to his pictures then or later: portraits in the Royal Collection and the Bedford Collection at Woburn Abbey, among others, were extensively labelled. The two known portraits of Thomas, first Baron Wentworth, also illustrate the point. What was probably the

Lumley label on the version in the National Portrait Gallery (No. 1851) has been painted out and a Wentworth label added, on which only the fragments of the original inscription remain; a similar label on the version with the family preserves the sitter's age and the complete inscription.[29]

Questions of provenance arise closer to home. Two entries in the inventory refer to portraits of Arundel himself. The first is listed as a 'statuary' but no full-length has survived except an inferior picture depicting him on horseback. The second entry, in the 'smaller scantlinge' category, includes the observation 'drawn twise by the famous paynter Steven'. But Lampton's precise meaning is unclear. He may have conflated the two entries and meant one full- and one half-length, or he may have meant two half-lengths as well as the full-length. In any case, four portraits of Arundel by 'Steven' are known and it may be that copies were provided to hang in all of Arundel's residences. In which case, Lampton's entry could be taken to mean that the one with the *cartellino* was Lumley's own for Lumley Castle and the other was Arundel's intended for Nonsuch Palace (the others would have hung in Arundel Castle and Arundel House).[30]

Other problems arise because many historical portraits have suffered over the centuries by overpainting, reattribution, and change of identity. Images have been lost because of decay or destruction arising from a lack of sympathy on the part of later generations. This collection is no different from many others which have been subjected to such vicissitudes and some portraits, especially of foreigners, cannot now be traced. Nonetheless, despite some difficulties, many portraits in the collection do yield the information to explain why and when they were acquired, and the provenances of others can be deduced from the biographies of the sitters, painters and collectors. Hence the origin and growth of this important collection can be established, in part positively and in part inferentially.

***

The foundations of the collection were laid during the period 1547-50. Arundel came to art partly of his own volition and partly through the generosity of Edward VI in respect of the work of Hans Holbein which figured prominently in the collection from the earliest stage.

Holbein worked in England 1526-8 and from about 1531 to his death in 1543. Eight portraits in the inventory are attributed directly to him: the cartoon of kings Henry VII and Henry VIII (one of their few authentic portrayals); Henry VIII; Sir Henry and Lady Guildford (a pair); Erasmus; Sir Thomas More; Sir Nicholas Carew and the full-length portrait of Christina, Duchess of Milan. The latter was in the palace of Westminster during the last ten years of Henry's reign, as confirmed by the inventories of 1542 and 1547, but it was not there at the death of Edward in 1553.[31] When the contents of the palace were compared with those in 1547, the absence of the portrait was explained thus: 'This Table Therle of Arundell hathe of the kinges maiesties gift as he saithe'. It also appears that the contents of Holbein's studio in Whitehall fell into Edward's hands when the artist died suddenly of the plague in 1543 because Arundel received another gift from the king which had had no previous royal connection:

> A great booke of Pictures doone by Haunce Holbyn of certyne Lordes, Ladyes, gentlemen and gentlewomen in King Henry the 8: his tyme, their names subscribed by Sr John Cheke Secretary to King Edward the 6 wch booke was King Edward the 6.

(The book was bound after Holbein's death, but clearly before Arundel was given it, between 1544 and 1553.) Cheke may have intended his labeling, incorrect in some cases, as an *aide memoire* for the young king. At any rate, Edward gave Arundel, his Lord Chamberlain, the sketchbook (when he had no further practical use for it) and the portrait of the Duchess of Milan at about the time the latter was beginning to collect pictures. The cultural disposition of the court was more austere than in King Henry's day and it is not unreasonable to suggest that the inaesthetic Edward might have given him other Holbein works as well; the cartoon would almost certainly have been in the king's possession before Arundel's.

Holbein's sketchbook contained eighty-five preparatory drawings for painted portraits and the sitters were mostly Henry's courtiers and their wives, practically all of whom were known to Arundel. Few of the paintings Holbein executed from the drawings remain, but in many cases a copy or studio work was made and survives. Apart from the eight pictures directly attributed to Holbein, twelve others in the inventory can be ascribed to his studio or as being derived from his drawings, one of which was of Arundel's mother-in-law, the Marchionness of Dorset (d. 1535). They could have come into Arundel's possession in one of several ways. Some may have been left in Holbein's studio and Arundel acquired them through royal patronage; or he had them painted by Holbein's erstwhile assistants from the book of drawings; or he (and or Lumley) had copies made. The early history of Holbein's portrait of Christina is of interest in this connection.

It has been discovered recently from an inventory of the house's contents that in 1562 the portrait of Christina was at Baynard's Castle, the London home of the earls of Pembroke. That evidence corroborates the sighting of the portrait there by Federigo Zuccaro in 1575, a report which has been doubted because it could not be substantiated and because Zuccaro's claim was not recorded until 1604, almost thirty years later. The painting was next listed in the Lumley inventory of 1590. The question arises as to why Arundel let the picture go to Baynard's Castle within ten years of being given it. A clue lies in the relationship between Arundel and William Herbert (1507?-70), first Earl of Pembroke. Like Arundel, Pembroke had held senior military positions and he was an important courtier under Edward VI. He was a key ally of Arundel against Northumberland in the power-struggles at Edward's death and he supported Mary Tudor's succession to the throne rather than Jane Grey, Northumberland's daughter-in-law. He remained in favour under Elizabeth, and although he was a Calvinist, he recognised the legitimate claim of the Catholic Mary Stewart to the English throne and he approved of her marriage to the Duke of Norfolk, Arundel's son-in-law. Pembroke died in March 1570 while in custody at Hampton Court on suspicion of being involved in the Rising of the Northern Earls. His portrait was in the Arundel-Lumley collection. It would have been entirely appropriate, then, for Arundel to sell, give or lend the portrait of Christina to Pembroke his friend, fellow courtier and political ally. Arundel was building up his own collection in the fifties and sixties and he is unlikely to have sold or have made a gift of the picture he had been given by the late king. And, if he had, it is difficult to envisage how Arundel, or Lumley later on, got it back except, of course, by re-purchase. Pembroke's heir Henry, the second earl (?1534-1601), would hardly want to dispose of such a remarkable picture, except that he was a militant Protestant who might have had an ideological objection to portraiture – art being seen as tainted with Catholicism. In which case, presumably the whole of the first earl's collection of sixty paintings would have been dispersed, but it was not. It seems more probable, therefore, that the portrait of Christina was lent to Pembroke for copying; other Holbein portraits may have been loaned for the same purpose; that of Sir Henry Guildford was in both of their collections. It is clear that no collector could rely entirely on original portraits to build up a sizeable collection, many would have to be borrowed and copied and this loan is simply an early example of the practice. The loan would have lapsed at Pembroke's death but at that point Arundel and Lumley were still in preventative custody following the Rising and they would be rearrested when the Ridolfi Plot was discovered shortly afterwards. Both of them had perforce to lie low for some time after the crisis passed in 1572 and it would be some time before it became opportune to recover the portrait. Since the picture was Arundel's in the first place, it would surely have been reclaimed during his lifetime, that is, before 1580. In short, then, the portrait of Christina was probably loaned to William, Earl of Pembroke, at some point in the 1550s and returned to Arundel in the late 1570s. Even if the precise dates and circumstances of the transaction remain to be explained, the close relationship between Arundel and Pembroke make their dealings in the matter entirely understandable.[32]

In any event, Edward VI's gifts to Arundel formed the basis of the collection and the earl soon acquired portraits of Edward both as prince and as king. They were painted by William Scrots [Stretes], a Fleming, who became King's Painter in 1545, two years after Holbein's death; Edward's pose is imitative of the famous stance of his father. Arundel also had Scrots's portraits of Lord Seymour and his wife Catherine Parr, Henry VIII's sixth queen, both of whom died before 1550; those were probably in Seymour's house when the earl bought it. His mannerist portrait of the Earl of Surrey was probably painted by Scrots after a Holbein drawing. Scrots appears to have left England at Mary's accession in 1553, the year of his death.

Arundel's first personal commissions, if not perhaps his initial acquisitions, comprise a set of five portraits of his military colleagues dated 1547 and 1550 painted by Hans Eworth, a Catholic Flemish artist who had fled Antwerp for London around 1545. The first was of Edward Shelley who came from a Sussex and Hampshire family which had local connections with the Fitzalans but, more pertinently, Shelley, had served with Arundel at Calais and had taken part in the Boulogne campaign during which he displayed a 'sober valiance of courage'; he was slain at the Battle of Musselburgh (or Pinkie) in 1547. The portrait is lost. James Wilford had also served with Arundel in France. His portrait is dated 1547 and is at Coughton Court. Sir John Luttrell, too, had served at the siege of Boulogne in 1544 with Arundel. Eworth's extraordinary portrait of him, dated 1550, which is in the Courtauld Institute, has been subjected to extensive iconographical analysis. Luttrell's uncle Thomas Wyndham was another famous soldier who had served with Arundel in France and Eworth painted him in 1550; the picture is at Longford Castle. The final portrait by Eworth in this group is that of Arundel himself. This is in medallion form depicting Arundel in threequarter profile in the pose of Emperor Marcus Aurelius dressed in gilded Roman field-armour and has been attributed with an elaborate political iconography. The absence of this portrait from the inventory suggests that it was given away by Arundel or Lumley, perhaps to one of Arundel's erstwhile associates.[33] These portraits, then, celebrate the military exploits of Arundel and his comrades in arms and they represent his own independent foray into the world of portraiture. They were, moreover, among Eworth's first English commissions.

Through Arundel, Eworth took Scrots's place as royal portraitist soon after Mary Tudor's accession and he gained widespread Catholic patronage; almost all of his identifiable sitters were in the queen's circle or sympathetic to Catholicism.[34] Altogether, there were eleven portraits by him in the collection, including one of Arundel's daughter Mary, Duchess of Norfolk (1555), a posthumous one of his son and heir Henry, Lord Maltravers (1557), based on John Bettes' portrait of around 1555, and one of Henry Lord Darnley on his seventeenth birthday (1562) painted for inspection by Mary, Queen of Scots, in support of his proposal of marriage. Eworth fell from favour at Mary I's death and it took thirteen years before he was accepted at the Elizabethan court. His last documented work is dated 1573. By far the most important resident painter until Hilliard, Eworth brought 'a sadness and beauty of observation as well as an incisive bite to his portraits', though Strong also describes him as 'a superb second-rater'.[35]

Other portraits painted in the 1550s probably entered the collection at once. The painter John Bettes I is represented by a portrait of Thomas, Lord Wentworth, Arundel's successor as Lord Chamberlain (c. 1549). Gerlach ('Garlicke' in the inventory) Flicke (c.1495-1558), a German painter who worked in England from around 1545 until his death (and whom Strong describes as 'a painter of meticulous dreariness',[36]) is represented by three portraits: a full-length of Thomas, first Lord Darcy of Chiche (1551), one of Arundel's predecessors as Lord Chamberlain (d. 1558), Thomas, third Duke of Norfolk (d. 1554), and Queen Mary I (d.1558). Only the latter is known to have survived.

A large proportion of Arundel's portraits up to this point had a personal significance for him; some portraits were gifts, and others were either of old colleagues, associates or members of his family. Curiously, however, the inventory does not list portraits of Arundel's parents or his first wife, Lady Anne Percy, daughter of the fourth earl of Northumberland,[37] though there was one of his mother in law, and he commissioned the companion and posthumous portraits of the first two dukes of Norfolk. But ensuing events would lead to a massive enlargement of the collection and a widening of its scope. Firstly, there was the series of deaths in both the Arundel and Lumley families which left Arundel and Jane his remaining daughter, Lumley's wife, bereft. Then Queen Mary died in November 1558 and Arundel's political importance, initially unaffected, gradually waned. At first, however, as we have seen, he had high hopes of marrying the new queen, and his recent purchase of Nonsuch Palace gave him the opportunity of impressing her with the completion of her father's pet architectural project. Arundel and the Lumleys were all of an artistic and historical turn of mind, in any case, and the opportunity to decorate and embellish a major palace to their own taste was irresistible; that doing so would facilitate Arundel's courtship of Elizabeth was a bonus.

The royal collection, already substantial, was housed almost entirely in the palace of Westminster (later in the new palace of Whitehall), the sovereign's principal residence. Nonsuch was virtually a storehouse and in the charge of Sir Thomas Cawarden when Arundel took possession. An inventory of the contents taken on that occasion showed that only four pictures were hanging there:

> One table with a picture of our Lorde and the iii kinges of Colleyn of alabaster.
>
> One table of wood burned with pictures of our ladie and aungells.

> One faire table of white and blacke of a kinge and Justices with the scripture audite illos et quod justum est judicate.
>
> One small folding black folding table with an obskure painting of th'emprouers.[38]

Arundel, who had been collecting pictures for about ten years, could do better than that and he transferred many of his pictures from Arundel House to the state rooms on the first floor of the palace where there was also a privy gallery. The Lumleys, then in their early twenties, might not have brought any pictures with them, but they eagerly supported Arundel's ambitions, and the decoration of the palace became their joint endeavour.

Arundel and Lumley concentrated on the contemporary and historical portraiture of the English monarchy and peerage, which was, of course, the milieu to which they belonged. Insofar as any custom of the kind had been established by this time, it was becoming standard practice for peers to hang a series of royal portraits in their country seats: the fourth Duke of Norfolk had 'eleven pictures of kings and queens' hanging in his house at Kenninghall in 1571. Arundel would certainly have commissioned a set, perhaps *en bloc*, immediately on taking over at Nonsuch for, after all, it had been a royal palace in the first place and it is likely that he intended them to be permanent fixtures in one of the state-rooms. Moreover, given his close relationship with Mary and her two predecessors, he was probably more enthusiastic about doing so than some others. The inventory lists portraits of all the English kings since Richard II (1367-1400) and some of their consorts. Obviously many of the likenesses of the earlier kings are artificial, and neither the painters or the dates of them are known, but Arundel's artists presumably worked from prototypes in the royal collection to avoid any divergent iconography. Ultimately, there were twenty-five royal portraits in the collection, culminating with Flicke's portrait (after Mor) of Mary I and the two panel-portraits and the only known contemporary marble bust of Elizabeth I.

The English upper classes formed by far the largest group of sitters in the collection; portraits of sixty-one peers and peeresses and twenty-seven of the higher gentry appear in the inventory. Nine of these are attributed to 'the famous paynter Steven' who has always been identified as Steven van der Meulen. Vertue visited the Lumley residence in

Grosvenor Square in 1735 and saw 'several old family pictures' painted by 'Steven' and was shown the artist's receipts for payment.[39] These attributions must now be revised following the discovery of two wills: one made by Steven van der Meulen in 1563 and the other made in 1566/7 by Steven van Herwijck, both of whom had been painting in England and each of whom could reasonably have laid claim to the title of 'famous paynter'.

Meulen is first mentioned in 1543 as a pupil of Willem van Cleve in Antwerp. He arrived in London around September 1560 and he was naturalised in February 1562 by which point he had become a well-established painter. His career in England lasted a mere three years, however, for he was among the large number of people in the capital carried off by the plague; his will, dated 5 October 1563, was proved on 20 January 1564. Herwijck, a Fleming, was a medallist, jeweller and painter who had travelled widely in Europe executing various commissions before settling in England from around 1562. He, too, enjoyed but a short career in this country, for he made his will on 22 August 1566 which was proved on 24 March 1567.[40] Since the working lives of these artists in England overlapped by two years (1562-4) at most, it is possible to revise the attributions of some of the portraits by 'Steven' in this collection on chronological grounds. The portraits of Elizabeth Fitzgerald (1560) and Dudley (1560/1) are by Meulen; Herwijck may be given the portraits of Norfolk (1565) and Egmont. The latter has no date but it is significant that Herwijck had earlier struck a medal of his brother George Egmont, Bishop of Utrecht. The remaining five portraits (of Arundel and the Lumleys) were executed during the overlapping period, but only three are dated: Arundel (December 1562); Lumley and his wife (a pair, May 1563).[41] Secure attributions of this group to one or other of the painters can only be made after detailed art-historical investigation, which is outside the scope of this study.

The collection included a substantial group of some forty portraits of rulers, statesmen and military figures involved in contemporary continental politics in which England took the closest interest. Holland was a Habsburg, and hence Spanish, possession and was governed by regents for Charles V, and then for his successor Philip II. Increasing resistance to the hispanicisation of the Netherlands culminated in the

Dutch Revolt of 1565 which led to some twenty years of hostilities. Elizabeth's policy was to acquiesce in Spanish suzerainty over the Low Countries but to neutralise any military threat to England by getting the Spanish army out without letting the French in and yet without acceding to Dutch independence. Her aim was partially realised with the Treaty of Nonsuch, concluded in August 1585 with the United Provinces, which gave her an armed presence (under the command of Robert Dudley, Earl of Leicester) at the key points of Flushing and Brill and a representative (also Leicester) on the Council of State in the Netherlands. Clearly, it would be fitting to have portraits of the main protagonists in this prolonged conflict on display in the palace which was visited frequently by the queen and her councilors and when foreign policy would be discussed. For that reason a large number of portraits were copied. In 1589 Lumley borrowed a portrait of Queen Elizabeth, wife of the French King Charles IX, from Mr More of Loseley to be copied.[42] Some portraits, however, appear to have been acquired rather late. The portraits of the Count of Hoorn and his brother the Lord of Montigny, who were executed by Alva in 1568 and 1570 respectively, did not join the collection until after 1590, yet Meulen's portrait of the Count of Egmont, who was executed with Hoorn, was acquired much earlier. Similarly, the portrait (after Anthonis Mor) of Antoine, Cardinal de Granvelle, Secretary of State to the Emperor and a key figure in the governance of the Low Countries until 1563, did not appear in the collection until some years after his death. It is likely that the late acquisition of some foreign portraits arose because copies by continental artists simply took longer to come by.

The group of foreign portraits is by no means comprehensive, of course, but it is almost evenly divided between Dutch, French and Spanish sitters whose images were required when they had reached positions of power and influence. Those of Emperor Charles V (perhaps after Titian), his principal adviser Viglius, the Duke of Savoy (both by Jacques de Poindre[43]) and his son Philip II (by Mor, the Habsburg court painter) were probably acquired at an early date in the period. Those of the regents would be obtained as they took office later on: the Duke of Alva (Mor) and the Duke of Parma (possibly after Titian) and his wife Margaret of Austria. Some portraits were obtained to celebrate a sitter's success in arms such as that of the Count de la Marche, leader of the Sea-Beggars who took The Brill, dominating the entrance into the lower

Rhine, on 1 April 1572. It hardly seems fitting for Arundel or Lumley to have celebrated the assassination of William of Nassau in 1584, but as well as his portrait they had one of his killer, Balthasar Gerards. There were also the matching portraits by Pieter Pourbus of Henri III and his victim the Duke of Guise. It was much more appropriate to hang portraits of three Polish princes who had gained prestige for keeping their kingdom outside the Habsburg empire. A small number of historical European portraits included Emperor Maximilian I (by Bernard Strigel), Pope Julius II (after Raphael) and a Raphael self-portrait. The foreign portraits form a varied selection, then, but it is clear that Arundel and Lumley kept up with the political changes among the continental leaders and generally sought portraits for the collection which would have a contemporary diplomatic relevance.

Four portraits in the inventory are attributed to an artist named 'Hubbert' 'Hubbard' or 'Hubbart'. He was Hubert (Huybrecht) Beuckelaer, a painter of Antwerp, whose life-dates are not known but whose career has been partially recovered. He appears to have been trained in the workshop of Agnolo Bronzino in Florence in the 1550s, after which he returned to Antwerp around 1560 to become assistant to Antonis Mor. In advance of the Spanish conquest of his native city, he fled to England around 1583/4 and immediately gained the patronage of the Earl of Leicester who had had military, diplomatic and artistic interests in Flanders for some time. Beuckelaer's known English portraits include ten which were executed between 1583 and 1591 (one of which is of Henry Percy the ninth, 'Wizard', Earl of Northumberland 1585/6 for which he was paid the extraordinary fee of £20), and one of c.1605. Four belonged to Lumley but only that of Sir John Hawkins (d. 1595) survives; it bears a *cartellino* and the date 1591. The lost portrait of Edward Dyer (d. 1607) is perhaps of a similar date but it is not possible to be sure. The dates of the portraits of Thomas, Lord Darcy and his sister, Lady Elizabeth Lumley, are also unknown, though since both of them married in 1582/3 it seems likely that they were painted within a year or so after the artist's arrival in England. (Beuckelaer is known to have lived in Greenwich in 1586, where the Lumleys, too, had a house.) His biographer remarks that Beuckelaer appealed to unorthodox political and religious tastes (Leicester the Puritan, Lumley the Catholic) and, despite the lack of extant paintings, 'whose style Flemish and Italian elements had blended' to 'become a distinctly cosmopolitan counterpoint to the dominant traditionalism of Elizabethan portraiture'.[44]

George Gower, the fashionable court painter between 1573 and 1596, painted the Kytsons in the best of his early style which shows a knowledge of French court portraiture. Three portraits attributed to him were in Lumley's collection: the Catholic martyrs Thomas Percy (1566) and Philip Howard (1575), and a marriage-portrait of Mary, Lady Darcy of Chiche (1583), also a Catholic. Lumley, however, did not offer the increasingly important Gower the major painting project he had in mind. We have seen that William Segar first gained Lumley's patronage because he was an accomplished heraldic artist, but Segar's sentiment that portraits and monuments enabled people to 'retaine in memory the excellent actions of such men as had lived honourably and died vertuously', was bound to have further commended him to Lumley, the genealogist and collector. Lumley also approved Sir Thomas More's description of the ideal society in which were erected statues of famous men as both testaments to their achievements and as an example to their posterity.[45] Nothing is known of the origins of the Segar brothers Francis and William, both of whom were painters. Since Francis spent much of his life abroad and is not heard of before 1590, it is with William 'Seigar' that Lumley was wholly concerned. In 1580 or thereabouts Lumley commissioned Segar to paint a series of fifteen full-length portraits of his ancestors 'lyneally descending from the Conquest' to hang in the great hall of Lumley Castle, the refurbishment of which was nearly finished.[46] Only one or two of the later portraits can be genuine and Segar had to exercise his imagination in portraying the earlier generations, for most of the images are obviously entirely manufactured. Indeed, their costumes have attracted derisive comment: 'Most of them have a sort of turban, and their fantastic robes give them a very Saracenic air'.[47] They are all armed with massive swords and shields, the latter displaying the Lumley heraldic arms which is the most obvious, not to say predominant feature of all the portraits. Segar completed the series in 1588 with portraits of Lumley and his second wife (making seventeen portraits in all).

Segar painted three other portraits for Lumley. Firstly, the lost portrait of his son Charles Lumley, who died in infancy. Secondly, 'Kinge Richard the seconde, delyvering the wryte of Parliament to Ralphe the first Barron of Lumley, called by him the eight yeare of his Reigne' (c.1590). This was a copy of the portrait in Westminster Abbey of the enthroned youthful and red-haired king in front of whom Segar superimposed a kneeling, elderly, stout, balding and grey-bearded Sir Ralph de Lumley; in fact the latter was aged twenty-three when he was made a baron in 1385. Secondly, there was the full-length portrait of Lumley in parliamentary (or academic) robes dated 1591, his last commission from Lumley. In all, thirty portraits in the inventory are by or attributed to Segar, twenty of which are of Lumley family members. It is not suggested that Segar worked in Durham throughout the fifteen-eighties (though he must have done so for a good part of the time), because ten portraits in this collection as well as four in others, by or attributed to him datable between 1585 and 1591, can only have been painted in London or thereabouts, including one of the queen in 1585. After he left Lumley's employment in 1591 Segar went on to paint at least four more portraits (including another of the queen in 1597) but he seems to have abandoned portraiture in 1598 to concentrate on his work as a herald. His neo-mediaeval style was, in any case, becoming old-fashioned and less sought-after (the Earl of Essex switched from him to Marcus Gheeraerts) At any rate, in terms of the number of paintings he completed and the length of time he was engaged, Lumley was Segar's earliest and principal artistic patron.[48]

A number of portraits reflected Lumley's wider interests. Aristocratic dabbling in alchemy, chemistry, medicine and so on had a long history (Lumley's contemporary the 'Wizard Earl' of Northumberland researched such matters). Lumley collected books on these topics and he had one or two portraits of the practitioners (Paracelsus and Sir Edward Kelley). There was a selection of literary portraits (Chaucer, Churchyard and the great mediaeval Italians) and one of George Buchanan, the Scot, by Arnold van Bronckhorst (fl. 1566-86). Bronckhorst was a Netherlander who first went to Scotland prospecting for gold but gave it up and became a painter. He was paid for a portrait of Buchanan in 1580 of which Lumley's was a copy. Lumley displayed a group of adventurers and explorers (Drake, Hawkins, Cabot, Cavendish, Stukeley). The law was represented by James Dyer and Julius Caesar, and his own church by recently deceased bishops and saints.

Arundel and Lumley acquired examples of the work of some twenty portraitists working in England during the sixteenth century; Dürer's Lord Morley of 1523 was probably the earliest. Around fifty of the ninety English non-royal portraits can be associated in one way or another with a named artist or his studio. Fifteen of the others are of historical personages and were probably not painted to order. It is unlikely that either Arundel or Lumley would have commissioned portraits of Jane Shore, Edward IV's mistress, or of William Sommers, Henry VIII's fool. Portraits of that sort may have entered the collection as gifts or serendipitously. The other portraits of peers and gentry were probably acquired deliberately and were commissioned from copyists as sitters reached positions of importance, or had their likenesses painted at the time of a marriage or on some other important occasion. In 1572 William Cecil was created Lord Burghley, appointed Lord Treasurer and made a Knight of the Garter; his portrait by an unknown artist, one of many depicting him in those capacities, appeared in the collection shortly afterwards. It has not been possible, however, to reconstruct the circumstances in which every portrait was acquired or to account for why some and not others were collected, hence it has to be assumed that Lumley built up the collection by acquiring pictures piecemeal.

There was one occasion when he is thought to have acquired a larger number of pictures in a single transaction. The Earl of Leicester died on 4 September 1588 very heavily in debt and his creditors, mainly the queen, required satisfaction. Inventories of his possessions were drawn up in April 1590 and sales were held in June. The Lumley inventory of that year included twelve pictures which correspond with pictures in Leicester's inventory and they may therefore have been bought by Lumley. In some cases, the correlations are plausible but others are less certain. Precisely named genre scenes and representations of the Old Testament stories are probably correctly identified, but pictures of the Nativity of Christ, St Jerome and Mary Magdalene were not unusual and may have been already in Lumley's collection. At any rate, interestingly, the pictures in this batch included only one portrait – that of Leicester – the others were religious or secular narratives and most were painted by Flemish artists.[49]

In summary, then, it is clear that the collection was formed by Henry Fitzalan between 1547 and 1550. At first he collected pictures which had personal associations but, after the purchase of Nonsuch Palace in 1556, his scope widened to include portraits of the most prominent English and continental statesmen of the day and of recent history. That development was almost certainly influenced by his daughter and son in law, who not only shared his enjoyment of the palace but who appreciated its political importance. The collection was not, therefore, just a compilation of portraits having a private significance for, unlike some other contemporary collections, it was not made up only of portraits of family and friends which were intended to form an ancestral pictorial record. But nor was it just a means of currying favour with the queen, who liked and frequently visited Nonsuch, for the collection came to serve as a public diplomatic and political tool. The collection was as objective and eclectic an assemblage of the most prominent people of the day in a long period of international tension and was as complete as was practicable or, at any rate, of those who chose to have their portraits painted. It betrayed no bias in either politics or religion. Indeed, one lacuna is the absence of a portrait of any of the popes after Julius II. But then, there were seventeen of them in the century after his death in 1513 and their portraits would have been difficult to come by, even if it had been decided to brave any hostility which would have arisen from putting them on display in Protestant England. On the other hand, the presence of the rabidly anti-Catholic Francis Walsingham may be thought surprising, but he was a major English politician who could hardly be ignored; he may even have presented a copy of his portrait be hung in the palace. The collection was built up steadily over the years except for a lull between 1569 and 1572 when both Arundel and Lumley were involved with Mary, Queen of Scots, and were in custody for some of that time. Arundel's death in 1580 brought another pause but Lumley presently resumed collecting and went on doing so more or less for the rest of his life.

A reorganisation of the collection became necessary following Lumley's surrender of Nonsuch to the queen in 1592. When he moved out of the palace he would have had to find new homes for around 190 pictures. (i.e., not including the acquisitions made after 1590 and the twenty-five family portraits, mostly by Segar, which had always hung in Lumley Castle). He left behind a few portraits and objects, perhaps in the presence chamber and gallery, given that Nonsuch continued to be a favoured royal residence. The library certainly remained *in situ* as did the collection of musical instruments, and it is likely that some of the royal portraits were left in place. The portrait of Richard II seems to have been a gift to the queen. Baron Waldstein visited Nonsuch in 1600 but he provides little evidence of the contents because he appears only to have been allowed into the hall where he saw a collection of sculptures representing stories from Ovid and portraits of Charles IX of France, Henry VIII and his wives, Elizabeth, Jane Seymour, mother of Edward VI who died in childbirth, and a picture of Medusa with snaky locks.[50] John Ernst, Duke of Saxe-Weimar, visited Nonsuch in 1613 and made the following note of the portraits he saw:

> The mother of Philip II, King of Spain
>
> The wives of several English gentlemen
>
> Portraits of many English gentlemen, and old English kings
>
> Bathory, King of Poland
>
> The Treasurer Cecil
>
> A carved bust said to be an exact image of Christ [*sic*][51]

Some of the named portraits can be traced in the inventory, and the last item was probably the 'special picture of Christ cast in mould' by Raphael. But the terms 'several' and 'many' in relation to the others he saw is maddeningly vague and there is no way of knowing the numbers involved. Even allowing that more than one copy of a portrait existed, the duke's note does, however, confirm that Lumley left some portraits in the palace.

Lumley Castle was intended as the principal home for his collections (and it was fortunate that his earlier restoration of the castle made it suitable for the purpose), but he did not have to move everything up to the north because he could have added to the contents of his other houses. There was Stansted, now his wife's dower house; his town-house on Tower Hill where the portraits of the older and younger Wyatts who had owned the house before him were already hanging; a house at Greenwich, which he used when the court was at Greenwich Palace; and then there was Keeper's Lodge, Lumley's official residence at Nonsuch. The lodge was described in a survey of 1650 as a

> timber building tiled overhead standing in the said Nonsuch park a pretty distance remote from Nonsuch house commonly called the keepers lodge, consisting of a hall, a parlour, a kitchen, a buttery, a larder, a scullery, a milkhouse, a bolting house, a deer house, a coal house, and ten chambers or rooms overhead, a stable, a little barn of three bays, a hay

> house, and a barn of five bays thatched, a garden or orchard very well planted and two little yards.[52]

Although the lodge was small and may not have been an entirely suitable building in which to display large pictures, his other properties were both appropriate and big enough and it is probable that items from the Nonsuch collections were placed in each of them. At any rate, so far as can be seen the collection remained substantially intact despite the upheaval of 1592. When Lumley's post mortem inventory was taken in 1609, almost twenty years after the compilation of the inventory, there were 233 pictures in Lumley Castle, though they were not identified individually. Hence, excluding the twenty-five family pictures, there were 208 pictures in the castle and there was an unknown number hanging in his other houses. Lumley had given little away.

Lumley has been described as an antiquary rather than a connoisseur, as a 'voracious' collector, and that his collecting was one of 'naive and unsophisticated accumulation'.[53] Certainly, the extent of his art-collection illustrates a propensity to collect as many portraits as possible and discrimination hardly entered into it, but, on the other hand, Lumley could only acquire what there was to be had and this was bound to include naive, even artificial portraits. The principal purpose of portraiture in his day was to provide a visual accompaniment to the written pedigree, hence the simulation of earlier generations was an obvious necessity. Moreover, in general a sophisticated or penetrating characterisation of the sitter was neither required or offered. Portraits were painted in the archaic style which was necessary to avoid the attentions of the iconoclasts. Portraiture as a genre could not achieve full aesthetic sophistication until more relaxed times came about – the age of Van Dyck.

In any case, the inventory documents all styles of portraiture executed in the Elizabethan age and is therefore a roll-call of most of the important contemporary painters working in northern Europe. Native English artists are well represented but they are heavily outnumbered by northern Europeans because England lagged far behind continental artistic standards. Renaissance Italy was cut off from post-mediaeval England after the Reformation and a century would elapse before full contact was re-established between them, hence English and Italian art of the period cannot be assessed on similar grounds to the former's detriment. (Segar, the neo-mediaevalist, is a special case for he was briefed to produce portraits appropriate to the setting of a mediaeval castle.) Lumley's patronage of the most eminent contemporary painters, his bookmanship and musicality, his preservation of the Arundel collections, and his building restoration at Lumley argues a more sophisticated than naive approach. Many of his pictures are unique and are of museum quality; they now hang in leading art-institutions across the world.

Ultimately, the collection outstripped in scope and size every other in England; that was partly because no other collector had so favourable a setting and appreciative an audience, but nor did anyone else have such ambition. Thus the development of English collecting and connoisseurship was well underway by the middle decades of the sixteenth century among a small band of English aristocrats and Lumley was their leading figure.[54] It has been said that he 'deserves to rank with Thomas Howard, earl of Arundel, among the great English collectors of works of art', but I would put him ahead. Indeed, Howard's most recent biographer has observed:

> But for Lumley, Arundel might not have sensed that he was one with his ancestors: that as a patron in later life, he was maintaining a family tradition, and that it was Lumley who introduced him to classical sculpture.[55]

Not only was Lumley the prototype of all English collectors, he was also the forerunner of the wealthy and well-educated Catholic gentleman who, excluded from public life, attended to his estates, became a dilettante and enjoyed art for its own sake, and who became expert in history, science, mathematics or some other branch of scholarship. Such would be found throughout the land during the following three centuries.[56]

Annexe: The Lumley Inventory of 1590

The following reprints the Lumley Inventory initially published by Lionel Cust in *Walpole Society* volume 6, pp. 15-35, 1917/8. Material from Mary Hervey, 'A Lumley Inventory of 1609', *ibidem,* pp 36-50 has also been embodied.

The inventory entry is given in **bold** letters. Additions after 1590 in same hand are shown in []. Additions after 1605 and in a different hand are shown in { }.

Each entry is annotated with a brief clarification of the sitter's identity, if one is necessary, followed by details of the portrait. Where inventoried portraits have not been identified it has been thought useful and of interest to add a note of the whereabouts in Britain of known portraits of the sitters, without necessarily implying a provenance to the Lumley collection.

References are to material in the Bibliography.

* * *

A Certificate from Mr John Lampton Stewarde of Howseholde to John Lord Lumley, of all his Lo: monumentes of Marbles, Pictures and tables in Paynture, with other his Lordshippes howseholde Stuffe and Regester of Bookes. Anno 1590

These sorted together for the memorye of yo[r] Lo: house.

Opening page of the Lumley Inventory (The Red Book)

A note of Pyctures caryinge the fowrme of the whole Statuary

Adam and Eve

Picture unidentified.

Statuaryes of xvi^{en} Auncestors of yor Lo: lyneally descending from the Conquest unto yor self

Lampton meant that there were fifteen full-length portraits of Lumley's ancestors and one of Lumley himself. There were, however, seventeen generations between Liulph and John and it is Sir Roger (Sir Robert's predecessor) who has been left out. The post mortem inventory of 1609 placed 'xv pictures of my Lord Lumley's ancestors with a pillar of his pedigree' in the 'Great Chamber' of Lumley Castle. It is 'almost certain' that the series was painted by William Segar or his brother Francis. [Cust 19] Painting began around 1580 and the set was completed in 1588. Each figure stands in a stone niche which is inscribed at the base with the name of the subject, his father, and wife where appropriate. All except the sixteenth carry a shield emblazoned with the Lumley heraldic arms which were six silver parakeets on a red background until Sir Robert (No. 6 below) adopted the arms of his wife's family (Thweng): three green parakeets either side of a red bar on a white background. The arms also appear at the top left of each portrait and a diamond-shaped lozenge impaling the wife's arms is shown at top right. Each portrait measured some twelve by eight feet, and in 1857 Fordyce saw them hung in plain black frames. The portraits, 'with the pedigree and arms of Lumley from Liulphus, Minister to William the Conqueror down to Elizabeth Darcey de Chiche', were bought in at the auction in Lumley Castle in 1785 for £8.10s. In 1807 they were again bought in for £16.16s. The first fifteen portraits belong to the Lumley Trustees and are on loan to Leeds Castle; those of John and his wife Elizabeth are at Sandbeck Park.

1.Liulphus. The portrait is inscribed with the date 1080 and, at the top: *Successiones Dominorum et Baronum de Lumley.*

2.Uchtred.

3.William de Lumley.

4.Sir William de Lumley (I).

5.Sir William de Lumley (II) (alive c. 1250).

6.Sir Robert de Lumley (d.c. 1325).

7.Sir Marmaduke de Lumley (1314-65).

8.Sir Ralph de Lumley (c1360-1400) Created Baron Lumley 1385 by Richard II attainted 1400.

Two other portraits are named Ralph. The first depicts his ennoblement and is listed separately. The second, which is not inventoried, was painted by an unknown artist in 1567. Warner said it was 'Marked 1567. Aetat. 78.' Pennant has: 'Small full length', and is described at auction in 1785 as 'whole length, of Ralph Lumley, 1567' when it was bought in for £2.12s.6d. No Ralph Lumley was living in 1567 and it may be a portrait of Roger, father of Richard Lumley, the chief beneficiary of John Lumley's will. It is now at Sandbeck Park.

9.Sir John de Lumley (1383-1421).

10.Sir Thomas de Lumley (1408-85).

11.Sir George de Lumley [(c.1445-1507); created Baron Lumley in 1480.

12.Thomas Lumley, who predeceased his father George in 1487.

13.Baron Richard Lumley (c.1477-1510), son of Thomas (No.12).

14.Baron John Lumley (1493-1544).

A portrait of John, by an unknown artist, not in the inventory, was described by Fordyce as of 'a small figure of a young man, with handsome delicate features, in a Spanish dress. On the back of the picture is written "Lumley who was in the batte of Flodden Field when King James of Scots was slain."' That was partly garbled by the cataloguer for the Lumley Castle auction in 1785: 'small life ¾ of Mr Lumley slain in the battle of Floddenfield'. Lumley was at Flodden in 1515 but he lived for a further thirty years during which time he attended the Field of the Cloth of Gold in 1520 and was a leader of the Pilgrimage of Grace in 1536. Strong identifies the costume as Italian c.1550 and concludes that the sitter was probably foreign. [*TJP* 203] It was bought in for £2.2s. at the 1785 auction and reappeared in the 1807 auction when it was again bought in (for £2.12s.); it is now at Sandbeck Park.

15.George Lumley. Attainted and beheaded in 1538 for taking part in the Pilgrimage of Grace during the lifetime of John his father.

16.John Lumley (1534?-1609). Succeeded his grandfather; restored in blood 1547; created Baron Lumley 1553. The portrait depicts Lumley 'in rich armour, a grey beard, dated 1588, aet. 54' (Pennant), 'in splendid steel armour, studded with gold' (Warner). [Pennant p. 322; Warner pp. 299/301]

yor eldest sonne Charles

Died in infancy. Portrait lost.

bothe yor Lo: wives

a. No full-length portrait of Jane Fitzalan, Lumley's first wife survives. Steven van der Meulen's 1563 portrait is almost a full length, but it was inventoried separately. A portrait of her was listed in the Northampton inventory of 1614. [*Archaeologia* vol. 42 (1869) p. 356]

b. William Segar's portrait, c. 1584-6, of Elizabeth Darcy, Lumley's second wife. It was painted in the same style as those of Lumley and his ancestors (Nos. 1-16 above) and was clearly intended to complete the series, making seventeen portraits in all. It is now at Sandbeck Park.

old tyme

This hung adjacent to a panel displaying a long meditation in Latin beginning: 'With winged shoulders, irrevocable time flies...' and is now untraced.

Kinge Richard the seconde, delyvering the wryte of Parliament to Ralphe the first Barron of Lumley, called by him the eight yeare of his Reigne

An imaginary and anachronistic reconstruction of the event, inscribed at the top: 'R.R.2 AN DNI 1384 Ao REG 8. The portrait of Richard is a copy of the painting in Westminster Abbey thought to date from c. 1388, onto which Lumley is superimposed; Lumley's *cartellino* is on the dais. The youthful king (supposedly seventeen years old) is enthroned and Lumley, depicted as a bearded old man of twenty-three, dressed in late Elizabethan parliamentary robes is kneeling at his feet. In 1735

George Vertue visited the Earl of Scarbrough's house in Grosvenor Square and remarked on 'a large picture of K Richard the second delivering a deed to Sr. Ralph Lumley an ancestor of that family, he is on his knees before the King ... painted much in the manner of Holbein but the painter's name on the picture and in this old inventory, taken about 1590, is ... Stephens'. The inventory does not mention Steven van der Meulen and the modern attribution is to William Segar, c.1590-1600; the depiction of Lumley is identical to that of No. 8 above in the series by Segar. It is on loan to Leeds Castle. [Vertue p. 81]

King Henry the eight and his father Kinge Henry the seaventh joyned together, doone in white and blacke by Haunce Holbein

Cartoon (paper mounted on canvas) for a wall-painting in Whitehall Palace, finished in 1537 but lost when the palace was burned down in 1698. The cartoon was among the pictures bequeathed to Robert Cecil, Earl of Salisbury, for it appears in the Salisbury House inventory of 30 June 1612. It was not included in the inventory of 1629 and may have been moved to another of the earl's houses. Since it is next found in the Devonshire collection at Chatsworth, it may have been given to the earl's second daughter Elizabeth who married William Cavendish, third Earl of Devonshire, in 1639. It was acquired by NPG (No. 4027) in 1957. [*Dynasties* No. 5; *TJP* 153-5; Susan Bracken, 'Holbein's Chatsworth Cartoon, Its possible location in the 17th century', *The British Art Journal* vol 1, no. 1 (1999), pp. 14/5]

Kinge Henry the eight alone doone in oyle colours

(1491-1547). This portrait was catalogued in the Sandbeck Park sale of 1807 as: 'in splendid regal costume, in high preservation, Holbein'. It is possibly the portrait now at Hampton Court which has been cut down all round to become a half-length. [Millar, No. 37.]

his sonne King Edward the sixt drawne by (blank)

(1537-53). The portrait, which bears Lumley's *cartellino*, is described by Millar as a

> good version of perhaps the most important official portrait of Edward VI, which has been convincingly associated by Dr. Auerbach [*Tudor Portraits* (1954) 77-8] with Guillim

> Stretes or Scrots. The type may have originated in 1550, when negotiations were set on foot for a marriage between the King and the eldest daughter of Henri II of France.

It was bought in at the Lumley Castle auction of 1785 but went for £3.15s. in the auction of 1807. It was recorded in the collections of William Beckford and the Duke of Hamilton before it was bought for Queen Victoria in 1882 (ascribed to Holbein) and is now at Hampton Court. [*TJP*, 94; *Icon* No. 6; Millar No. 49; Piper, p. 228]

Quene Anne Bulleyne

Anne Boleyn (1507-36) second queen of Henry VIII. This portrait was last recorded in the sale of James West's (d.1772) collection in 1773 when it was said to have been cut down due to damage by fire when in the Temple. [*TJP* 5-7; Davies]

Duches of Myllayne, afterwards Duches of Lorreyn daughter to [Christierne] king of Denmarke doone by Haunce Holbein

(1522-90). Christina, younger daughter of Christian II of Denmark and Isabella of Austria, sister of Charles V. Holbein visited Brussels in 1538 and painted this portrait of her (in mourning dress for her husband the Duke of Milan who died in 1535) in connection with her possible marriage to Henry VIII, but she was passed over in favour of Anne of Cleves. The portrait was in the palace of Westminster during the last ten years of Henry's reign, as is confirmed by inventories of 1542 and 1547. At the death of Edward VI in 1553, when the contents of the palace were compared with those of 1547, the absence of the portrait was explained thus: 'This Table Therle of Arundell hathe of the kinges maiesties gift as he saithe'. The portrait was probably kept at Nonsuch Palace and then in the Lumley house on Tower Hill from 1592 until Lady Lumley's death in 1617 when it passed into the ownership of Lord Darcy. He probably sold it to Thomas Howard, Earl of Arundel, in whose possession it was by 1627. It then passed to the dukes of Norfolk and it was bought by the National Gallery in 1909. Lumley's *cartellino* was removed during subsequent cleaning. [Shaw; BL, Lansdowne Roll 15; Ganz No. 98; Piper, p. 227; R. Strong, 'Some Early Portraits at Arundel Castle', *Connoisseur* (March 1978) 195; Hervey No. 193; E. Goldring, 'An important early picture collection: The Earl of Pembroke's

1561/62 inventory and the provenance of Holbein's 'Christina of Denmark", *Burl. Mag.* vol. cxliv, no. 1188 (March 2002) pp 157 ff.]

Duches of Parma, Regent in Flaunders, Base doughter to the Empero[r] Charles the fiveth

Margaret of Austria (1522-86). Sister of Philip II whom she followed as Regent 1559-1567. The portrait is unidentified but one was included in the Arundel Inventory of 1655. [Hervey No. 436]

King Phillip of Spaine

Philip II (1527-98). This was one of at least three copies in Britain of the portrait by Antonis Mor: at Ipswich, NPG No. 347, or in the Fitzwilliam Museum. The whole length of 'a gentleman in armour (Philip of Spain)' was in the Lumley Castle auction of 1785 and was bought in for £5.15.6d. It was put up again at Sandbeck Park in 1807 as 'Philip II, full length, in rich armour' (it is not known what it fetched; it may, of course, have been bought in again). [*TJP* 248; Wright 141, 182.]

Henry of Burbon King of Navarre and of Fraunce

Henri de Bourbon (1553-1610). Many portraits of him are known, including a full-length which was inventoried at Hatfield House in 1611 and is conceivably one of the pictures bequeathed by Lumley to the Earl of Salisbury ; a portrait also appeared in the Arundel Inventory of 1655. [Auerbach 69; Hervey No. 371]

Will[m] Nassau Prince of Orange, murthered by Balthazar Geraertez, a Burgunyan gent

William Nassau (1533-84), Prince of Orange 1544; gained the soubriquet: *'Le Taciturne'*. He was shot by the Burgundian Balthasar Gerard, a fanatical Catholic, on 10 July 1584 for suppressing Catholicism in Holland. Portrait not traced.

the Princes his last wife, daughter to Colligny Admyrall of Fraunce and widow of Telligny

Louise de Coligny, daughter of Gaspard de Coligny (1519-72) and widow of Charles Seigneur Teligny (c.1535-72). Portrait not traced.

the last old Earle of Arundell fitzallen, Lo: Chamberleyne to k: H;8 and K: Edw: 6 and Lo: Steward to Quene Mary and Q. Elizabeth

Henry Fitzalan (1512-80), last of the Fitzalan earls of Arundel, founder of the collection; Lumley's father in law. Two entries in the inventory refer to portraits of him: this and another (see below) which lists one, or perhaps two, half-lengths by Steven van der Meulen, but none of the known portraits is a full-length. There is, however, a portrait at Chatsworth which Davies deemed to be a full-length of Arundel by Hans Eworth. It depicts him mounted on a white horse; he is in armour, wears the badge of the Garter and holds a field-marshal's staff. In the background there is an unknown castle and hills with a river running into a bay with shipping. The dating and attribution of the portrait, however, are problematic. It has a latin inscription which translates as:

> Henry, Earl of Arundel, Lord Maltravers & Clun, Knight of the Order of St George, & & & Ancestor of the Most Honourable Lord Philip present Earl of Arundel & Surrey, Lord Mowbray Segrave Brewes [i.e., Broase] Maltravers & Clun 1581.

But the old earl's soldiering had ended many years before and he died on 24 February 1579/80 at least a year before the portrait was painted; in any case, Eworth's painting career had ended some seven or eight years earlier, and he may even have been dead by 1580/1. The Garter and staff are, however, appropriate attributes for the earl and the portrayal of the horse with a sprig of oak-leaves in its mane is an authentic Fitzalan emblem. But, this depiction of horse and rider is not unique; an almost identical portrait of François I of France by François Clouet, c.1540, is in the Uffizi Gallery, Florence. It is possible that Philip (first of the Howard earls of Arundel), who had been estranged from his grandfather for some time, had this post mortem portrait painted as an expression of remorse as well as respect for his grandfather's earlier military career. Moreover, since the old earl had left his collection of portraits to Lumley, the new earl might not have had a portrait of his grandfather and this picture remedied the deficiency. Whatever the provenance of this portrait, it seems unlikely that it was ever Lumley's for Lampton would probably have specified an equestrian portrait.

Willm Harbert first Earle of Pembroke, created by King Edward the sixt Lo: Steward to Quene Elizabeth

William Herbert (1507?-70), first earl (of the second creation) of Pembroke, 1551. This portrait, by an unknown artist (school of Eworth), bearing the Lumley *cartellino* and with the later inscription: 'AETATIS 66 1567' [*sic*] is at Wilton House. It was bought by the fourth or fifth earl around 1650 to replace a copy lost in a disastrous fire around 1647; it was seen at Wilton by Aubrey in 1655. [Piper p. 231; Sidney, 16th Earl of Pembroke, *Paintings and Drawings at Wilton House* (1968) 54/5; ODNB illus.]

Thomas first Lo: Darcy of Chiche created by King Edw: 6. Lo: Chamberleyne to the said K: Edw: drawn by Garlicke

(1506-58). Created baron and K.G. in 1551. The portrait, bearing the Lumley *cartellino*, and signed by Gerlach Flicke, 1551, was last seen in Irnham Hall, Lincs., in 1848; it disappeared when the house was sold in 1854. A copy, inscribed with the date 1554 and the name of the sitter, in Hengrave Hall, Suffolk, was sold in 1952 but its present whereabouts are unknown. [Mary Hervey, 'A Lumley Inventory of 1609', *Walpole Society*, vol. 6, p. 72; Piper, p. 228, n.13; *Icon*, No. 17]

Lo: Charles Howard of Effingham, Lord Admyrall of England

(1536-1624) English statesman and naval commander. He became lord high admiral in 1585 and commanded the English fleet in the defeat of the Spanish Armada. Since this portrait was in the collection before 1590, it may have been the lost full length Garter portrait of c.1585-90 based on Gheeraerts's engraved roll of the Garter Procession of 1576. All other known portraits of Howard are post-1596. [*TJP* 235-7; Millar, p 84]

Sir Christofer Hatton Knight, as he was being vice-chamberleyne to Q. Elizabeth [who afterward was Lo: Chancello^r^ of Englande]

(1540-91) Lawyer and statesman. Lampton's entry dates this portrait, (by an unknown artist possibly Cornelis Ketel), to 1578-87. Two identical full-length portraits of c.1585 are known: 1. In the City of Northampton City Art Gallery. 2. In the Inner Temple with a copy in NPG. [Davies; *TJP* 133-8; Wright 111; ODNB illus.]

Lorde Darneley [afterwards K: of Scott] and his brother Charles Stewarde in one table

Henry Stewart (1545-67). In 1565 he married Mary Stuart, Queen of Scots. This life-size portrait, in watercolour on fine fabric by Hans Eworth, is coincident with Darnley's seventeenth birthday which fell on 7 December 1562 and was probably intended to be taken secretly up to Scotland, conceivably by Lumley, on behalf of Darnley's mother, Margaret Douglas, Countess of Lennox. The portrait appeared in the inventory of Salisbury House in 1612. It passed to Charles I, was sold during the Commonwealth, but recovered by Charles II at the Restoration; it is now at Holyrood Palace, Edinburgh. [Millar, No. 57; *TJP* 60/1; *Icon* No 47; Auerbach, 18, S. Bracken, 'Holbein's Chatsworth Cartoon, its possible location in the 17th century', *The British Art Journal* vol. 1, no. 1 (1999) pp. 14/5; ODNB illus.]

Note. The entry: ~~**the Lord Darley , after King of Scotts**~~ appears earlier among the English royals but was removed by Lampton to this less elevated position in the inventory.

[Robert Dudley Earle of Leicester]

(1532?-88). He was one of the most frequently painted Elizabethans and three (possibly four) portraits of him are listed in the inventory, the last of which to be added to the collection is this full-length. The earl is depicted with full military accoutrements and was probably painted in 1585-6 when Leicester was in the Netherlands, possibly by William Segar, though Bruyn is not convinced that it was an *ad vivum* portrait; he also suggests it was a product of the workshop that produced the portrait of Ambrose, Earl of Warwick. It is now at Parham Park. [Bruyn, p. 110 n. 31; *TJP* 191-6.]

[Edwarde Earle of Oxfourde]

Edward de Vere (1550-1604) succeeded as seventeenth Earl of Oxford in 1562. Vertue said that a full-length by Cornelius Ketel was in the collection of the Countess Dowager of Strafford in Yorkshire. A full-length portrait of c.1585 is at Hatfield House. [[B.M. Add. 230618 p.18; *GEC*; NPG archive; E. Chaney, *The Evolution of the Grand Tour* (1998), p. 12]

[yor Lo^{p} selfe in yor Parlyament Robes]

Hutchinson saw this portrait of Lumley, which bears the Lumley *cartellino*, hanging in the Music Room of Lumley Castle. Fordyce describes him 'in full crimson robes, and holding in his hands a glove and a purse, as Baron of the Exchequer'. Pennant has Lumley 'in his robes, with a glove and handkerchief in one hand, a little black skull-cap, white beard, dated 1591. This, I believe, was the performance of Richard Stevens, an able statuary painter, and medallist, mentioned by Mr Walpole' [*Anecdotes of Painting* I, 161]. The painter cannot have been Steven van der Meulen, for his last work was completed some twenty-three years earlier. More reasonably, Piper has 'artist unknown ... conceivably by Segar'. It is now at Sandbeck Park. [Fordyce p. 612; Pennant p. 322; Piper p. 227.]

[Monseur brother to Valois laste Kinge of Fraunce in the robes of y^{t} order]

Henri, Duke of Anjou (1556-84), Knight of the Golden Fleece, brother of Henry III of France. Portrait not traced.

[Counte de Horne

in the Robes of their Order

Counte de Mounteny]

Phillipe de Montmorency, Count of Hoorn (1518-68) and his brother Florent de Montmorency, Baron of Montigny (1527-70), both in the robes of the Order of the Golden Fleece. The portraits have not been traced.

[Robert Earle of Sussex Anno 1593]

Robert Radcliffe (1560-1629), whose succession as tenth earl in December 1593 aged twenty is presumably celebrated in this portrait by Gheeraerts. Hutchinson, mostly copying Pennant, has

> Full length in white armour and gold brocade breeches, young and handsome, a staff in his right hand, his left resting on a sword. His helmet with an enormous plume placed on a table: this motto *amando e fidando troppo son ruinato.*

The picture was offered at auction in 1785 as a 'whole length portrait of Radcliff, Earl of Sussex, in armour' and was bought in at £10.10s. It was offered again in 1807 when it realised £6. It is now in the Tower of London. [Hutchinson p. 404; Piper p. 227n7; Pennant p.323; Brayley p. 192; NPG archives.]

[Thomas Lord Broughe in his Robes of the Garter]

Thomas, fifth Lord Burgh, (1562-97); he was made K.G. in 1593. No portrait answering this description has been identified. A full-length portrait in a private collection, by or after Segar, depicts him as a young man and inscribed with the date 1588 and 'The Lord Burroughs Deputy of Ireland'. He is in armour and does not wear robes or a Garter George. It has a *cartellino* but not of the Lumley type. [NPG archives]

Pictures of a Smaller Scantlinge

King Richard the Second

(1367-1400). The first King of England to sit for his portrait, c.1388. This could have been a 'shop' copy of the original portrait in Westminster Abbey, but it could also have been the portrait to which the following wellknown anecdote refers. William Lambarde, Keeper of the Records in the Tower, presented Queen Elizabeth with his *Pandecta Rotulorum* at an audience in the Privy Chamber at Greenwich on 4 August 1601. During their conversation she told him how the portrait came to be in her possession:

> The Lord Lumley, a lover of antiquities, discovered it fastened upon the backside of a door of a base room, which he presented unto me, praying, with my good leave, that I might put it in order with the rest of the ancestors and successors. I will command Thomas Knyvett, keeper of my house and gallery at Westminster to show it unto thee.

It is not known when or where the picture was found. If this is the portrait meant here, then, Lumley must have given it to Elizabeth after 1590, perhaps when he left Nonsuch Palace in 1592. It has been suggested, however, that Lumley's gift might have been a quite different portrait, now lost and known only from engravings. [G Harrison, 'A Last Elizabethan Journal (1599-1603)', *The Elizabethan Journals* (1938) p. 194; Millar, p.13; *TJP* 259-62; R.L. Poole, 'The Portraits of Richard

II', *The Antiquaries Journal* vol. 11 (1931), pp. 156-8]

King Henry the fourthe

(1367-1413). A version of the standard invented posthumous portrait in the Royal Collection and at NPG No. 310.[*TJP* 141/2]

King Henry the fiveth

(1387-1422). Painted posthumously in the late fifteenth century; other versions are in the Royal Collection and at NPG No. 545. [Millar No. 6]

King Henry the sixte

(1421-71). Presumably painted in the same workshop as the portraits of Henry V and Richard III, also in this collection, and the Royal Collection. Several closely related portraits exist, including that at NPG No. 546; a slightly different type is at NPG No. 2457. [Millar No. 8; *TJP* 145-8]

King Edwarde the fourthe

(1442-83). A number of portraits of a similar type exist, including one in the Royal Collection and at NPG No. 3542, NPG No. 4890 [Millar, No. 10; *TJP* 86/7; *Dynasties* No. 2]

King Richard the third

(1452-85). Probably one of the copies of the portrait in the Royal Collection which was frequently copied in later years, one of which is at NPG No. 148 [Millar No. 14; *TJP* 262-4]

King Henry the seaventh

(1457-1509). Several derivations of the portrait in the Royal Collection (c.1490-1500) are known. Davies places one at Christ Church and another in the Society of Antiquaries by an unknown artist c.1500. The portrait at NPG No. 416 by Michiel Sittow (1505) belonged to Margaret of Austria. [Millar No. 16; *TJP* 149-52]

Quene Elizabeth his wife

Elizabeth of York (1465-1503). Her portrait c.1502 was in the collections of Henry VIII and Edward VI (1542, 1547) and several later copies exist including that in the Royal Collection and at NPG No. 311 [*TJP* 97]

Prince Arthur their eldest sonne

(1486-1502). Henry VII's eldest son; first husband of Catherine of Aragon. A contemporary portrait by an unknown artist now in a private collection was the prototype for later copies, including those in Syon House and Weston Park. Two portraits in the Royal Collection are said to be of Arthur but the identity has been confused with his brother Henry. [*Dynasties* No. 1; Millar No. 20]

King Henry the eight

(1491-1547). This 'fine ancient portrait on panel' of Henry 'in winter costume' was auctioned at Sandbeck Park in 1807. It may be the original at Castle Howard (or one of seven recorded versions) depicting the king c.1542 in a surcoat, carrying gloves and a walking-stick, by an unknown artist (perhaps Lucas Horenbout, King's Painter 1534-44). [*TJP* 152-7]

King Edw: 6 being Prince

(1537-53). This portrait, which bears the Lumley *cartellino*, is closely related to the Holbein drawing of the prince and was painted c.1542-5: it was most recently catalogued as by 'a follower' of Holbein. It is now in a private collection in San Marino, California. [Weiss Gallery catalogue: *Illustrious Company: Early Portraits 1545-1720* (1998) No. 1]

Quene Marye drawne by Garlicke

Mary I (1516-58). This circular, head and shoulders portrait, 'Of a severe countenance' [Pennant], bears Lumley's *cartellino* and was copied by Gerlach Flicke in 1555 from the 1554 portrait by Antonis Mor which had been commissioned by Charles V for the betrothal of his son Philip. It was auctioned at Lumley Castle in 1785 and brought £5.5s. and is now in the Durham Cathedral Treasury. [*TJP* 207-13; *Icon* Nos. 18, 65; Piper, p. 228]

Quene Elizabeth as she was comying first to the Crowne

(1533-1603). Elizabeth was proclaimed queen in succession to Mary in November 1558. This is the first of two panel-portraits owned by Lumley and was presumably a copy of one of the earliest patterns of her as queen by unknown artists:

1. The 'Coronation' portrait, ?1559, now at Warwick Castle. 2. The 'Northwick Park' pattern, ?1558 and onwards, copies of which are at NPG No. 4449 and in the National Gallery of Ireland.

[*TJP* 109/110; R. Strong, *Portraits of Queen Elizabeth I* (1963) 54 ff.]. A portrait of Elizabeth which Pennant described as: 'Of a severe countenance' was auctioned at Lumley Castle in 1785, and was probably this rather than the next.

And agayne, as she was the xxxth yeare of her Reigne

This was the second panel-portrait of the queen owned by Lumley and ostensibly, depicted the queen as she was in 1588. A head and shoulders of the 'Cambridge' portrait-type, painted from 1575 onwards, bearing a Lumley *cartellino*, was bought at the 1785 auction in Lumley Castle for six guineas by Samuel Dickens, Archdeacon of Durham. He died in 1791 having bequeathed it to Westminster School, where it remains. (The prototype was given to Cambridge University in 1588/9.) [R. Strong, *Portraits of Queen Elizabeth I* (1963) pp. 63/4, no. 32; *TJP* 110; communication from Mr E Smith, Westminster School, 2003.]

[Stephen Batre Kinge of Poland]

Stephen Bàthori (1533-86), elected to the throne of Poland in 1575 and reigned as Stephen I. Portrait not traced.

[Sigismond Kinge of Poland sonne to John King of Swethland]

Sigmund Vasa III (1566-1632). He reigned from 1588. Portrait not traced.

[Sigismonde Batre Prince of Transsilvania a° 1595]

Sigmund Bàthori (1581-1602). Portrait not traced.

[Phillip sonne to the Kynge of Spayne that now is]

Philip III (1578-1621), son of Philip II. 'Philip Spain aeta 14' appears in Vertue's list of paintings at Lumley Castle in the early eighteenth century. Portrait not subsequently traced. [Vertue p. 42]

Duke of Richemond base sonne to K:H: 8

Henry Fitzroy (1519-36) the king's natural son by Elizabeth Blount, created Duke of Richmond in 1525. The only known portrait of him is a miniature, attributed to Lucas Horenbout, c. 1534, in the Royal Collection. [Davies; ODNB illus.]

Duke of Buckingham

Probably Edward Stafford (1478-1521), third duke. This portrait fetched £7.10s. at the Lumley Castle auction of 1807 but has not been traced. Half-lengths by unknown artists are at Magdalene College and at Longleat. [*DNB*; Davies; ODNB illus.]

first Duke of Northefolke Hawarde

John Howard (1430?-85). This portrait at Arundel, painted posthumously by an unknown artist and bearing the Lumley *cartellino*, is related by Piper to one at Windsor Castle of which Millar remarks:

> Probably painted in the second half of the sixteenth century ... A more painterly version at Arundel uses the same head, but is of a slightly different design and includes the hands and the Garter badge.

Strong notes that it is the companion to the portrait of the second duke (*next*), also at Arundel. [Piper, p. 228; Millar No. 2153; col. illus., Robinson opp p 32; Roy Strong, 'Some Early Portraits at Arundel Castle', *Connoisseur* (March 1978) 195/6.]

seconde Duke of Northfolke

Thomas Howard (1443-1524). Though without a *cartellino*, this is the companion portrait to that of the first duke (*previous*) and is at Arundel Castle. [Roy Strong, 'Some Early Portraits at Arundel Castle', *Connoisseur* (March 1978) 195/6.]

third Duke of Northfolke doone by Garlicke

Thomas Howard (1473-1554). No portrait of him by Gerlach Flicke survives. A portrait attributed to Holbein c.1538/9 was in the collection of Thomas Howard, Earl of Arundel (1655) and is now in the Royal Collection (Windsor Castle). Other versions are known, two of which are in Arundel Castle. [*Dynasties* p. 120; Millar No. 30; NPG archives; Hervey No. 198.]

Thomas Earle of Surrey

Actually Henry Howard (1517?-47), eldest son of the third Duke of Norfolk. Lampton followed the mistaken identification on two Holbein drawings of 1532-5. Strong remarks that Surrey sat for his portrait 'more times within the short span of his life than any other Tudor courtier'. This, by an unknown artist (possibly William Scrots), bears the Lumley *cartellino*. Vertue listed it and Pennant noted that 'the poetical Earl' was 'in black, with a sword and dagger, the date 1545'. It was offered at auction in 1785 and bought in at £7.17.6d., then in 1807 it was bought in for 5 guineas. A later Earl of Scarbrough gave it to the Duke of Norfolk and it is now at Arundel Castle. [Vertue, p. 42; Pennant p. 320; *TJP* 307/8; Piper, p. 228; Brayley p. 193.]

Thomas his sonne the 4 Duke of Northfolke

Thomas Howard (1536-72). The portrait, now at Castle Howard (with copies at Audley End and Arundel Castle), is dated 1565 and is attributed to Steven van der Meulen. Since Meulen died between 5 October 1563 and 20 January 1564 (the dates on which his will was written and proved), the portrait was probably finished and dated posthumously by his assistants; it also has the later inscription 'beheaded 1573'. [*TJP* 233; *Icon* Nos. 36, 37, 74; *Dynasties* p. 94]

Phillip his sonne afterwards Earle of Arundel

[St.] Philip Howard (1557-95), son of Thomas Howard, fourth duke of Norfolk and Mary Fitzalan, canonised in 1929. The portrait, at Arundel Castle, bearing the Lumley *cartellino*, is a head and shoulders of Arundel aged eighteen (c.1575). Strong considers it the most authentic likeness of Howard and attributes it to George Gower; Piper makes no attribution. [Strong, *Connoisseur* (March 1978) 195; Piper, p.228; see also Robinson, 69; ODNB illus.]

Charles Brandon the first Duke of Suffolke Lo: Gr M^{r}

(1484-1545), Master of the Household. The inventory confidently identified the sitter but certain inconsistencies explain why this portrait, as described, has not been traced. The only known portrait-type of him sitting alone is c.1540-5, after Holbein, depicting a seated, near full-length figure in a red brocade doublet and sleeves and a black coat with a broad brown fur collar, as at NPG No. 516 which Strong suggests was produced very late in the century. That would account for Pennant's late dating of this portrait: 'Duke of Suffolk, 1593. In a purple robe'. Although it is not listed among Lumley's 'statuaries', a whole length portrait of the Duke of Suffolk was incorrectly given a date of 1598 in the 1785 auction at Lumley Castle when it was bought in at seven guineas; the 1807 auction catalogue included the portrait: 'Duke of Suffolk, in purple robes, 1593'; it went for £3. [*TJP* 305/6; NPG archives; Cust; ODNB illus..]

Duke of Somerset Seyma^r Lo Protecto^r to King Edw: 6

Edward Seymour (c.1500-52). Known portraits include one at Sudeley Castle (1535), Longleat (1537-47 school of Eworth) and Syon House (1548). [*TJP* 295; NPG archives; ODNB.]

his brother Lord Admirall Seymer

Thomas, Baron Seymour of Sudeley (c.1508-49), appointed Lord High Admiral and a Privy Councillor in 1547. This may be the lost portrait, perhaps by William Scrots, which first hung in Seymour's house in Bath Place which was bought by Arundel in 1549. It was the forerunner of versions at Longleat, NMM and NPG No. 4571. [*TJP* 357/8; Davies]

the last Earle of Arundell Fitzallen, drawn twise by the famous paynter Steven

Henry Fitzalan (c.1511-80) twelfth and last of the Fitzalan earls of Arundel; Lumley's father-in-law. It is uncertain whether Lampton intended to include the full length of Arundel listed above or if he referred to two half-lengths. Lumley's portrait by Steven van der Meulen (1562-70?) is nearly threequarter-length and has a *cartellino.* It was seen by Vertue in London and by Pennant at Lumley and was offered at auction in 1785. It was bought in at £4.14s.6d but when it was put up again in 1807 it went for £1.10s. It was sold from Christies in November 1979 into a private collection. If Lampton meant there were two half-length portraits by Meulen, then the second was one of the following:

1. Inscribed 'Ao DNI, 1562/24 DECEMB.' at Castle Howard.
2. Inscribed 'Ao DNI, 1565/21 DECEMBRY', at NPG No. 5296.

(Other portraits of Arundel are at Knole, NPG No. 4693 and Longleat. [*Icon* Nos 69-71; Vertue, II p. 47, IV p. 42; Pennant, p. 322; Davies;

Brayley, pp. 193/4; NPG archives; ODNB illus.]

his sonne the Lord Mautrevers

Henry Fitzalan (1538-56). A portrait at Arundel Castle, with the Lumley *cartellino*, depicting Maltravers waistlength and dressed in black was tentatively attributed by Piper to Hans Eworth 1557. (Three variants are known.) Since that portrait was posthumous, it may have been based on a threequarter length executed c.1555, possibly by John Bettes I, which is also at Arundel Castle. (A threequarter-length of his father the Earl of Arundel dated 1558 and attributed by Roy Strong to John Bettes I based on the robust Holbeinesque quality of the characterisation is at Arundel Castle (a copy is at Petworth House). [Piper, p. 228; Strong, *Connoisseur* (March 1978) p.198]

the first Marques of Winchester, Pawlet, Lo: Treasorer

William Paulet (1474/5?-1572). The only known portrait-type is at NPG No 65 (1560-9), of which numerous copies are extant. [*TJP* 332; Marshall 118]

the Lo: Marques of Northampton Parre, Lo: great Chamberleyne

William Parr (1513-71), appointed Lord Great Chamberlain in 1550. The portrait is untraced but it probably derived from the half-length drawing in chalks by Holbein in the Royal Collection. [Davies; NPG archive; ODNB illus.]

Thomas Earle of Northumberland, executed at Yorke

[Bl.] Thomas Percy (1528-72), beatified in 1935. This portrait may have been that by George Gower at Petworth inscribed *Esperance Eu Dieu Ma Comphort, Ano Dni 1566 et die Deco. IVNI* depicting the earl kneeling at a prie-dieu. (A full-length of him in Garter robes by an unknown artist is at Alnwick Castle.) [NPG archive; M Merrick, *Thomas Percy Seventh Earl* (1949); ODNB illus.]

the first Earle of Southampton Writhesley, Lo: Chauncellor

Thomas Wriothesley (1505-50) first earl of the second (1547) creation; the first creation having become extinct at the death of William Fitzwilliam. Lord Chancellor 1544-7. K.G. 1545; an opponent of Protector Somerset and a political ally of Arundel. This portrait (after a miniature by Holbein), could be that at Woburn or the seated half length with the Garter George at Beaulieu. [*GEC; DNB*; Davies; NPG archive.]

Lo: Robert Dudley, M[r] of the horse to Quene Elizabeth

(1532/3-88), Master of the Horse 1559-87. Most portraits of him (and there are many) date from 1565 onwards, that is, after he was created Earl of Leicester in 1564. The picture inventoried here, then, must be or relate to one of two earlier half-lengths:

1. Inscribed on the sword: Aetatis 28 156[?] attributed to Steven van der Muelen c.1560-5, now in the Wallace Collection.
2. With his dog (of which there are several variants without the dog), by an artist of the Anglo-Netherlandish school, c. 1564, possibly van der Meulen, now in a private collection. [*Dynasties* No. 49; *TJP* 195]

of him after he was Earle of Leicester Lo: Steward, twise drawne bye Seigar

Dudley was created Earl of Leicester in 1564 and Lord Steward in 1584. Lampton's remark 'twise drawne by Seigar' seems to mean that this entry covered two portraits by William Segar. Bruyn takes that to be the case and suggests that they were acquired by Lumley from Leicester House after the earl's death in 1588. It is unexplained why Lumley would want two portraits of Dudley as an earl in addition to one of him as a baron, and then go on to acquire a full-length at some point after 1590 (qq.vv.). Only one of these two portraits had a *cartellino*. Pennant described it as: 'a three-quarter piece, dated 1587, with the collar of the garter, and a staff in his hand'. Warner has: 'in a very fashionable dress of Elizabeth's time, crouded with point'. Segar had been with the earl in the Netherlands and the portrait was probably painted after their return to England. It was bought in at the Lumley Castle auction in 1785 for £3.3s. and went for £2.6s. in 1807. It is now in a private collection, another is at Hatfield. [Brayley p. 193; Bruyn, pp. 110/111, n.31; *Icon* No 176; Pennant p. 324; *TJP* 196; Warner p. 304; NPG archive.]

the Earle of Southampton Fitzwill[m]s Lo: Privy Seale

William Fitzwilliam (1490-1542), created earl in 1537. This could have been the original portrait by Holbein, of 1537-40, (destroyed in a fire at Cowdray), or a copy, both of which were in the collection of Thomas Howard, Earl of Arundel in 1655. A small panel in the Wentworth-

Fitzwilliam Collection, Cambridge, derives from the original. (A head and shoulders at Hardwick Hall is wrongly inscribed *Thomas More.*) [NPG archive; Anon., *Holbein and the Court of Henry VIII* (Exhibition Catalogue 1978/9, Queen's Gallery) No. 26; Hervey Nos. 161, 190; M. Girouard, *Hardwick Hall*, (1976) p. 86.]

the first Earle of Bedfourd Russell Lo: Pryvie Seale

John Russell (c.1485-1555). Vertue listed the portrait in this collection and at the Lumley Castle auction of 1785 a portrait 'less half length John, Lord Russell, Earl of Bedford, 1555', was bought in for £3.18s. and was put up in 1807 when it went for £3. This was probably the head and shoulders with the collar of the Garter (after a Holbein drawing) now at Woburn Abbey with a Russell *cartellino*: 'John Russell ye first Earle of Bedford of that family'. [Vertue p. 42; *Dynasties* No. 97; *TJP* 21; NPG archive.]

the second Earle of Essex [Robert] Devereux, M^{r} of the horse, doone by Seigar

(1565-1601), appointed Master of the Horse in 1587. The portrait is inscribed on a Lumley *cartellino*: 'Robert Devereux Earle of Essex 1590'. Strong suggests that the portrait probably recorded his appearance at the Accession Day tilts in 1590. It may, however, be a marriage portrait; he married Frances, widow of Sir Philip Sidney in 1590 and her portrait of the same date is listed in the inventory. Pennant described Essex 'in full length, dressed in black, covered with white embroidery' but the portrait is not inventoried with the other full-lengths. Strong and Piper confidently identify the threequarter-length portrait in the National Gallery of Ireland as by William Segar. Piper remarks that the design 'rather suggests that it was originally a whole-length'. It is known to have been repaired in 1713 and that presumably is when it was cut down. (Vertue made a note of two portraits in the collection in the eighteenth century: 'Devereux Erl Essex no hat a beard 1590' which is the portrait meant here. The second, 'Ano. 1596 aeta. 33. Kt. Garter', was presumably acquired after Lumley's death.) It was auctioned at Lumley Castle in 1785 and bought in for £4.4s. and went for £4 in 1807. It was sold from the Earl of Stafford's collection in 1885 and later bought by the National Gallery of Ireland. [Vertue p. 42; Pennant p. 319; *TJP* 115-7; Piper pp. 231, 299-303]

Lo: Clinton, afterwards created Earle of Lincolne, Lo: Admirall

Edward Fiennes de Clinton (1512-85), created Earl of Lincoln 1572. He was drawn by Holbein and a large number of portraits in oil survive but, even if Lampton's wording means that the portrait was executed before Clinton was created an earl, the identification of this picture is no easier. There are in all:

1. NPG No. 2918, head and shoulders c 1560-5 by an unknown artist.
2. Ashmolean Museum: a half-length, attributed (wrongly *pace* Strong) to Hans Eworth, 1562.
3. Several copies of a threequarter-length as Lord High Admiral by an unknown artist, c.1568.
4. NMM, a head and shoulders by an unknown artist, c 1570-5. 5.
5. Two portraits dated 1584, one of which is at NPG No. 900 and another, bearing the Russell *cartellino*, is at Woburn. [*TJP* 200-2; NPG archive.]

Ambrose Earle of Warwicke, generall at Newhaven

Ambrose Dudley (c.1530-90). In 1562 he was appointed commander of an expeditionary force to take Le Havre (i.e., Newhaven) and he led the queen's forces against the northern earls in 1569. Vertue saw the portrait, undated and by an unknown artist, and Pennant described Warwick as dressed in 'a bonnet, furred cloak, small ruff, and pendant *George*'. A portrait corresponding to that description is at Woburn. It was offered at auction in 1785 and was bought in for £5.15s.6d; it went for £5.5s. in 1807 [Vertue p. 42; Pennant p. 320; NPG archive; Davies; *DNB*]

[the firste Earle of Shroesburie]

John Talbot (c.1387-1453), a soldier whose bravery earned him the earldom and the soubriquet 'the English Achilles'. A half-length is at Compton Wynyates together with the companion-picture of his wife. [NPG archive]

the Olde Earle of Lyneux

Matthew Stewart, fourth Earl of Lennox (1516-71). 'Olde' distinguishes him from his younger son Charles, the fifth earl, who died in London in

1576 aged twenty. A half length portrait, by an unknown sixteenth century artist, wrongly inscribed: 'Sir William St Loo ...' is at Hardwick. [Girouard; NPG archive.]

[Gilbert Earle of Shrewesburye that now is]

Gilbert Talbot (1552-1616). He succeeded as seventh earl in November 1590. Pennant saw:

> A threequarter length, unknown, dated 1596, aged 43. Dressed in a striped jacket, blue and white, garter', black cloak and breeches, white ruff, gloves on.

The date and age correspond only with Shrewsbury. A portrait by William Segar, or his studio, of that date and fitting the description in the Weiss Gallery in 1998 was catalogued with the observation that the portrait was 'not known by any other version'. It is now in a private collection. [NPG archive; *TJP* p.287; *Icon* No. 181; Weiss Gallery catalogue, *Illustrious Company: Early Portraits 1545-1720* (1998) No. 9.]

Pope Julius secundus

Giuliano della Rovere (1443-1513); elected to the Holy See in 1503; he became known as 'Il Terribile'. This portrait was probably a copy of the famous portrait by Raphael, 1511/2, which is now in the National Gallery, for which there was a cartoon and of which 'several surviving versions' are known. [John Pope-Hennessy, *The Portrait in the Renaissance* (1966) p.119.]

Cardynall Woolsey Lo: Chauncellor

Thomas Wolsey (1475?-1530). In 1515 he was created a cardinal by Pope Leo X and Lord Chancellor by Henry VIII. The portrait was one of many copies and variants of a standard pattern by an unknown artist, showing him in profile, dressed in cardinal's robes, including those at Hampton Court Palace, Auckland Castle and NPG No. 32. [*TJP* 334-6]

[Anthony Grandville Cardinall and Bishopp of Arras]

Antoine Perrenot de Granvelle (1517-86). Bishop of Arras 1538; raised to the cardinalate in 1561. A portrait by Scipio Pulzone (1550-98) is in the Courtauld Insitute, but best known is the portrait by Antonis Mor, 1549, now in Vienna. Woodall suggests that the latter may have been designed to hang with that of the Duke of Alva (who is represented in this inventory by a portrait with a *cartellino*), also painted in 1549, because of certain similarities in format, lighting and execution. The portrait may, therefore, have been copied for Lumley as a pendant to that of Alva, and that would explain why the picture did not enter the collection until after 1590. [Wright 167; J. Woodall, *The Portraiture of Antonis Mor* (unpub. PhD thesis, Courtauld Institute 1990) 609-12.]

Cardynall Poole

Reginald Pole (1500-58), Cardinal (1536), Archbishop of Canterbury (1556). This portrait was probably a half-length by an unknown artist, post-1556, of which a number were painted for English Catholic houses; one is at NPG No. 220. [*TJP* 250-2]

B. of Winchester, Steven Gardy^{n} Lo: Chauncello^{r}

Bishop Stephen Gardiner, (1483?-1555) A bust-length portrait attributed to Meulen depicting Gardiner as a young man and later inscribed 'A. More' (presumably meaning Antonis Mor) is in a private collection. Several half-length portraits by unknown artists are known: in Corpus Christi College, Oxford, Trinity Hall, Cambridge, Hardwick Hall and Plas Newydd. [NPG archive.]

B. of Rochester, Fissher

Bishop John Fisher (1469-1535). He was canonised with Sir Thomas More in 1935. Several workshop copies of a portrait based on a Holbein drawing of c.1528 were made for recusant houses. Copies are in three colleges at Cambridge: St. John's, Trinity, and Christ's. [*TJP* 119-21]

old Lo: Henry Morley, A^{o} 1523 done in water colo^{r} by Albert Duer

Henry Parker, Lord Morley (1480/1-1556). He signed the letter petitioning the Pope to annul Henry VIII's marriage but he remained loyal to the old faith. The *DNB* remarks: 'His writings display both his robust faith and his appreciation of classical and modern Italian literature. But his style is rugged: his verse shows no trace of an ear for metre, nor is accurate scholarship a conspicuous feature of his translations'. This portrait, by Dürer dated 1523, in chalk, heightened with white, on green-grounded paper, is in the British Museum. The portrait was listed in the 1655 inventory of Thomas Howard's collection. [Hervey No. 111; ODNB illus.]

Note. The following deleted entry appeared later in the inventory: ~~The old Morley Henry, doone by Albert Dure.~~

Vycount Mountague Browne

Anthony Browne (1526-92) created Viscount Montagu by Queen Mary in 1554. This is a threequarter-length portrait by Hans Eworth, inscribed 1569 (now covered over) described by Pennant as: 'A head of Sir Anthony Browne, a favourite of Henry VIII, with a bushy beard, bonnet, and order of the garter'. It was put up at the 1785 auction at Lumley Castle (Lot No. 11) and was bought in at £1.11s.6d. Then in the 1807 auction (Lot No. 35) it went for £1.7s. It is now at NPG No. 842. [*Icon* No. 50; *TJP* 224-6; Cust, 32/5; ODNB illus.]

yo r Lo: doone by Steven

John, Lord Lumley in a threequarter-length seated portrait by Steven van der Meulen, inscribed: 8 Maii Andni 1563/aetatis suea 30, and displaying a *cartellino*, the companion to a portrait of his first wife Jane. Vertue saw it, and Fordyce thought Lumley had 'a noble and expressive countenance'. The pair was put up for auction in 1785 and was bought in for £4.4s. Both are at Sandbeck Park. Two other portraits of Lumley by Meulen are known:

1. c.1560-3, also with a *cartellino*, depicting Lumley in a similar pose to the above but with acurtain top left and his arms top right, now at NPG No. 5262.

2. c. 1563-5, a variant of No. 1 without curtain or arms; sold from Sothebys in 1997.

[Vertue, II p. 47, IV p.42; Fordyce 612; *Icon* Nos. 66, 85; Piper, p. 227; NPG archives]

the first Lorde Sheiffeild, slayne at Norwiche

Edmund Sheffield (1521-49), slain at Norwich in an unsuccessful attempt to suppress Kett's Rebellion. A portrait attributed to John Bettes the Younger with a *cartellino* top right on which the partly illegible lettering reads *In ... fortuna ... Domina* was sold by Christies into a private collection in July 1991. [T. Fuller, *The Worthies of England* (1662) II 291; NPG archive.]

Arthure Lo: Gray of Wilton, Lo: deputie of Ireland, doone by Seigar

Arthur Grey, fourteenth baron (1536-93); Lord Deputy 1580-2. Segar's portrait is inscribed '1587/Aete 50/DEUM COLO FORTUNA SPERNO' [I worship God and spurn fortune] and is now at Helmingham Hall. Strong ascribed the portrait to Robert Peake the Elder but there is no reason to doubt Lampton's ascription to Segar; Peake's copy is at Badminton incorrectly called 'Edward, Fourth Earl of Worcester'. [E.K. Waterhouse, *The Collection of Pictures at Helmingham Hall* (1958) p.12; Strong *Icon* Nos. 190, 207]

the first Lo: Willoughbye [Perigrine] Bartue

Peregrine Bertie, Lord Willoughby de Eresby (1555-1601). Several half-length portraits with a view of Bergen-op-Zoom in the background are known: by Marcus Gheeraerts (in a Scottish private collection), Hieronimo Custodis (Rockingham Castle) and an artist of the English School (Ancaster Collection and the Tower of London). That in the Tower is untidily inscribed with an unknown motto: 'Vray Foy Acquerant', and what might be intended as a date: 'MCBI' [1581] on a pennant. [Davies; *GEC*; NPG archive; ODNB illus.]

Thomas the first Lo: Crumwell, Lo: pryvie seale, and vice-regent to K: H: 8

Thomas Cromwell (1485?-1540). This portrait, a roundel bust after Holbein and bearing a *cartellino*, is lost. Another portrait, of uncertain date, with an obliterated *cartellino* is at NPG No. 1727. [*TJP 113;* Piper, p. 228]

the first Lo: Wentworth, Lo: Chamberleyne to K: Edw: 6

Thomas Wentworth (1501-51). Two similar portraits were painted c. 1547-9 attributed to John Bettes I. A portrait, dated 1547, has had its Lumley *cartellino* painted over with a stiffer, heavier, and larger Wentworth one. It is now at NPG No. 1851. The other, also with a Wentworth label was sold in Suffolk by Sothebys in 1996. (The white rod of office which he holds was added after he succeeded Arundel as Lord Chamberlain in February 1550.) [J. Turner, *The Dictionary of Art* (1996); *TJP* 325/6; *Icon* No.3; Piper p 227n6; NPG archive; ODNB illus.]

the first Lo: Riche, Lo: Chancellor of England

Richard Rich (c.1496-1567). He was raised to the peerage in 1548 and served as Lord Chancellor until 1551. The portrait which probably derived from Holbein's chalk-drawing of 1536 in the Royal Collection is untraced. [The Queen's Gallery, Holbein Catalogue (1978) No. 75.]

Thomas the third Lo: Darcy of Chiche, doone by Hubbert

(1565-1640). Lumley's second wife bequeathed the Lumley house on Tower Hill to her brother, the sitter in this portrait. 'Hubbert' was Hubert Beuckelaer, an emigre from Antwerp. The portrait is lost. [Bruyn, *passim*; *Dynasties* p.69; *Icon* p.185]

the last Lord Braye

John Bray succeeded as second and last baron in 1539. Vertue listed a portrait at Lumley Castle of 'John Lesley Lord Brays'. A head and shoulders portrait with a cartellino was with Philip Mould Ltd., in 2008 (ex Stanford Hall). [Vertue, p. 42; NPG archive].

the first Lo: Burghley Cicill, Lo: Threasorer

William Cecil (1520-98). He was created Lord Burghley in 1571 and appointed Lord Treasurer in 1572. More portraits of Burghley exist than any other Elizabethan (except the queen) and most date from the last twenty-five years of his life. This portrait, seen by Vertue, was described by Hutchinson as 'a half length, in black, collar of the garter' It was, therefore, a version of the standard post-1572 portrait by an unknown artist, of which there are several surviving copies, including NPG No. 604. It was offered at auction at Lumley Castle in 1785 as 'Cecil, Lord Burleigh, Lord High Treasurer' and was bought in for £3.13.6d. It was taken to Sandbeck Park and put up in 1807 as 'Lord Treasurer Burleigh, ancient, on pannel' (the realised price is not given). [Vertue, p. 42; *TJP* 27-33; Cust 33]

[Sr Anthony Browne M^r of the horse to K:H:8 and K: Edward ye 6]

c.1500-1548. A portrait of Browne was destroyed in a fire at Cowdray in 1793, hence Lumley's must be the one by Hans Eworth c.1550. It was described by Brayley and Warner as 'a very curious half length', probably because it depicts Browne as a bust on a plinth with a very long inscription beneath It was probably Lot No. 12 in the auction at Lumley Castle in 1785 when it was bought in at £2.5s. and was the first picture in Lot No. 33 in the auction of 1807 when it realised £4.10s. It is now in NPG. [Pennant p.322; Cust pp. 32/35; Brayley p. 193; Warner p. 302; ODNB illus.]

Sr Nichls Carewe M^r^ of the horse to K:H:8

Nicholas Carew (c.1490-1539). This half-length portrait by Holbein 1532/3 has the Lumley *cartellino*. Vertue thought it was painted by Mor, and Pennant described the sitter as showing 'vast spirit in his countenance. In his hat is a white feather; his head is bound round with a gold stuff handkerchief'. It brought £10.10s. at the Lumley Castle auction of 1785 and is now at Drumlanrig. [Vertue II p. 47; IV p. 42; Pennant, p. 324; Piper, p. 227; ODNB illus.]

old Sir Thomas Lovell Threasorer of howseholde to K:H:7

(c.1449-1524). The portrait is lost. [*TJP* 202]

Sir Henry Guilford Coumptroller to K:H:8 [drawne by Haunce Holbein]

Henry Guildford (1489-1532). The portrait, on which the *cartellino* has been painted over, was executed in 1527. Together with the companion portrait of his wife, Lady Mary, it passed into the collection of Lumley's great-nephew Thomas Howard, Earl of Arundel in which they were recorded in 1655. The portraits were seen by Vertue in the collection of Howard's grandson William, Viscount Stafford in 1726. They were separated soon after Stafford's death in 1734 and Guildford was acquired for the Royal Collection; it is now in Windsor Castle. [Ganz No. 44; Millar No. 28; The Queen's Gallery, Holbein Catalogue (1978) No. 13; Hervey No. 185; ODNB illus.]

Sir Thomas Moore, Lo: Chauncello^r^ [drawne by Haunce Holbyn]

Sir Thomas More (1478-1535). Lord Chancellor 1529. He was Holbein's first patron in England. He was beatified in 1886 and canonised in 1935 (with Bishop John Fisher). This half-length portrait remained at Lumley Castle for two centuries. Pennant described More: 'dressed in that plainness of apparel which he used when the dignity of office was laid aside; in a furred robe, with a coarse capucin cap'. It was auctioned at Lumley Castle in 1785 as 'Sir Thomas Moore, Lord Chancellor' and was bought in for £6.6s. It was put up again in 1807 when it fetched £5.5s. It has not been traced but NPG No. 4358 is one of two documented versions. [Pennant, p. 320; *TJP 227-9;* S. Morison, *The Likeness of Thomas More* (1963), p. 13]

old sir Thomas Wyatt

(1503?-42). This portrait derived from either of two Holbein drawings. Roundels of Wyatt in half profile are known: NPG Nos 1035 and 2809 and another in the Bodleian Library. Since Lumley bought Wyatt's town-house on Tower Hill, it is highly likely that the portraits of Wyatt senior and junior *(next)* were already in the house and were left behind when the collection was reassembled at Lumley Castle in 1592. [*TJP* 338/9; M Conway 'Portraits of the Wyat Family', *Burlington Magazine* 16 (1909) p. 155]

the yonger sir Thomas Wiat executed

(1521?-54). He led the Kentish Rising in 1554 for which treason he was executed on Tower Hill. *DNB* refers to a portrait 'in profile on a panel', one of a group of Wyatt family portraits belonging to the fifth Earl of Romney, which Strong dates to c.1545-50 and suggests that it might be by William Scrots. A copy of an almost identical portrait, once in the collection of Charles I, is at NPG No. 3331. Like the portrait of his father (*previous*) this portrait was probably painted for the house on Tower Hill and remained there after 1592. [Conway *op. cit., TJP* 340; Davies; ODNB illus.]

Sr Thomas Hennege, Vice ch^{a}berleyne

Thomas Heneage (c.1532-1595), Vice Chamberlain to Elizabeth I 1589-95. A half-length portrait of him attributed to Segar, c.1590, was sold by Sotheby's in 1969 to the Palazzo Lapponi, Florence. [*Icon* No. 184; NPG archives.]

Erasmus of Roterdame, ~~all these eight~~ drawne by Haunce Holbyn

Desiderius Erasmus (1466-1536). Dutch humanist. Numerous versions and derivations after a Holbein portrait (1530/1) exist. This was a small-scale portrait and bore the *cartellino*; a piece of paper from Henry VIII's time is stuck on the back with the words: Haunce Holbein me fecit, Johanne(s) Noryce me dedit, Edwardus Banyster me possedit'. (Norris was the king's frame-maker and Banister was well-known at the English court.) The portrait appeared in the collection of Thomas Howard, Earl of Arundel (1655) and it then passed to the Howards of Greystoke. It is now in the Metropolitan Museum, New York. [Vertue p. 52; Piper, p. 228; Ganz No. 57; Millar No. 39; Hervey No. 428.]

Note. The deletion in the inventory entry indicates that Lampton or a later analyst realised that not all of the previous eight portraits were by Holbein.

Sir Willm Winter, doone by Siegar

d. 1589. (Wynter properly) Admiral. His portrait is lost and otherwise unknown.

sir Frauncis Walsingham Secretary

(1530-90). Secretary of State 1573-90. The painter John Critz the Elder gained his patronage in the 1580s and this was one of numerous copies of his threequarter-length portraits, c.1587-9, in private collections as well as that at NPG No. 1807 (reduced to half-length). [*Dynasties* No. 118; *TJP* 320-2; *Icon* 246; ODNB illus.]

sir Willm Petre Secretarye

(1505?-72). Secretary to Henry VIII, Edward VI and Queen Elizabeth. The fire-damaged original threequarter-length portrait by Steven van der Meulen is at Ingatestone Hall. This copy, bearing the Lumley *cartellino*, is inscribed separately: ANO DNI 1567 AETATIS SUAE 61. It was bought in at the auction at Lumley Castle in 1785 for 5 guineas. In 1802 Warner remarked: 'A very fine picture, but wilfully defaced by a scoundrelly broker, because it was not to be purchased'. It fetched £2.13s. when it was put up again in 1807. It was bought by NPG (No. 3816) in 1952. [Pennant p. 321; *TJP* 246/7; *Icon* No. 77; Piper, p. 231; D Piper, *Petre Family Portraits* (1956) No. 3; Warner pp. 303, 305; ODNB illus..]

his sonne sir John Petre

(1549-1613). This portrait was bought in for 3 guineas at auction in 1785 but it went for 10s.6d. in 1807 and is now lost. (Sir John is wrongly identified in a portrait at Ingatestone Hall; Strong has identified the sitter as William, second Baron Petre (1575-1637), the artist as Marcus Gheeraerts, and the date 1599.) [D. Piper, *Petre Family Portraits* (1956) No. 5; *Icon* No 264, of Lord William Petre.]

sir Willm Drury slaine in fraunce drawne by Seigar

(1527-79). In 1578 he went to Ireland as Lord Justice and died there; Lampton confused him with another knight of the same name who died in France. Piper suggests that this portrait may have been posthumous (and Drury's dates may be thought a little early for Segar to have painted him *ad vivum*) but Strong dates all of Drury's portraits to 1570-5 on the basis of costume. He does not mention Segar but discusses a threequarter length in armour in the Guildhall, Thetford, by an unknown artist, as the original from which copies at Courteenhall and a head and shoulders at NPG No. 1911 derive. A slightly differently posed portrait, perhaps by George Gower, c. 1570-5, is at Boughton. [Piper, p. 300n8; *TJP* 75, pl. 137; *Icon* No. 130; ODNB illus.]

sir Nichls Bacon Knight Lo: Keper of the great Seale to Q: Elizabeth

(1510-79). Lord Keeper 1558-71. A half-length portrait by an unknown artist, dated 1562, is at Corpus Christi College, Cambridge. At least seven copies are known of another half-length, inscribed *Mediocria Firma* (moderate things endure) by an unknown artist 1578/9, including that at NPG No. 164. [Davies; *TJP* 15/6; ODNB illus.]

Sir James Wilfourd Capten of Haddington

James Wilford (1516-50). Governor of Haddington in 1548 where he withstood a siege of some eighteen months. This portrait is the threequarter-length in armour with a view of Haddington top right, 1547, by Hans Eworth, at Coughton Court. [NPG archive; Davies; *DNB*; see also Boyle, art. cit. *EHR*; ODNB illus.]

sir Phillip Sidney, Lo: governo^r in Zealand

(1554-86). Governor of Flushing in 1585. In response to a request for his portrait from Hubert Languet in 1574, Sidney wrote: 'I shall have it done either by Paolo Veronese or by Tintoretto, who easily occupy first rank in this art.' This portrait was presumably a version of the half-length associated with John de Critz, c.1585, or the threequarter length at NPG No. 2096 by an unknown artist. [*TJP*, 291/2; *Icon* No. 247; D. Starkey, *Rivals in Power* (1990) p. 208; ODNB illus.]

sir Frauncis Drake the Great Navigato^r (doone by Siegar) [who sayled round about the worlde]

(1540?-96) This portrait was c.1590 but prior to the inventory's compilation. It hung in Trinity House, London, but it was destroyed by enemy action in the second World War. A copy attributed to Gheeraerts is in the Plymouth Art Gallery. [Davies; *TJP* 71; NPG archive]

Sir John Lutterel, who died of the sweat in K. Edw:6: tyme

John Luttrell (c.1518-51), military commander. This complex allegorical portrait of him by Hans Eworth, signed and dated 1550, was painted to celebrate the Anglo-French Treaty of Boulogne of 1550 and shows the naked Luttrell rising from a stormy sea being greeted by Lady Peace. It is now at the Courtauld Institute of Art. [*Dynasties* No. 23; *Icon* No 22; see also Boyle, art. cit. *EHR*]

[Sir John Haukins Treasurer of the Admiraltie drawne by Hubbert]

John Hawkins (1532-95). This heavily damaged portrait by Hubert Beuckelaer bears the Lumley *cartellino* and Hawkins's arms with the inscription 'Aetatis suae 58: Anno Domini 1591'. The portrait is not subsequently recorded at Lumley Castle; it is now in the National Maritime Museum, Greenwich. [Bruyn p. 99; Piper, p. 231; ODNB illus, attributed to Federico Zuccaro.]]

[Mr Thomas Candishe who sayled round about the worlde]

Thomas Cavendish (1560-92). He circumnavigated the globe (1586-8), the second Englishman to do so (i.e., after Drake 1577-80). A portrait attributed to John Bettes II, and dateable to 1588-91, was with the Weiss Gallery in 1992 (ex Hardwick Hall). The catalogue entry noted that the portrait at Welbeck Abbey was the only other to have 'any serious aspiration to being actually of Cavendish'. [Mark Weiss, *English and North European Portraits 1535-1715* (1992); NPG archive]

{Mr Churchyards picture}

Thomas Churchyard (1520/3-1604). He published a large number of volumes of prose and verse after 1560, many of which reflected his military background. *DNB* remarked that he 'lived quite long enough to see the greater part of his multifarious writings confined to oblivion'. His portrait is not otherwise known.

{An old man fancying a yong woman}

A Dutch genre picture which has been said to correspond with 'One of an old man looking on his booke and a Ladye by him entysing him from it, in a frame of woode' listed in the Earl of Leicester's inventory of April 1590 and that it was one of a group of a dozen pictures acquired by Lumley at about that time; but that does not explain why the other pictures were entered in this inventory immediately whereas this was not listed until after 1605, some fifteen years later. [Bruyn, Appendix p. 106]

Mr Edward Dyer of the Corte, drawne by Hubbert

Edward Dyer (1543-1607), alchemist. (Lampton confused him with James Dyer, a judge.) Hubert Beuckelaer's portrait is lost. [Bruyn]

Mr Edw: Shelley slayne at Mustleborough feilde, drawen by Haunce Eworthe

Edward Shelley, killed at the Battle of Musselburgh, 1547. His portrait by Hans Eworth is lost.[Boyle, art. cit. *EHR*]

Mr Thomas Wyndeham drowned in [the sea returninge from Ginney]

(1508?-1554). Vice admiral and navigator. His portrait is signed by Hans Eworth. Vertue mentions it and Pennant has: 'Good half length, aged 42 MDL a robust figure in green, with a red sash and a gun in his hand'. Although the gun is slung across his back not in his hand, the provenance to the Lumley collection seems secure from the inscription 'AETATIS XLII MDL HE/TW' It was offered at auction in 1785 and was bought in at 5 gns., but it went for £2.11s.6d. in 1807. It was bought by the Earl of Radnor in June 1813 and is now at Longford Castle. [Vertue p. 42; Pennant p. 324; *Icon* No 21; Piper p. 227n10; see also Boyle, art. cit. *HER*; ODNB illus.]

[Sir Edward Kelley rare for his knowledge in Alcumistrye]

(1555-97?), alchemist. The portrait has not been traced but an engraving of him in a biretta and fur-lined cloak appeared in the autobiography of the astrologer and prophet William Lilly (1602-81) and has been reproduced in most works on Dee and his circle.

Note. The following deleted entry appears at a later point in the Inventory: ~~**The picture of Sr Edward Kelley who was the of golde in before.**~~

the Earle of Salisburie, Cecill

Robert Cecil (1563-1612). Many portraits of him are known, all deriving from a single face type by John de Critz the Elder, 1599. In 1607 Salisbury paid de Critz for four further copies of his portrait which were to be given away. Vertue listed the portrait and Hutchinson described Cecil in this half-length portrait: 'dressed in black, a bell on the table, and a letter directed to him by all his titles, round the neck a green ribband, with the George: Above his head Sero sed serio' ('Late, but in earnest') which are common features of his portraits. The reference to Cecil's earldom presumably means that the portrait was one of the last to be inventoried by Lampton, and it was probably a version of the portrait at NPG No. 107, dated 1602, among others. It was put up for auction at Lumley Castle in 1785 and was bought in for £3.13s.6d. It was seen in the castle in 1807/8. [Vertue, p. 42; Pennant 323; Hutchinson p. 405; *TJP* 273-5; *Icon* No. 241; Brayley, p. 192]

{Julius Caesar}

(1558-1636), a judge. The Lumleys were in correspondence with him at the turn of the century. Strong remarks that his iconography is meagre; a portrait c.1610-15, probably by a Dutch artist at NPG No. 527 is *called* Sir Julius. Since it was not inventoried until after 1605, it seems unlikely that Bruyn's identification of this as 'A picture of Julius Caesar' owned by Leicester and acquired by Lumley in 1590 is correct. There is also a portrait at Rousham Hall. [Bruyn, Appendix p. 106; *TJP* 35; ODNB]

Henry the third Empo^r husbande to Mawd the Empresse

Henry III Holy Roman Emperor (1046-56). Lampton was historically confused: Empress Maud (or Matilda) (1102-67) married the *fifth* Emperor, Henry (d. 1125). A portrait of Henry is in Holyrood Palace.

Maximilian the Empo^r grandfather to Charles the Vth

Maximilian I (1459-1519); Holy Roman Emperor (1508-1519). Copies of the portrait by the Imperial court painter Bernard Strigel (1460-1528) are in the Bowes Museum, and at Upton Park. [Wright 177/8, 195.]

Charles the Vth Empour

(1500-58). Several portraits are to be found in British collections: Cambridge, Glasgow, Edinburgh (by Bernard van Orley), Petworth (after Orley), London (Wallace Collection) and Barnard Castle (by Coello). [Wright 74, 129, 147/8, 152, 182, 191]

Steven [Batere] King of Poland 1583

Stefan Bàthori (1533-86). This is the second portrait of him in the inventory and is untraced.

Duke of Savoy Regent in Flaunders doone by Jaques Pindar

No duke of Savoy was Regent in Flanders but this portrait was probably of Emmanuel Philibert (1528-80), Prince of Piedmont, who succeeded to the dukedom in 1553. This portrait by Jacob de Poindre (1527-70) of Malines has not been traced but a mid-16th century portrait of the North Italian or Spanish schools is in the Courtauld Institute. [Wright 101]

Duke of Parma, Regent in Flaunders

Alessandro Farnese (1555-92), succeeded as Regent in the Netherlands in 1578 and remained so until his death. A portrait was in the collection of Thomas Howard, Earl of Arundel, in 1655. There is one, after Titian, at Hatfield House once wrongly called Duke of Alva. [Hervey No. 365]

Duke of Alva, governo[r] in Flaunders, doone by Anthony Moorey

Fernando Alvarez de Toledo (1508-82). Governor in Flanders 1567-73. This portrait by Antonis Mor is signed and dated 1549 and has a Lumley *cartellino* showing the date of acquisition as 1557 (which is more likely to have been 1567 since that was when he was made Governor of the Netherlands, having been Viceroy of Naples previously). Vertue mentions the portrait and Pennant described Alva: 'in rich armour with his baton; short black hair and beard', and went on:

> I imagine that this portrait was painted when the Duke was young; for I have seen one (sent into England by the late Mr Benjamin Keen) now in possession of the Bishop of Ely, which represents him with a vast flowing white beard.

It was bought in for £15.15s. at the auction in Lumley Castle in 1785, but went for £10.10s. in 1807. It is now in the Hispanic Museum, New

York. [Vertue, p. 42; Pennant p. 325; Piper, p. 228. See also notes on the portrait of Cardinal Granville above.]

Duke of Askott 1583

Phillipe de Croy, third Duke of Aerschot (1526-95). Pennant and Hutchinson refer to an otherwise unidentified (and untraced) picture at Lumley Castle which might have been this one:

> a three quarter length of a man in a scarlet robe; and over his left shoulder a white mantle; a scarlet cap tied in the middle, and open behind; a narrow white ruff; and a collar of the fleece. The scarlet robe is furred with white: on it are several times repeated these words: *Ah! amprins au ra jay!* Oh! had I undertaken it!

[Pennant p. 324; Hutchinson p. 405]

[Duke of Sert]

Jerome Tseraerts of Brabant; Governor of Flushing in 1572. Portrait not traced.

County Egmond executed at Bruxels, drawne by Steven

Lamoral, Count of Egmont (1522-68). This portrait by Steven van der Meulen has not been traced.

Duke of Burbon, slayne at the sackinge of Rome

Charles, Duke of Bourbon (1490-1527), shot by Benvenuto Cellini on 5 May 1527 in an assault on Rome. Portrait not traced.

Henry Valoys last of that name, king of Fraunce, murthered

Henri of Valois (1551-89) Henri III of France (1574-89). Assassinated by the Catholic League in revenge for the murder of Guise (*next*). Three portraits of him, including a life-sized bust-portrait, possibly by Pieter Pourbus, were recorded at Hatfield in 1629. [Auerbach p. 65]

Henrye, Duke of Guyse murthered by the said kinge

Henri de Lorraine (1550-88), Henri III (*previous*) had him murdered. A life-size bust-portrait, possibly by Pieter Pourbus, was recorded in the Salisbury House inventory of 1629. [Auerbach p. 64]

Albertus, Cardinall of Austria now Governor of the Lowe Countryes'

(1559-1621) Archduke Albert, sixth son of Emperor Maximilian II and raised to the Sacred College in 1577; appointed Governor of the Netherlands in 1596. His portrait was painted frequently including that at National Gallery No. 3818, but Lumley's was likely to have been one of the bust-portraits of him and his wife (see below) by Guysbrecht (d. 1628) or Otto van Veen (1558-1629). Two pairs are known: one which was commissioned by the Earl of Salisbury in 1599; and one which was given to James I in 1603. [Auerbach Nos. 63 & 64; Wright 80, 136, 163/4, 178]

Andrew Dore Prince of Melph

(1468-1560). Vertue mentioned the portrait and Warner described it as 'a very fine half-length on wood'; Pennant has:

> Andrew Doria, a three quarter length, the great Genoese admiral, and patriot. He is dressed in black, in a cap, a collar, with the fleece pendant; a truncheon in his hand, and a dagger in his girdle. View of ships through a window.

Hutchinson adds a reference to his long beard. It was put up for auction at Lumley Castle in 1785 under its inscription: 'Pater Patrice Andreas Auria' and was bought in for £3.13s.6d. It was seen in the castle in 1807/8 but its present whereabouts are unknown. [Pennant p. 325; Hutchinson p. 405; Brayley, pp. 192/3; Warner p. 303.]

[Philip de Roye a councelor to the K. of Spayne]

Unidentified but possibly Philip de Croy, Duke of Aerschot, listed earlier, of whom this may be a second and later portrait. He died in 1595; King Philip died three years later.

Balthazar Geraertez gent, a Burgunyan, who murthered the Prince of Orange

Balthasar Gerard who assassinated William of Nassau on 10 July 1584. Portrait not traced.

President Viglius, a great Councello[r] to Charles the Vth, drawne by Jaques Pindar

Wigle van Aytta van Zuichem (1507-77). This portrait of 1560 by de Poindre was listed by Vertue, and Hutchinson described it as:

'threequarter length, in black gown furred in front, a black cap, sitting in a chair: A fine old face'. It was bought in at the auction in Lumley Castle in 1785 for £2.7s. and it went for £3.16s. in 1807 but its present whereabouts have not been traced. [Vertue, p. 42; Hutchinson p. 405]

Haward a Dutch Juellor[r], drawne for a Maisters prize by his brother Haunce Eworth

Portrait not traced.

Sebastian Gabote the great Navigator

Sebastian Cabot (1474-1557). This portrait has not been traced; two are known. The first was owned by James I, a copy of which was found in Scotland and bought by an American in whose home it perished in a fire in 1845 (and is known only from an engraving). The second is a 1763 copy of a full-length portrait attributed to Holbein in the ducal palace, Venice, but Holbein is not known to have painted him. [DNB; ODNB]

[Ignatius de Loyola first founder of the societie of Jesus]

(1491-1556), beatified 1609, canonised 1622. The portrait, probably early 17th century, is untraced.

[Franciscus Xaverius firste of the Jesuites whiche brought the Christian faythe unto y[e] Indians.]

(1506-52), beatified 1609, canonised 1622. The portrait, probably early 17th century, is untraced.

Sir Thomas Stukeley slayne wth the thre Christians kings.

Thomas Stucley (c.1520-78), a buccaneer. The portrait has not been traced. [J.E. Tazon, *Thomas Stukeley* (2003)]

{Bocchas}

Giovanni Boccaccio (1313-75), author of *The Decameron*. Portrait untraced.

{Petrarke}

Francesco Petrarch (1304-74), poet. A 16th century portrait of the Italian School is at Blickling Hall. [Wright 99]

{Dante}

Dante Alighieri (1265-1321) author of the *Divina Commedia.* A half-length which belonged to Edward Alleyn (1566-1626), who endowed Dulwich College, is at Dulwich Picture Gallery No. 537

{Oriosto}

Lodovico Ariosto (1474-1533), author of *Orlando Furioso.* Portrait untraced. (Perhaps a duplicate of a later entry in this inventory.)

sir Gefferey Chawcer knight

Geoffrey Chaucer (1340?-1400), poet. All known portraits of Geoffrey Chaucer derive from an illuminated manuscript of the early fifteenth century. Lumley's was presumably NPG No. 532 or a copy. Hutchinson noted: 'Doctor Stukeley, in his *Iter Boreale,* in 1725, says: "At Lumley Castle is a curious old picture of Chaucer, said to be an original". We could not find any such portrait, neither is it mentioned by Mr Pennant'. Evidently the picture left the collection in the mid-eighteenth century. [*TJP* 47/8; W. Hutchinson, *History of Durham* (1787) II, 408]

Buckenel the Scott

George Buchanan (1506-82), Scottish historian, scholar and poet. Several copies and variants of a portrait by Arnold van Bronckhurst dated 1581 are known, including NPG No. 524 and Scottish NPG No. 2678. [*TJP* 25-7; ODNB illus.]

Raphael de Urbino, the great paynter

Raffaello Sanzio (1483-1520). This picture, presumably a self-portrait, could be the original or a copy of that at Hampton Court c.1505-7, or of that in the Uffizi Gallery, Florence, c.1508. A copy of the latter by Giovanni Penni (1488-1528) is in the Royal Museum, Canterbury. [Wright 158]

Willm Somer, K:H:8: notable foole

William Somer (or Sommers) (d. 1560). This picture is unidentified. The ODNB refers only to a portrait of c.1545. DNB is discouraging about a painting at Hampton Court: 'A curious painting of a man's full face, grinning through a lattice window has been wrongly identified with Sommers and attributed to Holbein .... It was probably painted in the sixteenth century'. This may be *Boy looking through a casement* by an unknown artist, reproduced at R. Strong *Henry, Prince of Wales and England's Lost Inheritance* (1986) No. 96.

Theophrastus Paracelsus

(1493-1541). Pennant described the portrait: 'A half-length of the famous eccentric physician and chemist of the fifteenth century, *Philip Theophrastus* Paracelsus *Bombast de Hohenheim*: on the picture is added also the title of *Aureolus* ... He is represented as a very handsome man, bald, in a close black gown, with both hands on a great sword on whose hilt is the word *Azot*'. It fetched £3.10s. at auction in 1807 and but its present location is unknown. [Pennant p. 321]

[Margaret daughter to Duke of Anjoy and wife to K. Henry 6th.]

Margaret of Anjou (1430-82), daughter of the Duke of Lorraine; married to Henry VI in 1445. Probably one of a standard set of royal portraits, one of which is in Queen's College, Cambridge.

Elizabeth wife to King Edw: 4

Elizabeth Woodville (c.1437-92), daughter of Richard, Earl Rivers; married Edward IV in 1464. This was probably one of a standard set of English kings and queens in the Royal Collection (inscribed later with '1464'). An early 17th century copy is in Ripon Cathedral Copies are at Queen's College, Cambridge, and in the Royal Collection. [*Icon* p.47; Millar No. 12; illus. in D Baldwin, *Elizabeth Woodville* (2002).]

~~Elizabeth~~ {Margaret} Countesse of Richemonde and Darby and mother to K:H:7.

Margaret Beaufort (1443-1509) Countess of Richmond and Derby. Several versions of a posthumous portrait by an unknown artist in the collection of Henry VIII and Edward VI in 1542, 1547 and 1549/50 are known, including that in the Royal Collection (Windsor Castle) and at NPG No. 551 [Millar No. 15; *TJP* 18-21; *Icon* No. 236]

Quene Katheryn, mother to Quene Marye

Katherine of Aragon (1485-1536), and queen of Henry VIII. This was a version of a standard type, painted by an unknown artist c.1530 (derived from a threequarter-length by Johannes Corvus c.1510-20), several copies of which are known, including that in the Royal Collection (Windsor Castle) and NPG Nos. 163, 668. [Millar No. 41; *TJP* 39/40]

Quene Jane mother to K: Edw: 6.

Jane Seymour (1508/9-37), third consort of Henry VIII. Presumably Holbein's portrait of her, now in Vienna, or the copy from his workshop, now in The Hague. [*Icon* p. 6; See also Hervey No. 167; ODNB illus.]

Quene Katherin Parre, last wife to K:H:8

Katherine Parr (1512-48), sixth consort of Henry VIII. This portrait may have been NPG No. 4168, attributed to William Scrots, c. 1545/6, or a copy, or that by Master John c.1545, also in NPG, illus. at ODNB. [*TJP* 363-5]

[Isabel] wife to Charles the Vth Empo^r^, mother to K: Phillip

Isabella of Portugal (1503-39. Portrait not traced.

Mary Quene of Scottes, executed in Englande.

Mary Stuart or Stewart (1542-87). Lumley bequeathed a portrait of Mary to the Earl of Salisbury and its delivery in December 1609 is recorded: 'To my La: Lumleys man who brought your honor a picture of the Queene mother of Scotland - 40s.' [Hatfield Accounts] It is thought to have been the full-length portrait, by an unknown artist, dated 1578, now at Hatfield House, but doubts arise. Firstly, the Hatfield portrait corresponds in size to Lumley's full-length portrait of Darnley and his brother (q.v.) and Lampton would have inventoried them together, but, whereas the latter is listed in its proper place among the full-lengths, this image is inventoried among the smaller portraits – a mistake which Lampton was highly unlikely to have made. Secondly, the full-length portraits of Mary were all painted in the early seventeenth century, that is, after this entry in the inventory. Thirdly, on personal and politico-religious grounds Arundel and Lumley were bound to have had Mary's likeness from the early 1560s, when they began to be involved with her (the portrait of Darnley and his brother is dated 1562). Oil-portraits of Mary completed about that time, examples of which are in the Royal Collection and in the Victoria and Albert Museum, were based on François Clouet's bust-length drawing of 1560 in the Bibliothèque Nationale, France, known as the 'deuil blanc' ('white mourning') portrait. It seems clear, then, that the portrait inventoried here cannot have been the full-length of Mary, which was not inventoried at Hatfield in 1611, but a copy of the 1560 image. Hence it was probably one of the two small portraits of the queen hanging in the Wardrobe at Hatfield in 1629 which Auerbach mention, but only in passing. [Auerbach pp. 61-3; H. Smailes & D. Thomson, *The Queen's Image* (SNPG exhibition catalogue 1987) pp. 12/13, No. 15; Wright 140. An extensive bibliography on Mary's portraiture is at *TJP* 213-223.]

[~~Elizabeth~~] Q: wife to the Frenche Kinge, Charles the 9

Elizabeth of Austria, married in 1570 to Charles IX (1550-74). Presumably, this is the portrait of the 'French Queen' which Lumley borrowed from Mr More of Loseley in 1589, 'that he may take the like on't', though Lumley is not to be taken as the actual copyist. [A.J.Kempe, ed., *The Loseley Manuscripts* (1835) p 495]. The portrait is untraced.

[Isabel daughter to Phillip the second K: of Spayne]

Isabella Clara Eugenia (1566-1633). A portrait was in the collection of Thomas Howard, Earl of Arundel, in 1655; Dutch School companion portraits of her and her husband are at Hatfield House. [Hervey No. 433; Auerbach p. 64]

the Duchesse of Savoye

Catalina, sister of Isabel (*previous*). She married in 1585 and died in 1597. Portrait not traced.

a French Duchesse

Unidentified.

[the olde Countes of Salisburie behedded]

Margaret Pole (1473-1541). Created Countess of Salisbury by Henry VIII; she was beheaded for treason following the publication of *De Unitate Ecclesiastica* (1536) by her son Reginald, Cardinal Pole. This may have been the (extensively repainted) half-length portrait at NPG No. 2607 by an unknown artist working in the 1530s, or a copy. [Davies; *TJP* 271-3]

[the olde Marquesse of Dorcett syster to Sir Edw: Wootton]

Margaret Grey (née Wotton), Marchioness of Dorset,(d. 1535); mother of Arundel's first wife Catherine. This portrait, c.1532-5, after a drawing by Holbein, and showing the Lumley *cartellino*, is in a private collection in the USA. A copy is at Anglesey Abbey. [Piper, p. 228; Wright 91; *English Portaits 1530-1650* (Weiss Gallery catalogue 1986) No. 1]

[Counties of Shroesburie 2 wyffe to the first Earle of Shroesburie, eldest daughter to Richard Earle of Warwicke, Beauchampe]

Margaret Beauchamp, d.1473. Her half-length portrait, with a *cartellino*, the companion to that of her husband, is at Compton Wynyates. [NPG archives]

[Ladie Margaret Lenox]

Margaret Douglas, Countess of Lennox (1515-78). This portrait was NPG No. 401 c.1560-5 by an unknown artist or a copy [*TJP* 198-200]

Duchesse of Somersett, Stanhop

Anne (1497-1587), daughter of Sir Edward Stanhope, second wife of Edward Seymour, first Duke of Somerset (1506?-52).Portraits of her aged sixteen are at Syon Abbey and Petworth House; another of her as an adult is at Chevening. [NPG archives]

Mary Duches of Northfolke, daughter to the last Earl of Arundell [Fitzallen] doone by Haunce Eworth

Mary Fitzalan (c.1539/40-57), daughter of twelfth Earl of Arundel, wife of the fourth Duke of Norfolk. Her portrait by Hans Eworth is inscribed '1565/HE' but is datable to 1555 on grounds of costume; which is confirmed by the later inscription: 'aeta su 16'. From this collection the portrait passed to the Duke of Hamilton in whose inventory of 1704 it was described: 'A picture of the Duchess of Norfolk in Queen Elizabeth's time, down to the knees'. The picture has been reduced at the right and bottom and is now in the Cleveland Museum of Art. [NPG archives; *Icon* No. 26.]

Lady Marques of {~~Dorset~~ Northampton} borne in Swedelande

Helena Henriksson Snakenborg (1549-1635) of East Goathland, Sweden. She married the elderly Willam Parr (1513-71) six weeks before his death. A portrait of 'A young lady aged 21, possibly Helena Snakenborg, later Marchioness of Northampton 1569' is in Tate Britain. [G Sjogren,

'Portrait of a young lady, 1569, an identification', *Burlington Magazine* (1980) pp. 698-700; Tate Britain catalogue entry by Karen Hearn]

Countes of Huntington, daughter to the Duke of Northumberlande

Catherine Dudley (d.1620). In 1553 she married Henry Hastings (c.1536-95), third earl of Huntingdon. A photograph of a portrait, possibly by Federico Zuccaro, formerly called Katherine Pole but now thought to be of this sitter, is in the NPG archives.

Countesse of Lincolne, daughter to the Earle of Kildare

Elizabeth Fitzgerald (c.1528-90). Piper regards this portrait by Steven van der Meulen, which bears the Lumley *cartellino*, as so far the best authenticated portrait of Surrey's 'Fair Geraldine' and of 'considerable iconographic importance'. Pennant describes her: 'a lady in a singular dress of black and gold with a red and gold petticoat, dated 1560'. The portrait was bought in at the auction in Lumley Castle in 1785 for £4.14s.6d. but went in 1807 for £1.5s. It is now in a private collection in the USA. [Pennant p. 320; Piper, p. 228; *Icon* No. 72]

Countesse of Warwicke, daughter to the Earle of Bedford

Anne Russell (1548-1604), elder daughter of Francis, second Earl of Bedford. Three portraits of her at Woburn Abbey have the Bedford *cartellino* and have always been there. A head and shoulders is at Warwick Castle. (A portrait of her husband was auctioned from Lumley Castle in 1807.) [*Icon* Nos. 62, 129, 318.]

Countess of Essex wife to the 2 Earle of Essex and widow to sir Phillip Sidney

Frances Walsingham (1569?-1632), wife of Robert, Earl of Essex. This is perhaps the companion marriage-portrait with that of her husband by Segar c.1590. In the nineteenth century it was altered in three ways to suggest that the sitter was Mary Queen of Scots: the Lumley *cartellino* was painted over with *MARIA REGINA SCOTIAE*; another false inscription in English was added at the bottom; and a crucifix was painted hanging from her left hand. The portrait was auctioned from Lumley Castle in 1807 for £5.5s. It is now in the California Palace of the Legion of Honour. [*Icon* No. 183; Piper, pp.231, 300]

[Marye daughter to Sr William Candishe wyfe to Gilbert earle of Shrewsburye y^t now is.]

Mary Cavendish (1555-1632). In 1568 she married Gilbert Talbot, seventh earl, son of her stepfather the sixth earl. A threequarter-length portrait at Hardwick Hall (English School, 16th century) has the later inscription: *Queen Elizabeth*. A head and shoulders portrait is at St John's College, Cambridge. [NPG archives]

Lady Jane Graye, executed

Jane Dudley (1537-54), daughter of Henry Grey, Duke of Suffolk, husband of Lord Guildford Dudley, the 'nine-day queen'. This cut down and much restored half-length by an unknown artist, bearing the Lumley *cartellino* is the earliest known portrait of her and is now in a private collection. [*TJP* 79; NPG archives]

Lady Katheryn Graye, married to the Earle of Hertfourd

(1540-68). Second daughter of Henry Grey, Duke of Suffolk. In December 1560, in a private Catholic ceremony, she married Edward Seymour, Earl of Hertford (1537-1612). [HMC *Hatfield* xiii, 61-2] A portrait, perhaps by Gheeraerts, inscribed 'Ano 1562 aeta 22', was with Christies in 1950 but its present whereabouts are not known. [NPG archives]

Countesse of Arundell second wife to the late old Earle of Arundell [Fitzallen] daughter to Sir John Arundell of Lanherne in Cornewall.

Mary Arundell (d. 1557), she married Arundel in 1545. It is remarkable that no panel portrait of her has survived, but a miniature is at Castle Howard [NPG archives].

Countesse of Arundell, wife to Phillip Earle of Arundell, daughter to the Lo: Dacres of the northe.

Anne Dacre (1557-1630) eldest daughter of Thomas Lord Dacre of the North. She married Philip, Earl of Arundel and Surrey in 1571. A portrait of her (and her husband) was in the collection of Thomas Howard, Earl of Arundel, possibly that by Vorstermann (?) inscribed 'aetatis suae 52 A.D. 1613', but all that is known now is an unflattering engraving of her 'aet 69 Ao 16' by Hollar, though the dates are inconsistent in both cases. [NPG archives; Hervey Nos. 420, 421.]

yo[r] Lo: first wife daughter to the old Earle of Arundell [Fitzallen] drawne by Steven

Jane Fitzalan (d.1577), daughter of twelfth earl of Arundel and Lumley's first wife. This is the companion portrait to that of Lumley by Steven van der Meulen, inscribed: '8 Maii a.Dni 1563/ aeta suae 27', and has a *cartellino*. Vertue listed the portrait and Hutchinson described her: 'In black robes, a small ruff with gloves in her hand dress gracefully ornamented with strings of jewels'. In the auction of 1785 'a pair of half lengths of John, Lord Lumley and Jane his first wife, 1563' was bought in for £5.5s. In 1807 his went for £2.4s. and hers for £1.14s. They are now at Sandbeck Park. [Vertue p. 42; Pennant p. 322; Hutchinson p. 404; *Icon* No 67; Piper, p. 227]

my La: yo[r] second wife daughter to the Lo: Darcy of Chiche, drawne by Hubbart.

Elizabeth (d. 1617), daughter of John, second Baron Darcy and Lumley's second wife whom he married in 1582. Her full-length portrait by Segar was certainly in Lumley Castle, so this by Hubert Beucklaer may have been left in London or at Stansted in 1592 only to be lost after her death, perhaps in the razing of Stansted in 1644.

La: Darcy of Chiche wife to Thomas the third Lo: Darcy

Mary Kytson (d.1644), married Darcy in April 1583. A marriage portrait of her by George Gower inscribed '1583 AETATIS 17' was at Hengrave Hall until 1887; its present whereabouts are not known. [*Icon* No. 126]

La: Guilfourd wife to Sir Henry Guilfourd Coumptroller, drawne by Haunce Holbyn.

Mary Wotton, Guildford's Catholic wife. The portrait is inscribed: ANNO M D XXVII AETATIS SUAE XXVII. This is a companion portrait to that of her husband with which it remained until 1734/5. It is now in the City Art Gallery, St Louis, Missouri. [Millar, No. 28; Anon., *Holbein and the Court of Henry VIII*, Exhibition Catalogue 1978; Ganz No. 45; Hervey No. 186; Pollen 258.]

an Italian gentlewoman drawen by her selfe and presented to the olde Earle of Arundell in Italy.

Unidentified. This may have been one of thirteen known self-portraits by Sofonisba Anguissola (1532-1625) who was born at Cremona into a family of the minor nobility; she is the only female Italian artist of the period who might properly be termed a gentlewoman. Most of her portraits were completed when she was a young woman and living in Italy. When Arundel visited Italy in 1566-7, however, she had been in Madrid for some six years as lady in waiting and court painter to Queen Isabella, wife of Philip II. Nonetheless, the earl could easily have visited Cremona from Milan and have been presented with a portrait by her father. (Giorgio Vasari went out of his way to visit the Anguissola household in 1566 and included her in his *Vite* of 1568.) A self-portrait of her seated at a clavichord and with an aged servant (1561), is at Althorp House. [I.S. Perlingieri, *Sofonisba Anguissola* (1992) *passim*]

a Dutche Ladye

Unidentified.

an Italian Gentlewoman in great reputacon wth her husband for her beawty

Unidentified

Shores wyfe concubyne to K: Edw: 4.

Jane Shore (d.1527). She became one of the king's mistresses from about 1470 and she was celebrated in literature as 'the merriest' of them. Aubrey remarked upon 'a rare picture, viz. of that pretty creature Mrs Jane shore, an original' in the possession of Lady Southcot. A breast-length nude of the Fontainebleau School is at Eton College [illus. ODNB] and a flimsily clad waist-length by Bernardino Luini (d. 1532) is in the collection of the Earl of Halifax. An entirely proper portrait is at Magdalene College Cambridge. [NPG archives]

a bride of Constantinople

Unidentified.

Mary Magdalen drawen by Fraunсs Flores

Frans Floris de Vriendt I c.1519/20-70 was an Italianate painter of Antwerp; he is not known to have been in England. Bruyn identifies this picture as having belonged to the Earl of Leicester and was acquired by Lumley around 1590. Portrait not traced. [Bruyn, Appendix p. 106]

Lucretia drawne by {Cornelius Vancleave} of Anwarpe

Lucrezia Borgia (1480-1519) Duchess of Ferrara, Daughter of Pope Alexander VI. The portraitist and painter of devotional pictures, Cornelis van Cleve (1520-70) emigrated to England from Antwerp in 1555. He died insane through jealousy of Antonis Mor. Portrait not traced.

Pompeia

Portrait not traced; possibly one of 'Two pictures of Poppea Sabina with curtaines' acquired in 1590 from the Leicester collection. [Bruyn, Appendix p. 105]

Cleopatra in water colours

Untraced.

thre Italian Ladyes

Unidentified.

{Mary Medices daughter to Francise Duke of Thoscane and to Joan of Austria, and wife to Henrie of Borbon Kinge of France}

Maria de' Medici (1573-1642). She married Henri IV in 1600. A copy of Rubens's portrait is at Temple Newsham. [Wright 177]

Other Pictures and Tables

A Speciall picture of Christ cast in mould by Raphael de Urbino, brought into England from Rome by Cardynall Poole

Thre notable peics of hangings, One of Christ his passage with his Crosse to his Passion, The other of his passion, And the third of his Judgement doone by Henry Houmfrey, These were those especiall peices, y^t^ hong in S^ct^ Magnus churche at the bridge foote in London {gave away}

A large picture of o^f^ blessed Lady with Christ her sonne in her Armes.

A large table of the Passion of Christ crucified, doone by Mr Schoore of Utright

Jan van Scorel (1495-1562) of Utrecht. This may have been one of his altarpieces.

A table of the fower Evangelists, supporting Christ

A picture of S^ct^ Hierome

Possibly 'The Picture of St Jerome naked, with a curtaine of silke' acquired from the Leicester collection around 1590. [Bruyn, Appendix p. 105]

{The picture of our Ladie wth Christ in her armes togith^r^ with St Catherine and St Jhon Baptist on Canvasse}

{The Passion of Christ cutt in black stone}

{A great large table in folds of the Passion, very auncient and notable}

This was probably a mediaeval English triptych.

A table of Sainct Pawle preachinge

Notwithstanding the different saint's name, this could have been 'A Table of St. J. Baptist preacheing in the wildernes' acquired from the Leicester collection c. 1590 [Bruyn, Appendix p. 106]

A large table of Charite doone by Vincent of Macklen

Probably 'the picture of a naked woman with three babes about hir' by Vincent Sellaer of Mechelen [Malines], acquired from the Leicester collection c. 1590. Several versions are known. [Bruyn, Appendix p. 106]

A large table of Noe, doone by Fraunce Flores Anwarpe

Probably 'A very fayre picture of Noah and of the drowning of the whole world' acquired from the Leicester collection c. 1590. It is inventoried as by Frans Floris but a near contemporary source ascribes it to Cornelis Cornelisz. van Haarlem (1562-1638). [Bruyn, p. 95, Appendix p. 106]

A large table of Rape of {Helena}, drawne by Cleave Haunce of Anwarpe

Hans (Jan) van Cleve III, a member of a large South Netherlandish family of painters active in Antwerp from the late 15th to the early 16th centuries.

A table of a young man fancying the riche old woman

A large table of the maner of banquetting in Flaunders

A table of Anchises and Aenaeas

A table of Juno and Jupiter

A table of Venus and Adonis

A table of Dives and Lazarus

A table of the building of Babell

A table of Judith and Holofernes

A table of the sale of Joseph by his brethren

A table on the conyng pspective of death and a woman, doone by Hilliarde

Nicholas Hilliard (c.1547-1619), English court miniaturist. The picture is lost. [Auerbach *Hilliard* (1961) 273/6]

A table of the Ficlenes of Fortune

A counterfeyt of an old booke

A table of Cookerye

Probably 'A historie of Cookerie in a frame of woode all gilt about the border, with a curtaine of silk', acquired from the Leicester collection c. 1590 [Bruyn, Appendix p. 106]

Two large tables of China woork

A table of Hercules

The 9: worthies in roundels encealed

Traditionally the nine comprised three pagans: Hector, Alexander, Julius Caesar; three Jews: Joshua, King David, Judas Maccabeus; and three Christians: King Arthur, Charlemagne and either Godfrey of Boulogne or Guy of Warwick.

A great table of the birthe of Christ

Possibly a mediaeval altarpiece, and perhaps 'the picture of Christe how he was borne in an ox stall, with 2 leaves to fould and unfoulde' acquired from the Leicester collection c. 1590. [Bruyn, Appendix, p. 106]

A great table of the fower Evangelistes

A great table of the conversion of S^ct Pawle

This may have been 'A fayre large table of the Picture of Christ calling Peter out of the Custome house', acquired from the Leicester collection c.1590. But Peter was a fisherman and Paul was a rabbi; it was Matthew who was the tax-collector. Hence there is no good reason to doubt Lampton's identification as given in the inventory. [Bruyn Appendix p. 106]

A great booke of Pictures doone by Haunce Holbyn of certyne Lordes, Ladyes, gentlemen and gentlewomen in King Henry the 8: his tyme, their names subscribed by Sr John Cheke Secretary to King Edward the 6 wch booke was King Edward the 6

The book was bought for Edward at some date after 1547, as indicated by an (undated but contemporary) entry in the accounts of Sir Thomas Carwarden, Master of Revels and Keeper of Nonsuch 1544-59: 'for a peynted booke of Mr Hanse Holby making 6 li'. By Edward's death in 1553 the book had passed by gift to Arundel, his Lord Chamberlain, and at Arundel's death in 1580 it devolved on Lumley his son-in-law. At Lumley's death in 1609, the book went with his library to Prince Henry, at whose death in 1612 it passed to Prince Charles, his younger brother. Shortly after his accession in 1625, Charles exchanged it for Raphael's painting of St. George and the Dragon (now in the National Gallery, Washington DC) belonging to the Earl of Pembroke, his Lord Chamberlain. The latter gave the book to Thomas Howard, Earl of Arundel, who died in Padua in 1646. The book returned to the Royal Collection in 1675. In 1735 George Vertue recalled its Lumley provenance:

> In the inventory before mentioned dated 1590 amongst other things a book containing many pictures of Noblemen, Gentlemen, Ladies drawn by H Holbein, and the names put to them by Sir John Cheke, and that this book did belong to King Edward the 6th (this book not now nor has been time out of mind in possession of this Lord's [Earl of Scarbrough's] family). Query. if this be the very book the present Queen

> [Caroline] found at Kensington (Hampton Court) in one of the presses or chests. Which pictures are now framed put up at the Queen's house at Richmond, with glasses over them.

[Anon., *Holbein and the Court of Henry VIII* (exhibition catalogue The Queen's Gallery 1978-9, passim; 'Vertue's Notebooks IV', *Walpole Society XXIV* (1935-6) p. 81]

A great table of the temptacions of S^{ct}{~~Frauncis~~ Antony}

A great table of a Dutche woman selling of Fruyte.

Possibly 'A picture of a froe selling frutage' and acquired from the Leicester collection c. 1590 [Bruyn, Appendix, p. 106]

A pycture of St Francis

Picture of Lodovicus Orioustus the Poete [done by Lucios the payte$^{r.}$]

This may be a duplicate of the earlier entry on Lodovico Ariosto (1474-1533). Lucios was probably Lucas d'Heere (1534-84) of Ghent who is known to have worked in England.

Picture of Count de la Marche who wan Bryll in Holland for the Prynce of Orange

William de la Marck, leader of the Sea-Beggars who took The Brill, dominating the entry into the lower Rhine, from the Spanish on 1 April 1572. Portrait not traced.

{Other pictures in small of Christ, our Ladie and his Saints, wrought upon brass, and adorned wth marbles and marble Pillars}

Presumably these were embellished engravings; 66 pictures are listed.

{Sum of the valew of the picture 623£}

A SUMARYE of certayne stuffe within your Lo: houses the xxiith of May Anno 1590 the Inventoryes of the partyculers remaynyng in bookes subscribed by John Lambton, gentleman, steward of household to yor Lo: and under the handes of the severall wardropers there

{The Stuffe estemd 5380}

The Armo^{r} valewed iiii^{c} iiii^{xx} xvii viiid [£480.17.8.]

The Plate & sylver vessell [blank]

The Library Registred in a boke wryten by Alcocke, my L: of Chechester his L: servant, Ao 1596 with all the rest of my bokes myselfe have dyspersed sundery ways.

The history and contents of the library have been comprehensively treated in S Jayne & F R Johnson, *The Lumley Library* (1956). The original catalogue is lost but a fair copy, with corrections by Dennis Flemynge, made in 1609, at the time of the library's removal to St James's Palace, is at MS. O.4.38, in the library of Trinity College, Cambridge.

Lord Lumley by W Segar c. 1588

Chapter Five

The Last and Most Disastrous Sale[1]

By the turn of the century Lumley enjoyed an annual income of £1,799 including the rental from his estates in Sussex, Surrey, Kent, London, Yorkshire, Northumberland and Durham. The Lumleys maintained an impressive household and table: their annual expenditure on food amounted to £1,338.[2] They had also regained their social standing and they maintained a wide circle of friends, some of whom undertook buying commissions for them or sent them gifts: Sir Robert Sydney, Governor of Flushing, obtained gem-stones and Sir Oliver Manners sent four pairs of Roman gloves to Lady Lumley.[3] Lumley, who had conspired to bring about Burghley's downfall, courted Robert Cecil, Burghley's son. He sent Cecil gifts of a horse and vegetables from Nonsuch and had his young son William Cecil to stay. Lumley was confident enough to solicit Cecil's support in some legal matters on behalf of his dependents and servants.[4] The Lumleys had also regained a place in court life; in June 1600 the queen dined 'at My Lady Lomley's in Greenwich' and in December 1602 Lumley told Cecil: 'The state of my body hath made me unfit for the Court' but he hoped to see the queen shortly. He told Cecil that he desired to remain on the right side in the new reign and he was included in the Commission for Consideration of Coronation Claims by James I. In 1605 Lady Lumley held some minor position in the household of Queen Anne, James I's consort, for which she was paid £75 a year.[5]

Lumley died on 11 April 1609, aged seventy-five. He had outlived four sovereigns and survived the momentous political and religious changes of his times despite being on the wrong side for most of them and in an age when noble heads rolled for lesser conspiracies than his. His longevity, physical constitution apart, can be attributed to two interrelated factors. Crucially, his arrests in 1569 and in 1572 were precautionary and, since he was careful enough to leave no incriminating documentary evidence, he could not be charged with treasonable acts (though it would not have been an insuperable problem to arrange for a conviction) only with the lesser offence of misprision of treason. He was fortunate to get off with a temporary loss of liberty and a heavy fine. In any case, the leadership of the Catholic party was decimated by the executions of the Duke of Norfolk and of the Earl of Northumberland, the death in custody of the Earl of Pembroke, and the exile of the Earl of Westmorland. These served to intimidate the Catholic party to an extent that further executions, say of Arundel and his son in law, became unnecessary and might even have been looked upon as vindictive and hence counter-productive. Lumley's survival also testifies to a capacity to learn from historical experience as well as from his current difficulties. His grandfather had fallen from favour for his part in the Pilgrimage of Grace and his father had lost his life in the same cause. Doubtless Lumley would have persisted in trying to reverse the religious changes introduced by Edward and Elizabeth had there been the slightest chance of success, and there were some who tried to enlist him in subsequent plots, but he was by then persuaded of the futility of political intrigue and insurrection. He cannot have failed to appreciate that while his father, in the Pilgrimage, had delayed the implementation of the Reformation, he and the northern earls had expedited it.[6] As a result, both he and Arundel (who saved his skin because he, too, had been placed in custody before he could act) eschewed politics and retired to the safety of private life. Finally, Lumley seems to have developed a personal loyalty to Queen Elizabeth; they had, after all, been childhood friends and she had forgiven his involvement in the early Marian plots and spared his life, though it was a close-run thing. He did not, of course, receive any honours from her – the award of the Garter or a promotion in the peerage was hardly to be expected.

Since Lumley had no direct heir, his peerage became extinct. His testamentary dispositions are unclear; Surtees says (citing secondary sources only) that Lumley wrote three wills. The first, of 2 May 1597, preferred the issue of his sister Barbara but, having reflected on the danger to the continuity of his name (a characteristic consideration), he altered it in favour of his second cousin Richard Lumley despite a feud between their two branches of the family. Surtees dates the two alterations to 10 March 1606 and 28 January 1606, in that order, but the registered will is dated 22 January 1606.[7] Richard, son of Roger Lumley (about whom nothing is known), was baptised at Chester le Street in 1589. Details of his schooling are scant, although, having some misgivings about its quality or, more probably, its denominational character, (which may well have been the cause of the family feud) Lord Lumley took particular care to provide financially for the boy's upbringing. In February 1595 he executed a deed leaving his Durham estates to Sir Richard Lewkenor, M.P. and Serjeant-at-Law, and William Smith of London for fifteen years at an annual rent of £50 for the

> education and bringing up of Richard Lumley. If Lord Lumley dies during Richard's minority and Roger, Richard's father, or any other of his kindred or friends take upon them or sue to have the education, care and upbringing of Richard, the said rent to be suspended until they desist.[8]

This was reiterated at some length in Lumley's will. It seems likely that since Lewkenor had Catholic relations and that William Smith was undoubtedly a Catholic whereas Roger Lumley was not, Lumley wanted to ensure that Richard was brought up in the old faith. In the event, the question was never put to the test for Richard was aged twenty when Lumley died, and he remained a Catholic.

Lumley's will is nothing more than a formal document so banal is it in its dispositions considering the testator's social position, and wealth, which makes it all the more regrettable that the previous versions have not survived. At any rate, he left everything to his wife, his sole executrix, with the real estate entailed on his second cousin Richard Lumley at her death, but no other details were given. That some dispositions were made previously seems clear, for he left to Lady Lumley 'all the residue of my goods and chattels whatsoever *not before or otherwise given and bequeathed*' [emphasis added]. By the latter he would certainly have meant the bequest of the real estate to Richard Lumley, but he may also have referred to the gift of the library to Prince Henry (discussed earlier) and a bequest of some pictures to Robert Cecil, first Earl of Salisbury. On 4 July, within three months of Lumley's death, Salisbury's accounts show a payment to

> 'Lumleys man who brought to your Honour Pictures wch was given your Lo: as a legacye: 4l.

and in December that year:

> To my La: Lumleys man who brought your honor a picture of the Queene mother of Scotland – 40s.[9]

The number of pictures in the bequest is not known precisely (the high charge for delivery might indicate a substantial number), except that a portrait of Mary Stewart, Holbein's cartoon of Henry VII and Henry VIII and Eworth's double portrait of Darnley and his brother were delivered to Salisbury House in London and were subsequently transferred to Hatfield House, a new mansion which was nearing completion. Twenty-two portraits are common to the Lumley inventory of 1590 and the first Hatfield inventory of 1611, four of which can be traced at Lumley Castle until they were sold in the eighteenth century, but it would be imprudent to suggest that all of the others formed part of Lumley's bequest since both Lumley and Salisbury would have owned portraits of the same sitters.[10] Lady Lumley maintained the friendly relations with Salisbury which had been established by her late husband, and her brother Lord Darcy sent him a marble table from Italy with a head of Ferdinand, late Duke of Tuscany.[11]

Lady Lumley would have had to leave Keeper's Lodge at Nonsuch when her husband died and she probably removed any remaining pictures to her dower house at Stansted. She died on 4 February 1617 eight years after her husband and three months after writing her will. She was 'carried unto Cheam in Surrey to be buried' alongside her husband in the Lumley Chapel of the parish church.[12] As prearranged with her husband, she bequeathed the estates (Stansted and Lumley) with their contents to Sir Richard Lumley (who was knighted in 1616). Evidently, she was concerned about the future of her husband's collections for in her will she instructed Sir Richard that 'the marbles and pictures as shall be in the Castle of Lumley at the time of my death [are] there to remain as Airelooms to that house so longe as they will endure', and she said the same about the contents of her 'howse neare the Towerhill in the parish of St Olyffes in Hartstreete London' which she left to her brother Thomas, third Lord Darcy.[13] But her instructions were soon set aside.

Some time ago Mary Hervey surmised that those pictures which were listed in the inventory and which appeared in other collections soon after Lady Lumley's death, such as that of Thomas Howard, Earl of Arundel, were probably those left behind in the south, and she may well have been right, supposing Darcy was prepared to oblige.[14] On the other hand, Howard was aged twenty-four at the time of Lumley's death and he was probably familiar not just with the pictures left in Lumley's houses in the south but also with those in the main collection in Durham. It seems highly likely that at some point the young art-lover and antiquary would have travelled north to view his kinsman's great art-collection at Lumley and at the same time go the few miles further to Naworth in Westmorland to inspect the library and archaeological collections of his other kinsman, Lord William Howard.[15] It is quite reasonable to suppose that he would have earmarked certain items for purchase if they ever became available and if Sir Richard was happy to accommodate him. At any rate, wherever they came from, Holbein's Christina of Denmark was in Howard's possession by 1627; Dürer's watercolour of Henry Morley, Holbein's portraits of Edward VI, Erasmus, the Guildfords, Wyatt and the book of drawings appear in his inventory of 1655 as well as a dozen other pictures which could have been in the Lumley collection.[16] Similarly, pictures from the Lumley collection appear in the Salisbury House inventory of 1629; and eight portraits of members of the Norfolk family which are known to have been in Arundel House or Arundel Castle from the early seventeenth century were probably transferred following Lady Lumley's death.[17] It seems, then, that within a very short period after her demise, at least thirty portraits, not including a number at Tower Hill, had left the collection.

Sir Richard Lumley was elevated to the Irish peerage as Viscount Lumley of Waterford in 1628 and he held military command in the royalist forces during the Civil War under Prince Rupert. He garrisoned Lumley Castle but it was not involved in hostilities and suffered no damage. Stansted, however, was razed by parliamentary forces in 1644, in which action, presumably, most of the contents were destroyed. That would explain why some family pictures listed in the inventory cannot be traced: a full-length portrait of Lady Jane Lumley,[18] and Beuckelaer's portraits of Lady Elizabeth Lumley and her brother Thomas, Lord Darcy. Waterford's great-grandson Richard mortgaged his properties in Durham for £8,000 to finance the building of a new country seat at Stansted which was completed by William Talman in 1686. In September 1738 George Vertue went with the Earl and Countess of Oxford, Mr Caesar and others on a tour of Kent and Sussex. Their itinerary included Stansted Park but the earliest pictures noted by Vertue were Jacobean and post-dated those in the inventory.[19] The estate passed out of the family in 1766 and when Horace Walpole went there in August 1770 he saw nothing which might have belonged to Lumley. If perchance any pictures did survive, they perished in a disastrous fire in 1900.[20]

During the seventeenth century a number of important paintings were acquired for the collection at Lumley Castle, probably by Richard Lumley, Waterford's grandson, who was born around 1650 and was 'bred up in the Religion of his family, which had always been *Roman Catholic*'.[21] His governor was the Catholic priest Richard Lassels [?Lascelles] (1603-68) of a gentry family of Yorkshire. Lassels acted as tutor to several distinguished youths making tours of Flanders, France and Italy; he wrote *Voyage to Italy* (posth., Paris 1670) the first published guidebook for Grand Tourists and dedicated it to Lumley. Viscount Lumley, his mother, his brother and two sisters were granted a licence to travel abroad in October 1667 taking Lassels, twelve servants, six geldings and £60 with them.[22] It was probably this Richard Lumley who acquired three Van Dyck portraits, two of which were of Charles I, three pictures by Rembrandt, one of which, inevitably, was a self-portrait, four portraits by Lely, and *Joseph and His Brethren* by Velasquez, 'a great masterly composition'. While those, together with contemporary portraits of the family, were hung in Lumley Castle, it is clear that the number of historic portraits in the collection was further reduced. Around 1650 the portrait of the first Earl of Pembroke was either given by the then Lord Lumley or bought by the Pembroke family to replace its own portrait which was lost in a disastrous fire a few years earlier. Eworth's portrait of Mary, wife of the fourth duke of Norfolk was in the collection of the Duke of Hamilton by 1704.

Lumley was for a time in the household of James, Duke of York, and he accompanied the prince when James was exiled to Edinburgh. But it appears that Lumley became increasingly disenchanted with the zealous popery around him. James's Catholicism became known around 1668; then there was the 'Grand Design' of converting England to Catholicism as part of the Treaty of Dover of 1670; and James married the Catholic Mary of Modena in 1672. Some said that Lumley turned

Protestant at the time of the Popish Plot and Exclusion Crisis (1678-81) and it is perhaps unlikely that the English barony of Lumley would have been revived for him in May 1681 unless he was prepared to take his seat in the House of Lords as a Protestant. On the other hand, some were not convinced of his sincerity: Burnet remarked that Lumley, Norfolk and Shrewsbury 'had changed their religion during the late heats that had been against popery' but 'it was generally believed that they would be the first that would return'.[23] Moreover, although Lumley left the duke's service around 1680, he remained at court as Master of the Horse to Queen Catherine (of Braganza), a Catholic. On 22 January 1683 Sir John Reresby heard Lumley declare his speedy intention of quitting his place but that may have been only a preliminary to his appointment as Treasurer to the queen.

In March 1685 Lumley, aged about thirty-five, married the nineteen-year-old Frances Jones of Aston, Oxfordshire, who had Catholic forbears: her mother was a Bellasis, daughter of Lord Fauconberg. Lumley took his seat in the Lords in May 1685, a month after James's coronation. He was given a command at the Battle of Sedgemoor and it was his troop which discovered Monmouth hiding in a ditch and it was to Lumley that Monmouth surrendered. If Lumley's ecclesiastical allegiance was ambiguous during the early 1680s there was no doubt about it from 1687 though his resignation as Colonel of the 6th Dragoon Guards and his subsequent plotting against James II 'surprised many'. At any rate, he was one of the seven peers who signed the invitation to the Prince of Orange to come to England and he was the key figure in securing the north-east for William. He was rewarded with a number of civil and military appointments and he was created Viscount Lumley in the English peerage in April 1689 and raised to an earldom a year later. He chose Chichester for his title but when it was found that Charles Fitzroy, one of Charles II's natural sons had that title, Lumley chose Scarbrough instead. (The spelling is not that of the Yorkshire town Scarborough.)

Scarbrough was described around 1700 as a Whig and 'a Gentleman of very good Sense, a great Lover of the Constitution of his Country, and an improver of Trade, and his Genius lay very much this Way; a handsome Man, of a brown Complexion'. He held high office during the reigns of Mary, Anne and George I, and his wife served as Lady of the Bedchamber to Queen Mary and Queen Anne. In 1710 Pope wrote of him and a Mr Litton that he could 'not but be sorry two heroes of such a make should die inglorious in their beds'. Scarbrough died of apoplexy in London in January 1721. His three sisters Elizabeth, Frances and Mary remained Catholics; the latter two were unmarried and lived at Lumley and they probably maintained a priest in the castle or locality. Then in 1696 William Tempest, Scarbrough's agent and a Catholic, bequeathed £300 to the Benedictine Order for the maintenance of a priest in Chester le Street and that mission was the forerunner of that at Birtley.[24]

In 1720 Scarbrough decided to renovate Lumley Castle but it fell to the second earl to put the plans into effect. Sir John Vanbrugh was engaged on Seaton Delaval Hall and Castle Howard at the time. In the summer of 1721, Vanbrugh (like the new earl a member of the Kit-Kat Club) broke off from his work at Castle Howard to visit Lumley Castle which he found

> a Noble thing; and well deserves the Favours Lord Lumley designs to bestow upon it; in order to which, I stay'd there near a Week, to form a General Design for the whole, Which consists, in altering the House both for State, Beauty and Convenience, and making the Courts Gardens and Offices Suitable to it; All which I believe may be done, for a Sum, that can never ly very heavy upon the Family. If I had had good weather in the Expedition I shou'd have been well enough diverted in there being many more Valluable and Agreeable things and Places to be Seen, than in the Tame Sneaking South of England.

In April 1722 Scarbrough asked Vanbrugh 'to propose some things for him in order to begin his Works there'. Since economy was required, the alterations (Vanbrugh's only authenticated work in the county) were unusally modest and restrained for the architect of Blenheim Palace, Castle Howard and Seaton Delaval Hall. New state-rooms were formed: the Ballroom, the Dining Parlour, the Saloon and the Library. Externally there was a general refacing of the walls and the replacement of the old Gothic windows with modern lights; a new staircase to the first-floor Great Hall was also added.[25] The layout of the garden was probably the work of one of the founders of English garden design, Stephen Switzer, who had published *Ichnographia Rustica* (or *The Nobleman's, Gentleman's and Gardener's Recreation: An Introduction to Gardening, Planting,*

Agriculture and other Business and Pleasures of a Country Life (1715). He was at Lumley in 1729. Then in 1740 the Ballroom was redesigned by the Francini brothers as the Garter Room (the ceiling's centrepiece is a replica of the device of the Order of the Garter) and the plasterwork incorporated seven medallions of Roman emperors, which were all that remained of the thirteen recorded in 1590. The plasterwork has been attributed variously to 'two italians [who] came to do the room for Lord Richard Lumley'; to Francesco Vassalli and Martino Quadry, two itinerant Italian *stuccatori* who were active 1724-1763; or to Catezzi, Danielli and Franconi, who worked at Auckland Palace. [26]

A number of pictures were moved out the castle during these building-works and the opportunity was taken to have some of the Elizabethan portraits cleaned and restored. In 1725 Vertue noted that the portraits of 'Sir Nicholas Carew in Armour, by Ant. More [Mor], H. Erl of Surrey, John Ld Lumley 1563 aet. 30, Henry Fitzalan, Erl of Arundel' and other later portraits were at Cookfield Hall in Yoxfield, Suffolk in the possession of 'Sir H Sloane – Dr Harvey and his wife'. In 1732 Vertue listed twenty-four 'pictures repaired and sent to Lumley Castle (some of these painted by Sir Ant. More)' sixteen of which were in the inventory of 1590. Vertue also mentioned a panel portrait by van der Meulen of 'a Man's head well drawn and painted, and clean'd by Mr Sykes Junr.' The dates at which these restorations took place cannot be given, except that the portrait of the Earl of Essex in the collection is known to have been repaired and reduced in size in 1713. Vertue's observations show, however, that the family effected some conservation work on the collection in the early eighteenth century.[27]

Then in 1735 Vertue visited Scarbrough's house in Grosvenor Square and saw 'several old family pictures' painted by Steven van der Meulen and he was shown the artist's receipts for payment. He was given an account of the collection at Lumley Castle as well as the pictures in the London house. There were:

> several family pictures ... K. Hen. 8 on bord.
>
> An old vellum manuscript book containing the draughts of many marbles, fountains, chimney peces, tables.
>
> Monuments drawn belonging to that family and was at Lumley Castle - 1590 with an inventory of goods, pictures, &c.

> There is many pictures of the Kings of England from Ed. 3 &c. to Qu. Elis. or K. James, at that house many pictures of the great men in those reigns, and of this noble family and ancestors, many more amongst which is a large picture of K Richard the second delivering a deed to Sr. Ralph Lumley an ancestor of that family, he is on his knees before the King. John Lord Lumley painted much in the manner of Holbein but the painter's name on the picture and in this old inventory, taken about 1590, is ... Stephens. This Lord's picture was painted when he was 30 years of age about Ano. Dni. 1558, the beginning of Qu. Elisabeth's reign and he died in 1605, so that this painter ... Stephens was living [at] the beginning of that Queen's reign ... How long after? When Mr Jervaise saw this picture in Town he concluded that many pictures painted by Stephens passed for Holbein, it was so much like his pencil and manner rather softer and tenderer, but well coloured.
>
> in the inventory before mentiond dated 1590 amongst other things a book containing many pictures of Noblemen Gentlemen Ladies drawn by H Holben and the names put to them by Sr John Cheeke and that this booke did belong to K Edward ye 6th <this book not now nor has been time out of mind, in poses of this Lords family.> Qu. if this be the very book the present Queen found at Kensington <Hampton Court> in one of the preses - or chests. which pictures are now framed put up at the Queens house at Richmond with glasses over them.

The second earl shot himself dead at his home in Grosvenor Square in January 1740, a few days before he was to marry the Duchess of Manchester.[28]

Neither Vertue or Walpole travelled further north than York on their many tours and so they did not record the collection at Lumley, but there were one or two interested northern tourists later in the century. The traveller and naturalist Thomas Pennant of Chester toured Scotland in the summer of 1769 during the fourth earl's time. He intended to visit Lumley Castle because he had been told it was a place very well worth seeing:

> but, unfortunately it proved a public day (i.e., a day when the whole country is admitted, and the inquisitive traveller who may never pass that road again [is] alone excluded) and so I lost sight of it.

(Dr Johnson somewhere remarks of Pennant: 'He's a Whig, Sir; a sad dog. But he's the best traveller I ever read.') Pennant made a second tour in 1772, accompanied by the botanist the Rev. J. Lightfoot and the artist Moses Griffith, and on that occasion he managed to get into the castle. He made notes on the collection for his account of the tour and they were copied by William Hutchinson into his *History of Durham* of 1787. Pennant reprinted his *Tour* in 1790 but he omitted some of the pictures referred to in the first edition.[29] The context of these accounts shows that the whole of the collection was being described, not a selection, and they clearly indicate that the original collection had long since been decimated even taking into account the removal of a handful of portraits to Sandbeck Park (which was inherited in 1723 by Thomas Lumley who became third earl in 1740). In August 1772 Walpole visited Roche Abbey and wrote to William Cole: 'Lord Scarborough to whom it belongs, and who lives next door, neglects it as much as if he was afraid of ghosts'.[30] He did not call at Sandbeck.

When Pennant first visited, the total number of sixteenth-century portraits remaining at Lumley was fifty-two; he listed forty in 1790. No records survive to show precisely how, when or why the majority of the Elizabethan portraits were disposed of, but there can be no doubt that not only were no pictures bought in the eighteenth century but that there had been a continuous haemorrhaging from the historic collection due, perhaps to dislike, deterioration, to make room for newer pictures, for financial reasons, or as gifts. The antiquary William Stukeley had remarked in 1725 on 'a curious old picture of Chaucer, said to be an original' at the castle but Pennant did not mention it and Hutchinson could not find it.[31] Raphael's portrait of Pope Julius II was not seen by them either. A portrait of Shakespeare which was said to have been acquired by Lumley was not mentioned by Pennant, but the evidence for its existence is uncertain. It was not inventoried before 1609 and Fordyce said the portrait was auctioned from Lumley Castle in 1785, bought in and sold in 1807, but it does not appear in the auction catalogues.[32] Another portrait from Lumley's period was seen by Pennant but, since it is not identifiable in the inventory it might have been acquired later:

> *Garcia Sarmienta Cuna.* Full length in armour, a ruff, red stockings, white shoes, a white cross on his breast, a spear in his hand. Out of a window a view of the sea. He was captain of the guard to *Philip II*

Garcia Sarmiento de Acuna (1592-1624), son of the Conde de Gondomar, was a knight of the Order of St John of Jerusalem (the insignia of which was a white cross on a red ground.) The portrait was auctioned in 1807 and brought £5. Its present whereabouts have not been established.

By the 1760s, Richard, the fourth earl owned not only the Lumley estate in Durham but the Sandbeck estate near Rotherham in Yorkshire and the Glentworth estate in Lincolnshire which had been inherited from his Saunderson relatives. Rebuilding and emparking those properties, as well as outlays on electioneering, enclosures, colliery development, social and court expenditure and providing for a large number of offspring gave rise to considerable expenditure. Between 1755 and 1775, Glentworth House was enlarged; the mansion at Sandbeck was rebuilt by James Paine and the grounds were landscaped by 'Capability' Brown; Lumley Castle was also extensively repaired although one visitor remarked in 1781: 'Lord Scarbrough's 2 places in one of which is a fine Abbey in ruins, the other Lumley Castle hardly worth seeing'.[33] Winning new collieries in the Great Lumley area required an investment of some £17,000 between 1777 and 1783. When the fourth earl died in 1782, his successor inherited debts of some £70,000. The disposal of assets became necessary. On her way north to Dalkeith Palace, the Duchess of Buccleuch stopped at

> Lumley Castle to see if there was anything worth bidding for at the auction. I never saw anything so completely melancholy and neglected as the place. The House is a very good one and many tolerable pictures but none very good - A great many Scarbrough family which will sell for nothing I daresay.[34]

Mr Christie conducted the auction at the castle in August 1785 for George Lumley, the fifth earl. Forty-five early portraits were put up but only three were sold outright; the rest were bought in, including twenty family portraits. In November 1807, six months after succeeding his brother as sixth earl, Richard Savile ordered another auction. Mr Dawson disposed of a further four portraits of the historic collection at Sandbeck Park, and then in December Mr Dawson held what has been described as 'the last and most disastrous sale' at Lumley Castle:

> Tapestries of probably priceless value, pictures of the utmost interest, furniture of probably every date, and smaller objects of interest beyond description were brought to the hammer. For twenty-one days this ruthless sale continued.[35]

Forty pictures were put up but the family pictures were bought in. The catalogues for both the 1785 and 1807 auctions at Lumley Castle give the price realised alongside each picture, and in many cases the name of the buyer or dealer is noted.[36] It was at this point, then, that the great Arundel-Lumley Collection patiently built up in the sixteenth century and augmented in later periods was broken up. The family portraits, the Lumley Horseman and the four marble busts of kings and queens remained in the hall but almost immediately local historians noticed and regretted the dispersal of the main collection. Travellers later in the nineteenth remarked that, other than the hall, the castle was almost entirely unfurnished and neglected:

> There was hung about it a hush and solitude that told you as plainly as an enchanted place of old romance could that it was deserted. That it had long ceased to be the abode of its ancient line. That the high, the brave, and the happy who had so long made it alive, and filled it with a thousand memories, no longer inhabited it.[37]

The tenth earl refurnished and restored the castle at the beginning of the twentieth century and it was subsequently leased to the University of Durham. The remaining family portraits were removed in mid-century and Lumley Castle became a hotel. It had ceased to be, as was intended, a great treasure-house of the visual arts in the north.

A postcard view from around the beginning of the 20th century.

Appendices

1. The Will and Inventory of John, Lord Lumley (1606)

Register of Wills vol vii, 1586-1613, pp 292r-60. (University of Durham, Special Collections)

In the name of God Amen. The 22nd day of January in the third year of the reign of our sovereign Lord James by the grace of God King of England, France and Ireland, Defender of the Faith &c. That is to say of England, France and Ireland the first and of Scotland the 39th.

I John Lord Lumley knight Lord Lumley being in health of body and of perfect memory and understanding for which I give God thanks most heartily, do make and declare this my last will and testament in manner and form following:

First I yield and commend my soul to almighty God my maker and redeemer and will than my body be buried in the church at Cheam nigh unto Nonsuch in the county of Surrey whereof I am patron with as little extraordinary charge as conveniently may be. And I do give to every one of my servants which shall serve in my house at the time of my death one whole year's wages over and above all the wages which shall be due then unto them.

And I give and bequeath to every one of my halfe sisters vidlt. my sister Ridgley, my sister Savage and my sister Willoughby to every of them some piece of plate of the value of twenty pounds a piece of good and lawful money of Englande.

And whereas I have made a lease in trust to Sir Richard Lewkner knight sergeant at the law and chief justice of Chester &c and William Smith Esquire my old and trusty servant of divers manners lands and tenements in the counties of York, Durham and Northumberland bearing date the 27th day of January in the 32th year of the reign of Queen Elizabeth by and under the yearly rent of fifty pounds now forasmuch as the manors lands and tenements in the same lease comprised of greater value than the rent reserved upon the same lease amounts unto my meaning and will is that the said Sir Richard Lewkener and William Smith shall dispose and employ all the residue of the rents profits and issue of the premises over and above the said yearly rents of fifty pounds in manner and form following. That is to pay to the Lady Elizabeth my wife during the minority and nonage of Richard Lumley son and heir apparent of Roger Lumley Esquire and until the same Richard shall accomplish his full age of 21 years if the said Richard Lumley so long live or if the said Richard Lumley do die before the said age then the said surplus of rent shall be paid unto the said Elizabeth my wife during the minoritie and nonage of such heir male as shall by virtue or force of any conveyance by my mind have the castle of Lumley and until the same heir male shall accomplish his age of 21 years, if she the said Elizabeth so long shall live she using her liberality at her good pleasure towards the said Richard Lumley in that his minority and to the rest of his brethren and sisters But if it should happen the said Elizabeth to die during the said minority and nonage of the said Richard Lumley or any such heir male to whom the said castle of Lumley should come or remain as aforesaid then my will and meaning is that the custody education bringing up finding and maintenance of the said Richard Lumley during his minority and nonage shall remain and come to the beforenamed Sir Richard Lewkner and William Smith and to the survivor of them who shall have the surplusage of the said rents of the said manors lands and tenements and hereditaments in the counties of York, Durham and Northumberland aforesaid for and towards the maintenance education and bringinge up of the said Richard Lumley or if he die during his said minority for and towards the bringing up and maintenance of such heir maile as shall then have the castle of Lumley as aforesaid during the minority of the same heir maile as the said Lady Elizabeth my wife should have had if she had lived until the full age of the said Richard Lumley our heir male as aforesaid.

And I do further will and devise appoint and earnestly require William Smith Esquire my trusty servant to assign convey and set over all the remnant of the years which shall remain and be to come unexpired at the time of my death and in the lease of the manor of Hailinge or of the scyte and demesnes of the said manor by virtue of one lease made by me heretofore unto Thomas Stourton and Humphrey Lloyd Esquires unto my kinsman Richard Lumley eldest son and heir apparent unto the beforenamed Roger Lumley son of Anthony Lumley brother to John Lord Lumley my grandfather, he the said Richard Lumley and his assigns during the said term yielding satisfying and paying unto Anne now Countess of Arundel during her life and after her decease to person or persons unto whom the inheritance of her said manor shall remain descend or come the yearly rent or sum of fifty pounds of good and lawful money of England to be paid yearly at the two most usual feasts or days of payment in the year that is to say at the feast of St Michael the Archangel and the Annunciation of the Most Blessed Virgin Mary by even and equal portions.

And I do ordain constitute and make the aforesaid Lady Elizabeth my wife my sole executrix of this my last will and testament unto whom I do give and bequeath all the residue of my goods and chattels whatsoever not before or otherwise given and bequeathed for and to her own use and towards the performance of this my last will and testament.

And I do give and bequeath the sum of two hundred pounds of good and lawful money of England to be given distributed and disposed amongst and to poor people the residue to be delivered and paid by my executrix unto my trusty and wellbeloved servants William Smith Esquire and George Smith his son or one of them to be by them or one of them given and distributed at their or one of their discretions.

And I do appoint the beforenamed Sir Richard Lewkner to be overseer of this my said last will and testament desiring and earnestly requiring him to use his best care and diligence and assistance for and towards the performance of this my said last will and testament according to my true intent and meaning which he best knows because he was the first drawer and writer thereof by my special direction upon and after many conferences had between him and me therein.

And I do give and bequeath unto him the said Sir Richard Lewkner for the pains and travail which he shall take therein the sum of fifty pounds of lawful English money.

And do revoke and repeal by these presents all former wills and testaments by me before made or declared at any time before the day of the date of these presents. And in testimony thereof I have unto every sheet or leaf of these presents subscribed my name and have put to my seal the day and year first above written. Lumley

In the presence of George Smith Philip Lloyd Christopher Hopper.

***

2. A true Inventory of all such moveables as were found in Lumley Castle after the decease of the Lord John Lumley late husband to the Lady Elizabeth Lumley now living whom he left sole executrix by his last will and testament prized and valued the 24th day of April AD 1609 by us the praisors thereof whose names are underwritten. Vidlt.

Imprimis:	
7 pieces of hanging of Arras with gold of the story of Troy	£80
7 pieces of hanging of Queen Hester like the other	£80
5 pieces of fine hanging of Cipio and Hannibal	£80
6 pieces of hanging of Jason and Medea of a large ancient making	£80
6 pieces of hanging of the story of King Pluto	£80
4 pieces of hanging of the story of the Amazons	£60
3 pieces of hanging of the story of Paris	£40
12 pieces of Buskin hangings	£100
21 pieces of hangings of the story of King Saul and David	£120
4 pieces of hanging of the story of St George	£40
7 pieces of hanging of the story of Amadis	£70
4 pieces of hanging of gilt leather	£3
8 pieces of bed of gold and silver and silk with their furnitures	£200.13.4
3 beds of broad cloth viz. one purple, one carnation and one green	£20.13.4.

2 standing bedsteads of wainscott with their furnitures	£3
1 large traverse of purple taffeta	£6
3 chairs of cloth of gold and silver with a long cushion of the same	£15
1 purple cloth of gold chair with a long cushion	£3
2 needlework chairs with two long cushions	£3
2 chairs one of crimson silk and gold the other of crimson silk and silver and two little stools	£3
2 green velvet chairs 2 long cushions of the same 2 little stools	£3
2 purple velvet chairs and three purple velvet cushions and a little stool	£5
1 chair of tissue of silver and gold one long cushion and a little stool	£3.13.4.
2 crimson velvet chairs	40s
2 chairs one of purple cloth of gold the other of crimson cloth of gold of Bodkin with two long cushions and little stool of purple velvet	£3
1 chair inlaid with bone of crimson velvet and cloth of Bodkin	40s.
1 chair and two low stools of ash colour of cloth of gold	40s.
2 damask chairs three low stools of damask and two long cushions of damask	50s.
5 black velvet chairs two low stools of black velvet and one little square cushion	40s.
1 crimson velvet printed chair with 2 low stools and 1 long cushion	40s.
1 old black velvet chair embroidered with gold and silver with a long cushion suitable to it	10s.
1 yellow velvet chair with a long cushion	10s.
1 purple cloth chair with a long cushion and 2 low stools of the same	20s.
1 long needlework cushion with a little cushion suitable to it, 1 long Arras cushion with my Lady Arundel's arms, 1 long crimson velvet cushion embroidered with cloth of tissue & 1 long Turkey cushion of crolle	£3
12 little crimson velvet cushions wrought and stripped, 8 square cushions of crimson plain	£8
1 carpet of crimson damask fringed with gold	40s.
5 square velvet carpets 3 purple and 2 green	£10

1 Turkey carpet of silk and gold	£6
1 carpet of purple cloth fringed with purple silk	10s.
4 square Turkey carpets of silk	£7
15 Turkey carpets of crolls of divers sort	£11
5 long Turkey carpets of crolls	£25
3 long carpets of green cloth	40s.
11 caises and cushions of gilt leather	10s.
19 pallet beds and 18 bolsters and 20 pillows	£20
9 pairs of large cushions	£3
6 pollonia rugs 3 green 1 white 1 orange 1 red	40s.
10 spanish rug blankets	20s.
13 coverlets for pallets	40s.
5 livery beds	40s.
4 wool beds	40s.
8 mattresses	10s.
8 close stools and 12 chamber pots	15s.
6 pewter basins	6s.8d.
2 pair of racks 1brandreth 6 brotches 1 boiling iron 3 brass kettle and 4 brass pots	20s.

In the Hall

2 long tables vizt. 1 of walnuttree the other of fir	£3
a deerhead that came out of Ireland	2s.6d.
13 old Emperors heads of Rome	13s.
a written table called the Theatre of the world in golden letters	5s.
Raphael Orbinus his picture	6d.
Henry the eighth Edward the 6 Queen Mary Queen Elizabeth cut in marble the pictures of Aristotle Plato my Lord of Arundel crest the Birth of Christ in alabaster	40s.
6 old emperors in marble	10s.
the stories and pictures of Mars and Venus	3s.4d.
Hercules picture and the picture of Time	5s.

In the Great Chamber

15 pictures of my Lord Lumlies ancestors with a pillar of his pedigree	£8
a picture of the story of the Passion with a secret [sarcanet?] curtain, the picture of my Lord Lumley in armour, with his two wives, his son Charles, and the old Earl of Arundel, the story of the Birth of Christ, and the 9 worthies neiled in glass together with picture of Christ and 2 globes in plain	£13
2 long drawing tables of walnuttree one folding table of wainscot and a little table of wainscott	£5
1 marquetry table with the frame	40s.
2 fine marquetry cupboards and two livery cupboards	£13
6 walnuttree forms and 24 stools of walnuttree	50s.
6 walnuttree chairs	30s.

In the Saule [Saloon]

76 little pictures	£12
15 great pictures	£5
10 marble tables with frames	£30
1 fountain	£10

In the Drawing Chamber

9 pictures	£6.6s.8d.
3 other pictures viz. Queen Mary Queen Elizabeth and Constantine the great	10s.
8 pairs of brass landirons and three pairs parcel copper	£6.13s.4d.
1 chimney piece of white marble with cherubims	40s
10 square oak and elm tables and their cupboards suitable	£3.6s.8d
6 pair of fire shovels and tongs	3s.
one steel glass	12d.
6 standing bedsteads and two parver bedsteads 1 gilt the other plain	£8
91 pictures in the gallery and 4 in the wardropp	£40
1 wainscott table in the gallery	20s

References

Introduction: pages 1-8

1. G Akrigg, *Jacobean Pageant* (1962) p. 128; R. Strong, *The English Icon: Elizabethan & Jacobean Portraiture* (1969) p. 45; D. Matthew

2. M. Hervey, *The Life, Correspondence and Collections of Thomas Howard, Earl of Arundel, 'Father of Vertu in England* (1921) p. 266; E. de Beer (Ed.), *The Diary of John Evelyn* (1959) 440; D. Howarth, *Lord Arundel and his Circle* (1985) pp. 1, 2, 33.

3. Hoby had first intended an English translation in the 1550s. It was reprinted in 1577, 1588 and 1603. J. Sears & F.R. Johnson, *The Lumley Library: The Catalogue of 1609* (1956) No. 1643. Henry Howard, Earl of Northampton annotated his Italian edition of 1541 (P. Burke, *The Fortunes of the Courtier* (1995) esp. pp. 55-64).

4. L.B. Smith *A Tudor Tragedy: The life and times of Catherine Howard* (1961) p. 12.

5. L. Stone, *The Crisis of the Aristocracy 1558-1641* (1965) p. 715, on which much of the following discussion of the English peerage is based.

6. In the mid-seventeenth century the virtuoso gave way to the dilettante - which has been 'the curse of the English governing classes ever since': Stone pp. 715ff; W. E. Houghton, 'The English Virtuoso in the Seventeenth Century'. *Journal of the History of Ideas* iii (1942) pp. 62, 66/7.

7. K. Hearn (ed.), *Dynasties: Painting in Tudor and Jacobean England 1530-1630* (1995), p. 11; Stone, pp. 52, 59; Membership of the House of Commons rose to 400 in the same period. M. Graves, *The House of Lords in the Parliaments of Edward VI and Mary I* (1981), pp. 18, 43/5, 51, Appendix A.

8. Historical Manuscripts Commission, Calendar of the Manuscripts of the Marquess of Salisbury [HMC *Salisbury*] vol. I, p. 476, has Cumberland at Oxford, but V. Gibbs, et al. (eds.), [GEC] *The Complete Peerage,* (1910-40), places him at Cambridge, 1571-4, and taking an MA in 1576.

9. Calendar of State Papers [CSP] relating to English affairs preserved at Rome vol. I, pp.265, 400 (1 Mar 1571 and 411/2 (n.d., 1571); J.H. Pollen, The English Catholics in the Reign of Queen Elizabeth (1920), 171; Nichols, *Gentleman's Magazine* (1833) p. 493 [see Ch 1, n.14]. See also Stone p. 729 citing SP 12/157/90 (1582), and p. 741.

10. E. Fellowes, *William Byrd* (1947) p. 66.

11. Stone, pp. 54, 725.

12. A. Morey, *The Catholic Subjects of Elizabeth I* (1978) pp. 41, 139.

13. E. Reynolds, *Campion and Parsons* (1980), pp. 17/18.

14. Stone, pp. 97-9, 251/6, 266, 624. In 1575 the heralds recorded the pedigrees and arms of 56 families but in 1615 the number had almost doubled. M.E. James, *Family, Lineage and Civil Society* (1974), pp. 7, 11, 71; R. Surtees, *The History and Antiquities of the County Palatine of Durham,* vol. I (1816) p. clii ff. The number of peers rose to 121 in 1621 and 127 in 1629. In 1641 something like a fifth of the peerage were Catholics. Graves, pp. 18, 43/5, 51, Appendix A; J.E. Neale, *The Elizabethan House of Commons* (1967) pp. 140/1; Matthew, *Jacobean,* p. 240; Matthew *Charles I* p. 143n2; B. Magee *The English Recusants* (1938) pp. 127-8.

Chapter One: pages 9-28

1. Don Guerau de Spes, CSP *Simancas* II 185.

2. *GEC*; (Ed. E. Benham), E, Milner, *Records of the Lumleys of Lumley Castle* (1904), Ch. 1.

3. M. Hislop, 'Lumley Castle, its antecedents and its architect', *AA* (5) vol. XXIV 1996).

4. M Bush & D Bownes, *The Defeat of the Pilgrimage of Grace* (1999) p. 57n; James (1974) p. 48.

5. H. Miller, *Henry VIII and the English Nobility* (1986) p. 219, where Westminster is given rather than Westmorland; James (1974) p. 44.

6. R.W. Hoyle, *The Pilgrimage of Grace and the Politics of the 1530s* (2001)

p. 428; M. Bush, *Durham and the Pilgrimage of Grace* (Durham County Local History Society, 2000) passim.

7. M. Bush *The Pilgrimage of Grace* (1996) pp. 13-15, 18, 26-31.

8. J. Gillow, *Bibliographical Dictionary of the English Catholics* (4 vols 1884-1902) IV, 346; Milner p. 48.

9. James (1974) pp. 44/6. Hoyle, passim; Bush & Bownes, passim.

10. VCH *East Riding* (1923) vol.2, p. 326; Milner p. 30. The only registers to survive from Thwing date from 1692; Nichols (1833) (see n.14 below) p. 495 puts him at 17 years of age in 1550.

11. Graves 49; Stone (1965) p. 209; J. Raine *History and Antiquities of North Durham*(1852) pp. xxxii-iii; Nichols, p 495, quoting Nicholas Udall's dedication to Queen Elizabeth of Erasmus's *Paraphrase of the Gospels*.]

12. Graves 49; J.G. Nichols, *Literary Remains of King Edward the Sixth* (Roxburghe Club reprint, 1857) pp. lvii-lxiv; C Cross, *The Puritan Earl* (1966) p. 9; A. Weir, *Children of England* (1996) pp. 9, 14/5.

13. *Journals of the House of Lords*, vol. 1, 1509-77, p. 308 (1 Ed. VI, c.18). PRO E175/11/84 conflates this with the last year of Henry VIII's reign. 38 Hen. VIII.

14. The principal source for Fitzalan's life is an anonymous post-1580 account in British Library: Royal Mss 17 A IX. Internal evidence suggests that it was written by his Catholic chaplain. It was edited by J.G. Nichols and reproduced serially in the *Gentleman's Magazine* Part II (1833) pp. 10-8, 118-24, 209-15, 490-500.

15. Nichols (1833) p. 211 n6; C.L. Kingsford, 'Bath Inn or Arundel House', *Archaeologia* vol. 72 (1921-2) pp. 250 ff

16. J. Dent, *The Quest for Nonsuch* (1962) p. 144; Nichols (1857) II, p. 245; *DNB*.

17. Stone (1965) ch XII; ibid p. 687.

18. Stone (1965) p. 652.

19. British Library, Royal Mss. 17A xlix, dated 1550 and dedicated to Arundel by 'Your Lordship's obedient son J. Lumley, 1550.'

20. British Library, Royal Mss. 15A ix; reprinted in *Malone Society Reprints*, 1909.

21. The claim is made in S. Cerasano & M Wynne-Davies (eds.), *Readings in Renaissance Women's Drama: Criticism, History & Performance 1594-1998* (1998), esp. pp. 125-139. But see D.H. Greene, 'Lady Lumley and Greek Tragedy', *Classical Journal* vol. 36 (1940-1) pp. 537-47; F.D. Crane, 'Euripides, Erasmus and Lady Lumley' *Classical Journal*, vol. 39 (1943-4) pp. 223-8. Manuscripts written by Mary Fitzalan are at British Library Royal Mss. 12 A I-IV and 7 D IX. See also J. Stevenson, 'Women Catholics and Latin Culture', R. Corthell (et al Eds.), *Catholic Culture in Early Modern England* (2007).

22. S. Doran, *Monarchy and Matrimony: the courtships of Elizabeth I* (1996) p. 18.

23. N. Williams, *Thomas Howard Fourth Duke of Norfolk* (1964) p. 32

24. J.M. Robinson, *The Dukes of Norfolk* (1982) pp. 52, 84.

25. Stone (1965) p. 760.

26. HMC, National Register of Archives: Lumley Mss., MTD/A8/8 (1&2 Philip & Mary, 28 Feb. 1555/6). The area of the county is 679,040 acres, hence Lumley's land-holdings amounted to some 14%. In 1569 a general muster of inhabitants between 16-60 years of age in the Durham palatinate showed 7,773. Using the usual multiplier of four results in a population of 30,000. None of the county's towns had a population of more than 3,000.

27. *Journals of the House of Lords* vol. 1, 1509-77, p. 449.

28. J. Bossy *Under the Molehill* (2001) p. 47; Stone (1965) pp. 391 ff; J. Stow, *Survey of London* (1603, repr. 1908) I, pp. 129, 148, II, p 293; C.L. Kingsford, 'Bath Inn or Arundel House' *Archaeolgia* 72 (1921-2) p. 250; N Williams, *Thomas Howard* (1964) pp. 26ff; Milner p. 338; D. Price, *Patrons and Musicians of the English Renaissance* (1981) p.10.

29. Stone (1965) p. 760.

30. J. Carley, *Books and Collectors 1200-1700* (1997) p. 385 n. 83; *The History of the King's Works*, vol IV, 1485-1660 (Part II) (1982) pp. 179-205.

31. M. Whinney, *Sculpture in Britain 1530-1830* (1964) p. 2. Cure's son would work at Nonsuch in 1616 (cf Dent, pp. 110/1); Cornelius Cure was working at Ingatestone (cf. J. Turner, (ed.) *Dictionary of Art* (1996). Vasari presumably meant Nonsuch when he said that Nunziata (who was aged 21 in 1519) had made for Henry VIII his 'principale palazzo' (cf. E Chaney, *The Evolution of the Grand Tour* (2nd ed. 2000) p. 48).

32. Nichols (1833) p. 123; Dent, p. 58. Hearn (1995) p. 105.
33. Nichols (1833) p. 122; Dent, p. 56. Royal patronage of architecture virtually ceased until the Banquetting House was begun in 1619; Stone (1965) p. 703.
34. Dent, ch. 7.
35. Nichols (1833) p. 213 n.14.
36. British Library, Cotton Mss. Vitellius, F. v, reprinted by Nichols (1833) pp 493/4, although the date of her funeral is given by him as 26 October.
37. British Museum, Y5-153; Dent, pp. 52/6/8, 63, 96; de Beer pp. 483/4.
38. Nichols (1833) p. 210.
39. N. Williams *All the Queen's Men* (1972) pp. 35ff; Historical Manuscripts Commission, Calendar of State Papers, Simancas [CSP Simancas] vol 1, 8, 18, 28 & 29 Dec 1558; Milner, p. 51; W. Camden, *Annals*, 1615. Gomez Suarez de Figuera (1520?-71) fifth count and, from 1587, first Duke of Feria, was one of Philip II's leading councillors and in 1558 was Captain of the Spanish Guard; he married the English Catholic Jane Dormer in December 1588 and returned to Spain in 1559. He wholeheartedly supported the Ridolfi Plot.
40. Nichols (1833) p.123.
41. Doran pp. 21/2; Nichols (1833) p. 122n.
42. M.J. Rodrigues-Salgado and S. Adams (eds.), 'The Count of Feria's Dispatch to Philip II of 14 November 1558' *Camden Society* (4) vol. 29 (1984) p. 331; CSP Simancas, vol. I, pp. 95/6; CSP Simancas XIII, p 439, 12 Nov 1558.
43. A. Plowden, *Marriage with my Kingdom* (1977) pp. 76, 83, 98.
44. J. Lowers, *Mirrors for Rebels* (1953) p. 12.
45. W MacCaffrey, *The Shaping of the Elizabethan Regime* (1969) p. 111.
46. MacCaffrey, pp. 30, 31, 38; N Williams (1972) pp. 35ff. gives a full account of the dismissals.
47. MacCaffery p. 36, with names.
48. Historical Manuscripts Commission, Calendar of State Papers, Foreign [CSP Foreign] 1564/5, no. 1159.

49. CSP Simancas, I, pp. 414, 458.

50. CSP Simancas, I, pp. 126, 136, 212, 293/6; MacCaffrey, p. 125 citing Lansdowne Mss. vol. cii f.103; *Acts of the Privy Council 1558-70* (1893) p. 290; Nichols (1833) p.210.

51. CSP Simancas I pp. 392/8, 402; Nichols (1833) p. 211 n.4].

52. MacCaffrey, p. 111; CSP Simancas p. 431.

53. Historical Manuscripts Commission, Calendar of State Papers, Scotland [CSP Scotland], 1547-1603, vol. II 1563-9 (1900) p. 229, 24 Oct. 1565; CSP Simancas I, pp. 505, 515.

54. HMC Salisbury I 338/9, Christopher Rooksby to Cecil, June 1565; Stone (1965) p. 251. HMC Salisbury I 338, June 1566.

55. HMC Pepys Mss (1911), p. 70; CSP Scotland, pp. 235, 235-9, Nov. 1565.

56. CSP Simancas I, p. 533.

57. Stevens (1982), p.176; J. Woolfson, *Padua and the Tudors, English Students in Italy 1485-1603*, 5/6, 123/4; CSP Foreign (1566-8), p.166.

58. The full letter is given at Dent p. 161.

59. Chaney, p. 78.

60. CSP Simancas I, p. 623.

61. Sears & Johnson, No. 2189; CSP Simancas I, p. 636; Nichols (1833) p. 211.

62. J. Pollen, *The English Catholics in the Reign of Queen Elizabeth* (1920) p. 121.

63. K.J. Kesselring, *The Northern Rebellion of 1569, Faith, Politics and Protest in Elizabethan England* (2007) pp. 7/8.

Chapter Two: pages 29-48

1. HMC, Salisbury I, No. 1506 (Earl of Bedford to William Cecil 23 Jul 70).

2. CSP Scotland II, p. 670; J. K. Lowers, *Mirror for Rebels* (1953) pp. 12/16; HMC Salisbury I, 339; W. MacCaffrey, *The Shaping of the Elizabethan Regime* (1969) p. 221. J.H. Pollen, *The English Catholics in the Reign of Queen Elizabeth* (1920) p. 121; CSP Scotland II, pp. 668,

873; CSP Domestic [CSPD], Additional, xiv p. 17.

3. CSP Foreign, 1569-71, no. 568.

4. M. James, *Society, Politics and Culture* (1986) p. 306.

5. Welford 353; CSPD Additional xiv 42(1); CSP Scotland No. 259; AA(4) xlii (1963) 133.

6. M. Bateson (Ed.) 'A collection of original letters from the bishops to the Privy Council 1564', *Camden Miscellany*, ix 1895, pp. 65-7; CSP Foreign, vii pp. 266, 533; Lowers p. 14; MacCaffery p. 131.

7. He was appointed on 26 December 1560, cf. CSPD 1547-80, p. 187. Fletcher & MacCulloch, *Tudor Rebellions* (1997), document no. 23; C. Menmuir, *The Rising of the North* (1907) p. 4; J. Raine (Ed.) *Depositions and other Ecclesiastical Proceedings from the Courts of Durham* (Surtees Society vol 21, 1845, p.121).

8. CSP Foreign 1564/5, no. 1159. Northumberland himself said that he had been reconciled to Catholicism 'by one Master Copley, *two years and more,* [emphasis added] before our stir' [i.e., the rising of 1569] (cf. C. Sharp (Ed.) *Memorials of the Rebellion of the Earls of Northumberland and Westmoreland* (1840 reissued 1975) p.204). Others have incorrectly taken that to mean 1567, e.g., S. Keeling, 'The Church and Religion in the Anglo-Scottish Border Counties, 1534-72' (Durham PhD 1975), p. 384. A Jesuit was said to have celebrated Mass in Warkworth Castle, which belonged to the earl: *Calendar of Border Papers* I, p. 126. W Murden (Ed.), *Burghley's State Papers* II (1740-59) p. 52; CSPD 1566-79, Addenda XXI, no. 56.

9. Lowers p. 16; Sharp, p. 215.

10. HMC Salisbury I, p. 339.

11. A. J. Loomie, *The Spanish Elizabethans* (1963), pp. 35/38, 254/5; CSPD Eliz. Addenda XLV No. 104. The fifth earl died in 1563/4; his will was dated 18 August 1563, cf. W. Greenwell (Ed.) *Wills and Inventories from the Registry at Durham*, Pt II (Surtees Society vol. 38, 1860, p. 4.) His chaplain was Sir Nicholas Forster, Rector of Brancepeth from 1552; surprisingly, Forster retained that living until 1571 when, presumably, he died.

12. NRA Lumley Mss. MTD/A8/9; Milner 63/4; T.W. Beastall, *A North Country Estate* (1975) p. 6; M.J. Tillbrook, 'Aspects of the Government and Society of County Durham 1558-1642' (Liverpool PhD 1981) pp. 596/7; CSPD 1571; CSP Simancas I, p. 505.

13. CSP Simancas II, p. 36; CSP Scotland II, p. 873; Pollen, pp.120, n3, 131/2, 140.

14. Pollen, p. 169.

15. The obvious impediment of Mary's marriage to Bothwell seems to have been ignored: it was never nullified by the Holy See and he did not die until April 1578 – in a Danish prison.

16. Nichols, p. 211 n8; HMC Salisbury I, 1264.

17. CSPD Simancas II, 1568-9, No. 70; Pollen, p. 134 n.1. Pollen doubts if this was ever written down.

18. CSP Simancas II, p. 111; CSPD Eliz. Add., XXI Nos. 29, 56; 70, 80, 95, 102, 107; HMC Salisbury I, Nos. 1456, 1671, 1677; Black 131; Lowers, p. 17; Pollen 140.

19. CSP Simancas II, pp. 142 (23 April 1569), 145 (9 May), 145, 152, 156, 164 (June).

20. HMC Salisbury I, Nos. 1463, 1696, pp. 458, 554; HMC Simancas II, p. 185. But in his confession of 1572, the earl of Northumberland said: 'we should have aid from the Duke de Alva within twenty days', cf. Sharp 190/1.

21. Newcastle was already well-developed for the coal trade and only Whitby and Hartlepool were at all frequented by shipping. VCH *Durham* III (1928) p.267; W C Mitchell, *History of Sunderland* (1919, repub. 1972) p. 53; Bowling 32/3; PSAN (NS) 8, 140. 232]. Sharp, pp. 79, 96, 122, 363.

22. Williams (1964) p. 161.

23. HMC Salisbury I, Nos.1340, 1451. Dent remarks, p. 165, that their creditors took this opportunity to seize certain manors which had been security for a loan of £1,900.

24. CSP Simancas II, pp. 224, 236; HMC Salisbury I, No. 1433; CSP Scotland II, pp. 684/686 (which show that Arundel was interrogated on 10 Oct.)

25. *State Trials* I col. 977; HMC Salisbury I, Nos. 1349, 1356, 1368/9, 1388, 1397, 1456, 1677, 1696, 1699.

26. Midnight, 10 November, cf. Sharp pp. 15-18.

27. 15 November, cf. Sharp pp. 35-7, 41/2; HMC Salisbury I, No. 1407.

28. Sharp, pp. 64, 79-80, 83.

29. Raine, *Depositions* (Surtees Society 21) pp. 127-205, summarised in Sharp 252-263. See also A Forster, 'Bishop Tunstall's Priests', *Recusant History* vol 9, no.4, (1968) pp. 175-202.

30. Sharp p. 103. Sir Henry Gates took possession of Hartlepool, cf. Sharp p.79.

31. N Williams, *Norfolk Archaeology* 32 (1961), p. 73; *GEC* IV 25/6; Sharp, appendices. A half-length portrait, probably by Eworth, of Richard Norton dressed in black with a crucifix hanging on a cord around his neck and inscribed '1566 aet. suae 68' is in Lord Grantley's collection. Cf. Walpole Society III (1913) p. 35, no. 1566.

32. HMC Salisbury I, 1433, 1504. Arundel was brought to Hampton Court on 27 March (cf. HMC Simancas II, p. 240] but Lumley was confined in Mrs Hampden's house at Stoke Poges near Staines, Bucks until April. (PRO SP12/18/44; *State Papers* 1871 p 284. Arundel kissed hands on Good Friday. Williams (1964) p. 167. MacCaffrey pp. 251/2/5. Some twenty ballads on the Rising were printed in London, almost all of which were against the earls. 'Newes from Northumberland' by W Elderton attacked the sympathisers in London but does not name them. (Harleian Miscellany vol. X (1813) p. 267.)

33. Pollen pp. 138/9; James (1986), pp. 293, 354.

34. *GEC* IV, pp. 19, 23.

35. The earls wrote to Rome on 7 November 1569; the request was received on 16 February 1570 and the Pope acknowledged receipt on 20 February. The bull was issued on 25 February, and was sent into England in the hands of Dr Morton. Ridolfi received one copy via the nuncio in Paris and then eighty copies, some printed. It was published in London on 25 May when a copy was affixed to the Bishop of London's door by John Felton, a Catholic layman. Cf. Morey p. 55; Pollen pp. 149, 152/3.

36. Keeling p. 315. James (1974) pp. 50/1 citing CSPD Add. 1566-79, xv pp. 128, 134; xviii 276; Raine, *Depositions,* pp. 141, 167, 176, 188.

37. MacCaffery p. 266. The bull led to another outburst of ballads: C.H. First, 'The Ballad History of the Reigns of the Later Tudors', *Transactions of the Royal History Society* [*TRHS*] (3) vol. 3 (1909), p. 79.

38. CSP Rome I, pp. 346/7; HMC Salisbury I, 542.

39. The latter was preferred by Norfolk, cf. N Williams, p. 77; HMC Salisbury I, No. 1616; MacCaffery p. 273; Pollen p. 161.

40. Williams, p. 121; HMC Salisbury I, 1697. Norfolk had stood guarantor to Ridolfi for the debt and when this fell due made himself liable for a new figure of £3,000. By a legal agreement of 22 August 1570, Arundel, Lumley and Norfolk were bound conjointly and separately to pay Ridolfi the last-named sum if they failed to pay the £1,800 by 13 July 1571. De Spes could collect the debt. F. Edwards *The Dangerous Queen* (1964) pp.212/98/9; Williams p. 110. An audited list of Norfolk's debts was compiled by Mr Dix in September 1571 when it was shown that he owed a total of £8,000, (of which there was 'owing to Alderman Jackman's executors £2,150, part of Lord Arundel's debt, which the duke is to discharge'). The duke's annual income was £4,500, cf. Williams pp. 124/5; HMC Salisbury I, 527.

41. CSP Simancas p. 338. At some earlier point Norfolk was told that Lumley was in the Tower on a date by 1 October (HMC Salisbury I, 1641).

42. HMC Salisbury I, pp. 528, 532, 536. Symbols for Arundel, Tower of London, Berwick and Tynemouth were included in Mary's cyphers. Norfolk's bible was found to contain cyphers in three different places, and included symbols for Arundel and Lumley (Williams, illus. facing p. 131).

43. CSP Scotland vol. iv, p. 35, 10 Nov. 1571; HMC Salisbury I, pp. 540 556, 562.

44. HMC Salisbury I, pp. 535, 540/1.

45. The castle measured 256 feet long by 88 feet at its west end, tapering to no more than fifty feet wide at the east, projecting, end. It is now in ruins; for details of its structure see VCH *North Riding,* II, (1914) pp. 327-331; J.C. Atkinson, *History of Cleveland, Ancient and Modern* (1874) pp. 336-40; W.M. I'Anson, 'Kilton Castle', *Yorkshire Archaeological Journal* 22 (1913) pp. 55ff. In a list of estates (NRA Lumley Mss. No. 2291) in the North Riding belonging to Lumley dated 1583 there occurs 'Kilton, Cottam, Little- Morsome, Greate-Morsome, Skingre-Towne, Thormombye, Thornton'.

46. PRO, Roman Transcripts Series 1 No. 71, quoted at H Willaert, *History of an Old Catholic Mission* (1928) p. 21. CSPD Add. Eliz. xv pp. 30, 32; xxi pp. 67/8. In a remarkable gesture of reconciliation, he named Cecil guardian of his children. Cf. Stone (1965) p.60.

47. CSP Simancas p. 455; MacCaffery p. 289; R.B. Manning, *Religion and Society in Elizabethan Sussex* (1969) pp.227/8.

48. M. Biddle, 'The Vanished Gardens of Nonsuch', *Country Life*, Oct. 26, (1961) pp. 1008-10.

49. J.M. Robinson, *The Dukes of Norfolk* (1982) p. 79; Nichols pp. 214-5; Biddle p. 1008; M.A. Tierney, *History of Arundel*, (1834) II, p. 619; for an illustrationof the mural slab to the two earlier earls. See also 'Sussex Ornamental Brasses', *Sussex Archaelogical Collections* vol. 76, pp. 72/3.

50. Philip Howard had led something of a dissipated life as a young man and had fallen out with the family and with the queen. As an older man he turned to religion and antiquarianism and he would die a prisoner in the Tower. HMC Various II (Buxton) p. 236n; J. Pollen & W MacMahon (Eds.) 'The Ven. Philip Howard, Earl of Arundel 1557-1595', *CRS* 21 p. 23; Williams p. 122.

51. CRS 1, *Miscellanea I*, p. 59; Morey p. 179. MacCaffery, p. 292, has Lumley in attendance until 8 May 1572. Harley, p.103, places Lumley in the Marshalsea from Oct 1571 to April 1573.

52. James (1986) p. 370.

53. CSP Scotland II, p. 979; VIII, pp. 160, 189, 267, 678; HMC Salisbury III, nos. 215, 274, 1586; Milner pp. 74/5.

54. CSP Scotland IX, pp. 44, 83, 308, 346, 352.

55. HMC Foljambe, p. 11; *CRS* 21, p. 25; Manning p. 228.

56. HMC Foljambe, pp.40-44, 84/5.

57. *State Trials* I, cols. 1162 ff. (esp. 1167, 1189); col. 1229 ff; col. 1335 ff; HMC Bath V, pp. 73/4. *GEC* IV sub Derby (1572) p. 211n(e). HMC De Lisle & Dudley II, p. 397; HMC Rutland I, 370/1.

58. F.W. Steer, 'Lord Lumley's Benefaction to the College of Physicians', *Medical History* II, no. 4 (1958) p. 298. In addition to the manors of Westbourne with Stansted Park, Arundel also left a town-house in Chichester, cf. VCH *Sussex* III (1935) pp. 75-6, IV p. 127; The Earl of Bessborough, *Enchanted Forest, The Story of Stansted in Sussex* (1984) p.30.

59. *Letters and Papers Foreign and Domestic of the Reign of Henry VIII, 1515-8*, No. 950; CSPD 4 Nov 1574; Matthew (1970) p. 93; Dent pp. 166/7; Stone pp. 151, 528, 542: 'Improvidence piled up the £13,000 debt of Fitzalan in 1579'. Ridolfi held on to the papers relating to the Florentine debt as security for a loan of £1,825. Milner pp. 63-74.

60. Stone pp. 610/670; VCH *East Riding* II (1923) p. 326. Darcy was

married to Mary, daughter of Sir Thomas Kytson, whose family was Catholic and had many cultural interests, especially musical cf *GEC* IV 78 n (b).

61. NRA Lumley Mss. nos. 2289 & 2291; HMC Salisbury III, no. 215. C. Sharp *History of Hartlepool* (1816, repr. 1851) puts the purchase to 1586. At Lumley's request the queen granted a charter to the burgesses of Hartlepool in 1593 and he built a pier there for £2,000 as an outlet for his salt-pans. Lumley became the most important coal-owner in the aristocracy: his Durham estates produced the country's finest coal which was transported to the capital from the river Wear. Lumley and the Bishop of Durham went to arbitration over their respective rights in the manors which was unresolved in 1598. Hartlepool had gained something of a reputation for being 'much given to Popery' at this time: Sharp (1816) pp. 54-7; J. Nef, *The Rise of the British Coal Industry* I (1923) p. 30; Stone pp. 282, 341. Lumley employed stewards to collect rents and fines and generally maintain his estates; in 1583 the receivers were: Roger Marshall in Surrey (the receiver-general), John Gifford in Sussex, John Lambton in London, and Robert Hallyman for Durham and the other scattered estates.) NRA Lumley Mss. EMA/1/8. See also EMA/1/12 for the names in 1592.

62. It seems that in 1584 the Earl of Huntingdon took over the debt in return for a series of payments to ease his own cash-flow problems. Elizabeth approved provided she got £600 a year for nineteen years and Huntingdon agreed. He was receiving cash payments from Lumley as late as 1588. C. Cross, *The Puritan Earl* (1966) pp. 76/7, 109, citing Huntingdon Mss 5369 & 5409, at San Marino, USA, from which it appears that Lumley made two payments of £1,000 in 1584. (PRO C 54/1251).

63. HMC De Lisle & Dudley III, xvii, xxiv; *Notes and Queries* 16 Aug 1941 87 citing CSP Foreign xxi, p. 595; Dent pp. 163, 168-70.

64. Stone p. 420. He raised her jointure to £1,000; cf. HMC Salisbury V, 227.

Chapter Three: pages 49-70

1. S Kaushik, 'Resistance, Loyalty and Recusant Politics: Sir Thomas Tresham and the Elizabethan State', *Midland History* 21 (1996), pp. 37-72.

2. William Camden, *Brittania* II (1586) p. 136.

3. Stone p. 23.

4. H. Murray, *The Great Chamber at Gilling Castle*, (Ampleforth Abbey, St. Laurence Papers VIII (1996) passim; E. Berry, 'Henry Ferrers, an early Warwickshire antiquary 1550-1633', *Dugdale Society Occasional Papers*, No. 16, (1965).

5. *DNB*; R. Cust, 'Catholicism, Antiquarianism and Gentry Honour: the writings of Sir Thomas Shirley', *Midland History* 33, (1998) pp. 40, 53; Berry pp. 4, 5, 22.

6. Camden III, p.121; see also M. Hislop, 'Lumley Castle, its antecedents and its architect' *Archaeolgia* (5) vol 24 (1996) passim.

7. Surtees *Durham* I, p. 397; Surtees *Durham* II, pp. 139, 154/5; Camden, *Brittania* 742; W. Hutchinson *History of Durham* (1787) II, p.397; W.M. I'Anson, 'Mediaeval military effigies of Yorkshire' *YAJ* 28 (1926) pp.369/70, figs. 45/6; Milner pp. 8/9 (referring to Collins's *Peerage*), 322-7. NRA Lumley Mss MTD/A8/15, 30 Apr. 39 Eliz. I; James (1974) p. 109; N Pevsner, *The Buildings of England: County Durham* (1953) p. 67.

8. *DNB*; N. Pevsner, *The Buildings of England: Surrey* (2nd ed. 1971) p.145.

9. H. Dunk, 'The Lumley Monuments in the Ancient Church of St. Dunstan, Cheam, Surrey', *Ancient Monuments Society's Transactions* NS2 (1954) pp. 93 ff.

10. An illustrated account of Jane's funeral is given in British Library, *Royal Mss.* 35, 324; Dent p. 163; Dunk p. 102.

11. R. Strong, *Tudor and Jacobean Portraits* (1969) p. 217; *Dictionary of Art*; Dent pp. 51, 110/1. See also R. Stong, 'Some Early Portraits at Arundel Castle', *Connoisseur* (1978) p. 198.

12. References in *Faerie Queene* (Book III, canto xi, stanzas 29-46) and *Muiopotmos* (II, 270-340) have been held to indicate this familiarity. *Notes & Queries* No. 181 (1941) pp.86/7.

13. British Library, *Royal Mss.* 17A xxiii; S. Jayne & F.R. Johnson, *The Lumley Library* (1956) item no. 2208; James (1986) p. 369; E. McCutcheon, 'Sir Nicholas Bacon's Great House Sententiae', *English Renaissance Supplements* No. 3 (1997).

14. J. Evans, *A History of the Society of Antiquaries* (1956) pp. 1-13, citing in part *Archaeologia* I, (1770) p. xx; Evans pp. 14-9; Stone p. 502; D. Starkey *Rivals in Power* (1990) p. 110, dates the foundation of the Antiquaries to about 1586.

15. Robinson (1982) pp. 80 ff.

16. Robinson (1982) p. 95; A.L. Rowse, 'Nicholas Roscarrock and his Lives of the Saints', J.H. Plumb (ed.) *Studies in Social History* (1955) pp.10-14. See also G. Ornsby (Ed.), *Selections from the Household Books of the Lord William Howard of Naworth Castle &c.* (Surtees Society vol. 68 (1878).

17. Cust (1998) pp. 40-70; James (1974) p. 108; A.I. Doyle, 'William Claxton and the Durham Chronicles', J.P. Carley & C.G.C. Tite (eds.), *Books and Collectors 1200-1700* (1997).

18. Dent p. 59.

19. J. P. Carley, 'Sir Thomas Bodley's Library and its Acquisitions', Carley & Tite (1997) pp. 367/8. Carley's is a more plausible account of Arundel's acquisition of Cranmer's library than those given by Jayne & Johnson or D. Selwyn, *The Library of Thomas Cranmer* (1996). The former say that Arundel suggested its confiscation for Nonsuch; the latter says that it was presented to Arundel by the queen in 1553. But Arundel did not have an interest in Nonsuch in 1553. Moreover, some fifty volumes seem to have left the collection before Arundel took possession of the palace three years later (Carley, n. 80.)

20. Nichols, p. 123. The original catalogue is lost but a fair copy, with corrections by Dennis Flemynge, made in 1609, at the time of the library's removal to St James's Palace, survives at MS. O.4.38, in the library of Trinity College, Cambridge and is dated 1596. It is unclear why the books were catalogued after everything else was inventoried in 1590.

21. Jayne & Johnson p. 16; Selwyn p. xxxiii n.85.

22. *GEC*; Surtees I, p. 159 note d; Jayne & Johnson p. 12; Selwyn p. xxxii.

23. Jayne & Johnson p. 9; Stone p. 705.

24. Jayne & Johnsoon p. 13.

25. Surtees II, p. 159/60; R. Strong, *Henry Prince of Wales and England's Lost Renaissance* (1986) pp. 52, 200; G. Parry, *The Golden Age Restor'd: The Culture of the Stuart Court 1603-1642* (1981) pp. 81-4.

26. Dent p. 19 citing James Cleland, *The Institution of a Young Noble Man* (1607) which, it seems, was almost certainly written at Nonsuch. See also Susan Cole, 'So Sweet a Star as Harry', *Royal Stuart Papers XXXIX* (1992), p. 3.

27. Dent pp. 185 ff; p. 7.

28. E. Chaney, *The Evolution of English Collecting* (2003) p.40.

29. Account for 22 October 1609 at CSPD 1603-10 LVII, p. 87; Jayne & Johnson pp. 13-5; HMC Salisbury V, p. 250.

30. CSP Venetian 1610-3, p. 106.

31. Jayne & Johnson p. 17; Selwyn p. xxxv; T.A. Birrell, *English Monarchs and their Books: from Henry VII to Charles II* (The Panizzi Lectures 1986) pp. 30-40.

32. The full indenture is reprinted at Steer pp. 301/2; NRA Lumley Mss. EMA/1/13-19 is a record of Lumley's payments of his £20 share from 1596 to 1606.

33. C. Warren, 'Music at Nonesuch', *Musical Quarterly* vol. 54 (1968) p. 52.

34. J. Blezzard, 'The Lumley Books', *Musical Times* vol. 112 (1971) p. 128. The music section of the Lumley Library published by Jayne and Johnson in 1956 has been revised and fully annotated by J. Milsom, 'The Nonsuch Music Library', C. Banks et al (eds.), *Sundry Sorts of Music Books* (1993) pp. 146-182. Burney's first volume was published in 1776, the same year as John Hawkins' (1719-89) five-volume *History of Music*].

35. Price p. 32; British Library, Royal Mss, Appendix pp. 36-40; Warren p. 57; A. Boyle, 'Hans Eworth's Portrait of the Earl of Arundel and the Politics of 1549-50', *English Historical Review* vol. cxvii no. 470, p. 36. See also here for Lumley's writings in 1550.]

36. D. Stevens, 'A songe of fortie parts, made by Mr Tallys', *Early Music* (1982) p. 176; J. Harley, *William Byrd: Gentleman of the Chapel Royal* (1997) pp. 84, 293, 319; E.H. Fellowes, *William Byrd* (2nd ed. 1948) p. 6.

37. 'Humberston's Survey', *YAJ XVII* (1903) p. 154.

38. Harley pp. 48, 77; Fellowes, p. 71; F. Emmison, *Tudor Secretary* (1961) pp. 213/4.

39. Harley p.102;, Price p. 160; Fellowes p. 71; Warren p.56.

40. Harley p. 229; J. Kerman, *The Masses and Motets of William Byrd* (1981) p. 42; Price p. 160.

41. Robinson p. 77.

42. Matthew (1970) pp. 76/7; HMC Salisbury VI, pp. 62-3; X, pp. 202, 204-5; J. Sykes, *Local Records* (1833) p. 82; James (1974) pp. 157/8.

43. Information about Leaver was given by a courier in the rising of 1569, cf. HMC Salisbury I, p. 491. In a note of January 1580/1, presumably in the hunt for recusants, one bishop advised the spymaster Walsingham to look for where 'a brother - either natural or in law - of Lord Lumley dwells'. CSP Scotland vol. v. p. 599.

44. Gillow *Bib. Dict.*, I, p. 414, citing Strype.

45. PRO SP 12/154/62; J. Pollen (Ed.), *Documents Relating to the English Martyrs* (CRS vol. 5 (1908) pp. 30/1, 39; E. Burton & J. Pollen, *Lives of the English Martyrs* I (1914), pp. 22-31. Professor T A Birrell kindly informs me that the spy 'PHW' is in fact PH in CSPD (the W is a notarial squiggle). A facsimile of the initials 'PHW' is printed at *Yelverton Mss* (CRS vol. 53 (1960) pp. 188/9) where they are attributed to Robert Woodward, servant to Robert Eare, Steward to the Earl of Shrewsbury.

46. 'Names of knaves & papistes & harbourers of prestes', PRO SP 12/195/107, calendared as '1586?' at CSPD Eliz. (1581-90) vol. 2, p. 376, n. 107. In a personal communication, Michael Hodgetts dates the paper before 19 Nov. 1587 from internal evidence in other parts of the report.

47. PRO SP12/248/102 (CSPD vol 3, 11 May 1594); Harley p. 103; Price p. 157.

48. G. Anstruther, *The Seminary Priests* vol. 1 (nd) 1 *sub nomen;* Manning p. 228 n. 3) quotes the Harleian Mss 2143 fo. 12v as saying that in 1587 Lumley and Philip Howard were each fined £1,000 by the Star Chamber for harbouring seminary priests. But Howard was fined £10,000 in May 1586 for a variety of offences; he was in the Tower from April 1585 until his death in April 1595; in 1571/2 Lumley was fined £1,000 for misprision of treason.

49. P. Caraman, *A Study in Friendship* (1995) p. 34. A document in the Jesuit Archives in Rome, of c.1609 entitled *Oedipus schedularum*, [Archivum Romanum Societatis Iesu, Anglia 36/II, ff.268r-v.] lists the Jesuit '*ecclesia*', or mission-stations, and the principal families attached to them. Lumley is listed among those of the Scot Thomas Abercrombie (c.1567-1644) who was sent to England in 1602 after his ordination in Rome that year. He lived in England, apart from a short absence in Scotland in 1610, until his death. [H. Foley, *Records of the English Province of the Society of Jesus* (8 vols. 1877-83) VII, pt. I, pp. 2-3, but T.M. McCoog, *English and Welsh Jesuits 1555*-1650 (CRS Records Series vol. 74, 1994) p. 98 has Abercrombie in England only from 1609. See also T M. McCoog, 'The Society of Jesus in England 1623-1688: an institutional study', (doctoral dissertation University of

Warwick 1984) p. 194. In a communication, Fr McCoog, S.J., says that the *schedularum* was compiled in the context of the renewed attempt to get bishops for England. Each Jesuit ecclesia is abbreviated with two initials and the names of the principal families contained within that ecclesia. A. Dures, 'Recusants in London c.1580-1629', *Essex Recusant* vol. 10 (1965) p. 77, gives the number of recusants in the Tower Ward as 7 and 24 in the Aldgate Ward.]

50. HMC Salisbury XII, p. 570; McCoog (1994) *sub nomen.*

51. CSPD 1601-3, vol. 6, p. 211; CSPD Add. 1580-1625, p. 356; Anstruther I, p. 270.

52. CSPD James I, vol. 8 p 442; Milner p. 84; HMC Salisbury XIX p. 335.

53. Dent p. 188; W. Bannerman (Ed.), *The Registers of St Olave, Hart Street, London 1563-1700* (Harleian Society vol. 46 (1916) p. 141; *Journals of the House of Lords*; *GEC*; CSPD 1603-10, XLIV, 75; Surtees *Durham* II, 155-70. J. Bossy, *The English Catholic Community 1570-1850* (1975) pp. 140-1 for burial of Catholics between dusk and dawn 'when the most distinctive visual feature of a Catholic funeral, the carrying of candles or tapers, must often have proved both useful and picturesque'. Stone, p. 577, has it that c.1615 noblemen began to be buried at night for economy.

Chapter Four: pages 7-162

1. S. Foister. 'Paintings and other works of art in sixteenth-century English inventories', *Burlington Magazine* May 1981, pp. 273 ff.

2. In the overwhelmingly majority of cases there is no reason to doubt the attributions of Lampton and Lumley, as has been done by J. Bruyn, 'Hubert (Huybrecht) Beuckelaer, an Antwerp portrait painter, and his English patron, the Earl of Leicester', S. Groenveld & M. Wintle (Eds.), *Britain and the Netherlands XI: Relgion, Scholarship and the Arts in Anglo-Dutch Relations in the Seventeenth Century* (1994) pp. 95/7]

3. L. Cust, *The Lumley Inventories,* (Walpole Society 1918) pp. 15 ff. & plates. Reproductions of some plates are at G. Jackson-Stops, 'Riches of a Renaissance Courtier: The Lumley Inventory', *Country Life* (5 June 1986) pp. 1586-88.

4. M. Whinney, *Sculpture in Britain 1530-1830* (1964) p. 2; J. Speed, *Theatre of the Empire of Greate Britaine* (1611) Bk 1, ch vi, p 11.

5. The seven are: Augustus, Claudius, Nero, Galba, Otho, Vespasian and Divi ivli (?Julius).

6. Hutchinson *Durham,* II, p. 402n gave it as his opinion that 'by the letters we think it has been painted since this time'.

7. Edward died in 1377; the licence to crenellate the house was granted by Bishop Skirlaw in 1389 and building was completed c.1392 in the reign of Richard II.

8. Whinney (1964) p.3; K. Hearn, *Dynasties: Painting in Tudor and Jacobean England 1530-1630* (1995) Nos. 36-9. M. Aston, 'Gods, Saints and Reformers: Portraiture and Protestant England', L. Gent (Ed.) *Albion's Classicism: The Visual Arts in Britain 1550-1660* (1995) p. 197. The horseman and the four large busts are at Leeds Castle but the six small busts appear not to have survived. Cust remarked on their loss in 1917.

9. HMC Salisbury XVI, p. 376; Hutchinson, *Durham* II, p. 408.

10. E. Auerbach *Nicholas Hilliard* (1961) pp. 273/6. Glover made a visitation of Yorkshire in 1584/5; he died in 1588. The roll is listed at Jayne & Johnson, catalogue no. 1452. See also C.H. Hunter Blair (Ed.), *Visitations of the North, Part iv, 1575,* (Surtees Society vol. 146, 1932), pp. ix-xii; Surtees *Durham* I, p. 5; James, pp. 109/110.

11. NRA Lumley Mss EMA/1/12. He was buried 'before the reading pew' in the chancel of St Olave's, Hart St., Tower Hill, on 5 April 1605. Lumley's cook was also buried in the chancel on 18 April 1606, cf. Bannerman p. 138.

12. Barkley (1982); see also S. Morison & N. Barker, *The Likeness of Thomas More* (1963) pp. 51/2.

13. 'Cecil, one of the keenest art patrons, had an extensive collection of paintings (of those recorded only Lord Lumley's was larger), many of which can no longer be traced ... Whereas other collections consisted principally of portraits, Cecil's was unusual in the number of religious and mythological paintings ... His position ensured the presence of portraits of foreign rulers and statesmen and these far outnumbered family portraits ...' Hearn (1995) pp. 152, 175 Stone pp. 714-6.

14. The portraits were of family members and Richard III but mostly of foreign royalty, including Louis XI, Francis I, Charles IX, Ferdinand of Spain, the Queen of Hungary and the Count of Nassau, cf. Williams p. 43; see also A. Weir *Children of England* (1996) p.160.

15. R. Strong 'Some early portraits at Arundel Castle', *Connoisseur* (March 1978) p. 198. The 1655 inventory of Thomas Howard lists the latter (Lady Anne Percy) at No. 419.

16. M. Aston, *The King's Bedpost:Reformation and Iconography in a Tudor Group Portrait* (1993), p. 97.

17. D.W. Tough, *The Last Years of a Frontier* (1928) p. 66; R. Wendorf, *The Elements of Life: Biography and Portrait-Painting in Stuart and Georgian England* (1990) p. 79.

18. For an extended discussion of the laws against the importation of Catholic art from abroad and the dangers of possessing it, see R. L. Williams, 'Collecting and Religion in Late 16th Century England', E. Chaney, *The Evolution of English Collecting* (2003) pp. 181 ff.

19. Chaney (2003) pp. 34/5; Plowden (1977) p. 93.

20. Stone p. 713.

21. British Library *Royal Mss.,* B IX (1565); McCutcheon pp. 9/10.

22. Strong: (1986) p. 200; Strong (1969) p. 45; M. Biddle, 'The Vanished Gardens of Nonsuch', *Country Life* (October 26, 1961) pp. 1008-10.

23. PRO *Calendars of Patent Rolls, 1556-9,* nos. 381, 611, 627, 635, 710, 721, 772, 1727; 1569-72, nos. 1262, 2211.

24. [J. Strype, *Annals of the Reformation...* vol 1, pt II, p. 119 (Oxford 1824). Maximilian was invested with the Garter in Vienna by the Earl of Sussex in January 1568, cf. CSP Foreign (1566-8) p. 527. See also *GEC.*

25. Stone p. 701; Chaney (1998) p. 24 , see also ch. 3 for the difficulties of Italian travel at this time.

26. Cf. A.J. Loomie, *The Spanish Elizabethans* (1963) p. 3. William Barker, a Cambridge graduate had travelled to Italy as a young man and published a collection of *Epitaphia et Inscriptiones Lugubres, ab eo collecta cum in Italia animi causa, peregrinaretur* (1566) Lumley Library No. 1819. He became one of the duke of Norfolk's secretaries and confessed to having been involved in the Marian plots, whereupon his master repudiated him as an Italianated Englishman. *DNB.*

27. The books are those which introduced the history and art of Italy to the English cited in chapter 1 of J. Hale, *England and the Italian Renaissance* (1954).

28. Strong (1969) p. 49; *Archaeologia* XXX (1844) pp. 1-30.

29. D. Piper, 'The 1590 Lumley Inventory: Hilliard, Segar and the Earl of Essex – I' *Burlington Magazine* XCIX (1957), p. 227n6. This article reproduces several portraits having a *cartellino.*

30. Strong (1978), p. 198.

31. W.A. Shaw (Ed.), *Three Inventories of the years 1542, 1547 & 1549-50 of Pictures in the Collections of Henry VIII and Edward VI. (1937).* The second includes Nonsuch Palace *temp.* Edward VI.

32. See references given in the inventory and E. Goldring, 'An important early picture collection: The Earl of Pembroke's 1561/62 inventory and the provenance of Holbein's 'Christina of Denmark'', *Burlinton Magazine* vol. cxliv, no. 1188 (March 2002) pp. 157 ff.

33. The portrait, now in the Denver Art Museum, is reproduced in E. Chaney, *The Evolution of the Grand Tour* (1998) p.8; and its iconography is discussed at length by Andrew Boyle in 'Hans Eworth's Portrait of the Earl of Arundel and the Politics of 1549-50', *English Historical Review* cxvii.470 (February 2002), though its whereabouts at and since its completion are not conjectured.

34. Aston (1993) p. 191.

35. R. Strong, 'Hans Eworth Reconsidered', *Burlington Magazine* CVII (1966) p. 107.

36. Strong (1969) p. 8.

37. Her portrait was in the collection of Thomas Howard, Earl of Arundel in 1655, cf. M. Hervey, *The Life of Thomas Howard, Earl of Arundel* (1921) Appendix V, p. 490, no. 419.

38. Shaw, p. 58.

39. 'Vertue's Notebooks II', *Walpole Society* XX (1932) p. 26.

40. B. Grosvenor, Philip Mould Fine Paintings: Catalogue (2008), pp. 18-23.

41. 'Vertue's Notebooks II', *Walpole Society* XX (1932) p. 26.

42. Strong attributes twenty-four 'realistic if somewhat stern' portraits to Steven van der Meulen. R. Strong, The Elizabethan Image, (Tate Gallery exhibition catalogue 1969), nos. 39 & 40. Surtees, II, p. 155.

43. Poindre (1527-70) was listed as 'Pindar' in the inventory. He was born in Malines and went to Denmark to paint imaginary portraits of the early Danish kings].

44. Bruyn, passim, & nn. 9/10; the Leicester inventory of 1588, *Archaeologia* vol. 73 (1923), p. 29; *Notes and Queries* (3), II, (1862) p. 225.

45. *Utopia* (1516) ch 8.

46. Segar is anachronistically termed Sir William in the literature dealing with this period though he was not knighted until 1616; he died in 1633. Strong (1969) pp 29, 215. Piper is not entirely confident in attributing the series to the hand of Segar: cf. (1957) p. 299 n2.

47. W. Howitt, *Visits to Remarkable Places* (2 vols. 1856) II, p. 138.

48. Strong (1969) No. 177. A portrait of Sir William Drury c.1570-5 has been attributed to Segar, though it might be posthumous; cf. Inventory; Hearn (1995) pp. 77, 179.

49. Bruyn, Appendix. A thirteenth picture, though apparently having belonged to Leicester was not inventoried by Lumley until after 1605.

50. G.W. Groos (Ed.), *The Diary of Baron Waldstein* (1981) p. 157.

51. W.B. Rye, *England as seen by Foreigners in the Days of Elizabeth and James I* (1865) pp. 163/7.

52. Dent p. 292, spelling and punctuation modernized.

53. Bruyn, p. 104; D. Matthew, *The Jacobean Age* (1938) p. 141. (Anthony Blunt dismissed the 'distressing style' of English sixteenth-century portraits as 'mere furniture pieces': *The Spectator* 16 Nov. 1934.

54. Goldring p. 160; Stone (1965) pp. 710-22; L. Stone, *The Family, Sex and Marriage in England, 1500-1800* (1977) pp. 62-91, 179, 285; R.L. Williams 'Collecting and Religion in Late 16th Century England', E. Chaney, *The Evolution of English Collecting* (2003) pp. 176/7; L. Cust, 'Notes on the Collection formed by Thomas Howard, Earl of Arundel and Surrey, K.G.', *Burlington Magazine* xix (1911) p. 278]

55. D. Howarth, *Lord Arundel and his Circle* (1985) pp. 10/11.

56. L. Gooch, '"The Religion for a Gentleman": The Northern Catholic Gentry in the Eighteenth Century', *Recusant History* vol. 23 no. 4 (1997) pp.543-568.

Chapter Five: pages 163-176

1. Milner p. 276.

2. Milner pp. 338/9; Stone pp. 760, 782/3.

3. HMC De Lisle & Dudley II, p. 163; III, p. 138; HMC Rutland I, p. 412.

4. Salisbury III, pp. 356, 490, 618; V, p. 529.

5. HMC De Lisle & Dudley II, p. 468; Salisbury XII, p. 509; XVI, p.

376; XXIV, p.67; CSPD James I (8) (1603-10), p.19.

6. Kesselring, p. 25.

7. Surtees, *Durham,* II, pp. 159/60; Durham Probate Records (Durham University Library) 1606, See Appendix.

8. NRA Lumley Mss. MTD/A16/1.

9. E. Auerbach & C.K. Adams, *Paintings and Sculpture at Hatfield House* (1971) p. 62; HMC Salisbury XIX, p. 121.

10. For example, nine royal persons and the Cardinal Archduke Albert and his wife the Infanta Isabella (a pair, 1599); a similar pair was given to James I in 1603. Auerbach & Adams, pp. 70/1.

11. HMC Salisbury XVI, p. 376; Auerbach & Adams, p. 62.

12. Bannerman p. 149.

13. NRA Lumley Mss., MTD/A10/3, dated 6 November 1616.

14. Hervey (1921) pp. 56-8; the view is repeated by S Foister, ' "My Foolish Curiosity", Holbein in the collection of the Earl of Arundel', *Apollo* (August 1996) p.18. A list of pictures common to the Bedford and Lumley collections in 1619 is given by K. Hearn, 'Lucy Harington, Countess of Bedford, as Art Patron and Collector' (MA thesis Courtauld Institute, 1990) pp. 48-50.

15. Howarth p. 12.

16. M. Hervey, 'A Lumley Inventory of 1609', *Walpole Society* 1918 p. 39; see also Hervey (1921), Appendix V.

17. Auerbach & Adams pp. 20 ff.

18. Her portrait was listed in the Earl of Northampton's inventory of 1614, cf. *Archaeologia* vol. 42 (1869) p. 357. (It may be noted that Howard's mansion at Greenwich burned down in 1617 and one or more of the lost pictures might have been consumed in the fire.)

19. 'Vertue's Notebooks IV', *Walpole Society* XXIV (1936) p. 148.

20. P. Toynbee, (Ed.) 'Horace Walpole's Journals of Visits to Country Seats &c.' 'Vertue's Notebooks V', *Walpole Society* XVI (1928) pp. 68/9; Earl of Bessborough, *Enchanted Forest: The Story of Stansted in Sussex'* (1984) p. 88.

21. [Macky, *Characters* Roxburghe Club, p63].

22. Anstruther 2, p. 184; Milner pp. 115/6; Gillow IV, p. 143, no. 2

23. *GEC* p. 508 note (a) quoting Burnet, Macky and Reresby;

24. *GEC* p. 509 note (e); p. 510 notes (a) (b); Milner pp. 90-121; T.W. Beastall, *A North Country Estate* 1974) pp. 1-4.

25. K. Downes, *Sir John Vanbrugh* (1987) pp. 456/7; R. Hugill, *The Castles and Towers of the County of Durham* (1979) pp. 68 ff.

26. *Country Life*, 18 June 1910; Howitt (II, p. 144); *Practical Builder* (1848).

27. 'Vertue's Notebooks, II', *Walpole Society* XX (1932) pp. 26, 47; 'Vertue's Notebooks, IV', *Walpole Society* XXIV (1936) p. 42.

28. Vertue II, p. 26; IV p. 81; W.S. Lewis, W.H.Smith, G.L. Lam (Eds.), *Horace Walpole's Correspondence with Sir Horace Mann*, vol. 22 (1960) p. 312; see also vol. 30 p 313.

29. T. Pennant, *A Tour in Scotland 1769* (Chester, 1774) p. 30; *A Tour in Scotland, 1772* Part II (London, 1776) pp. 321 ff.; Hutchinson, II, pp.403-8; Hutchinson occasionally referred to Pennant (II pp. 319 ff.). The material also appeared in an undated edition of the journal *The Literary Cabinet* but no copy has survived; the British Library has only 3 editions: February to March 1827. Cust (1917/8 p. 30, refers to the *Cabinet* and he used the first edition of Pennant; Hervey (1918, pp. 43 ff.) used the 1790 edition.

30. Toynbee (1928) p. 74; Lewis *et al* vol. 1 (1960) p. 275.

31. Hutchinson p. 408.

32. The portrait is supposed to have been bought by Ralph Waters of Newcastle and given, after his death, to George Rippon of North Shields. At the death of Rippon's widow the portrait was sent for auction by Christie, Manson & Co., but its provenance could not be verified. It was sold eventually to Lady Burdett-Coutts, in whose possession it was thought to be in 1893; its present location is not known. Milner, p. 327; W. Fordyce, *History of Durham* (1857), p. 612n; Strong (1969) pp. 285/6; G. Neasham, *North-Country Sketches* (1893) pp. 6/7.

33. Lady Carlow to Lady Stuart, 7 July 1781, quoted at Milner p. 337.

34. To Lady Louisa Stuart 3 August 1784, quoted at Milner p. 338. Beastall pp. 34, 78, 108.

35. Milner p. 276.

36. The reproduction of the auction catalogues by Cust (1918, pp. 31 ff.)

is selective, indicated by his omission of certain lots, and incorrect or missing sums. These errors and omissions have been corrected here from a copy of the original auction catalogue. The lots omitted by Cust from the 1785 catalogue are: 8. Gent. ½ length £2.2.0; 9. Gent. ½ length £2.5.0; 18. Unknown £1.11.6.; 27. Portrait of a lady & 2 heads £2.2.0; 43 Unknown £4.14.6; 44. Unknown £3.3.0; 58. Six old portraits and a view in Venice £3.13.6; 60. This lot included 'An allegorical subject' £1.11.6.

37. Howitt, II, p. 144; *Handbook for Travellers in Durham and Northumberland 1873* (1873) p. 68; Surtees *Durham* II, pp. 154/5.

Bibliography

Abbreviations

AA	Archaeologia Aeliana
BM	The Burlington Magazine
CRS	Catholic Record Society
CSP	Calendars of State Papers
HMC	Historical Manuscripts Commission
PRO	Public Record Office [The National Archives]
TRHS	Transactions of the Royal Historical Society
YAJ	Yorkshire Archaeological Journal

Primary Sources: Manuscript

'A Certificate to John, Lord Lumley, of All His Monuments of Marbles, Pictures & Household Stuff, anno 1590'. Parchment, i + 40 ff. [The inventory known as the 'Red Velvet Book' because of its binding.]

Register of Wills vol. vii, 1586-1613, pp 292r-60. (University of Durham, Special Collections)

Primary Sources: Printed

A Catalogue of all the ... Tapestry Hangings ... A Most Capital Collection of Fine Old Portraits by Holbien, Vandyck, &c. [sic] to be sold at Lumley Castle by Mr Christie August 8th 1785.

Acts of the Privy Council 1558-70 vol. 7 (PRO 1893)

W.B. Bannerman (Ed.), 'The Registers of St. Olave, Hart Street, London, 1563-1700', *Harleian Society Registers* vol. 46 (1916)

M. Bateson, 'A Collection of Original Letters from the Bishops to the Privy Council 1564', *Camden Miscellany* vol. 9, 1895

C.H. Hunter Blair (Ed.), *Visitations of the North*, pt. IV: 'Visitations of Yorkshire and Northumberland in A.D. 1575', *Surtees Society* vol. 146, 1932

Calendar of Patent Rolls 1556 et seq (PRO, 1936-86)

Calendars of State Papers (PRO):

Border Papers, 2 vols. 1560-1603 (1894-6)
Domestic [CSPD], Edward VI, Mary I, Elizabeth, James I, 1547-1625, with Addenda 12 vols. (1856-1872)
Foreign, vol. vi 1564/5 (1869)
Rome, vol. i 1558-1571 (1916)
Scotland, 2 vols. 1509-1603 (1858)
Scotland & Mary Queen of Scots, vol. ii 1563-1569 (1900)
Spanish (Simancas), i, ii, 1558-1603 (1892-9)
Venetian, vol. xii, 1610-13.

L. Cust, 'The Lumley Inventories', *Walpole Society* VI (1917-8)

W. Greenwell (Ed.) 'Wills and Inventories from the Registry at Durham,' Pt II (*Surtees Society* vol. 38, 1860)

HMC Reports and Calendars:

Bath, vol. V
De Lisle and Dudley vol. II
Foljambe
Rutland vol. I
Salisbury vols. I - XIX
Various Collections (Buxton)

HMC, National Register of Archives, (64), Lumley, Earls of Scarbrough.

T.B. Howell (Ed.), *A Complete Collection of State Trials and Proceedings for High Treason* vol. 1 (1816)

Journals of the House of Lords, vol. 1, 1509-77.

Letters and Papers Foreign and Domestic of the Reign of Henry VIII vol. ii, *1515-8* (PRO 1864)

W Murden (Ed.), *Burghley's State Papers 1571 to 1596* vol. II (1759)

G. Ornsby (Ed.), 'Selections from the Household Books of the Lord William Howard of Naworth Castle &c.,' *Surtees Society* vol. 68 (1878).

J.H. Pollen (Ed.), 'Documents Relating to the English Martyrs', *CRS* Records vol. 5 (1908)

J.H. Pollen & W MacMahon (Eds.) 'The Ven. Philip Howard, Earl of Arundel, 1557-1595', *CRS* Records vol. 21 (1919)

A. Pough, *The Annals of the Parishes of St. Olave, Hart St., & All Hallows, Staining* (1894)

J. Raine (Ed.), 'Depositions and other Ecclesiastical Proceedings from the Courts of Durham', *Surtees Society* vol. 21 (1845)

M.J. Rodrigues-Salgado and S. Adams (Eds.), 'The Count of Feria's Dispatch to Philip II of 14 November 1558' *Camden Society* (4) vol. 29 (1984)

C. Sharp (Ed.), *Memorials of the Rebellion of the Earls of Northumberland and Westmoreland* (1840) reissued with intro. by R. Wood as *The Rising in the North* (1975)

'Vertue's Notebooks', *Walpole Society* vols., 18, 20, 22, 24, 26, 30 (1930-1955) (1935-6)

Secondary Sources: Books

G.P.V. Akrigg, *Jacobean Pageant* (1962)

Anon., *Handbook for Travellers in Durham and Northumberland 1873* (1873)

G. Anstruther, *The Seminary Priests* vol. 1 (1968)

M. Aston, *The King's Bedpost: Reformation and Iconography in a Tudor Group Portrait* (1993)

J.C. Atkinson, *History of Cleveland, Ancient and Modern* (1874)

E. Auerbach & C.K. Adams, *Paintings and Sculpture at Hatfield House* (1971)

E. Auerbach, *Nicholas Hilliard* (1961)

C. Banks, et al (Eds.), *Sundry Sorts of Music Books* (1993)

H. Barkley, *Likenesses in Line* (1982)

E.S. de Beer (Ed.), *The Diary of John Evelyn* (1959)

T.W. Beastall, *A North Country Estate: The Lumleys and Saundersons as Landowners 1600-1900* (1975)

Earl of Bessborough, *Enchanted Forest, The Story of Stansted in Sussex* (1984)

T.A. Birrell, *English Monarchs and their Books: from Henry VII to Charles II* (The Panizzi Lectures 1986)

J. Bossy, *The English Catholic Community 1570-1850* (1975)

J. Bossy *Under the Molehill* (2001)

E.W. Brayley, *The Beauties of England and Wales*, vol. V, (1808)

J. Bruyn, 'Hubert (Huybrecht) Beuckelaer, an Antwerp portrait painter, and his English patron, the Earl of Leicester', [Eds.] J. Roding et al, *Dutch and Flemish Artists in Britain 1550-1800* (Leids Kunsthistrorisch jaarboek 13, Leiden 2003)

P. Burke, *The Fortunes of 'The Courtier'* (1995)

E. Burton & J. Pollen, *Lives of the English Martyrs* vol. I (1914)

M. Bush, *The Pilgrimage of Grace* (1996)

M Bush & D Bownes, *The Defeat of the Pilgrimage of Grace* (1999)

M. Bush, *Durham and the Pilgrimage of Grace* (Durham County Local History Society, 2000)

W Camden, *Brittania* vol. II (1586)

W. Camden, *Annales, or, The History of Elizabeth* (1615)

P. Caraman, *A Study in Friendship* (1995)

J.P. Carley & C.G.C. Tite (Eds.), *Books and Collectors 1200-1700* (1997).

J.L. Caw, *Scottish Portraits* (1963)

S. Cerasano & M Wynne-Davies (Eds.), *Readings in Renaissance Women's Drama: Criticism, History & Performance 1594-1998* (1998)

E Chaney, *The Evolution of the Grand Tour* (2nd ed. 2000)

E. Chaney (Ed.), *The Evolution of English Collecting* (2003)

H.H. Child, *Iphigenia at Aulis Translated by Lady Lumley* (*Malone Society* 1909)

H.M. Colvin (Gen. Ed.), *The History of the King's Works*, vol. IV, 1485-1660, Part II (1982)

R. Corthell (et al Eds.), *Catholic Culture in Early Modern England* (2007)

P. Croft (Ed.), *Patronage, Culture and Power: The Early Cecils 1558-1612* (2002)

C. Cross, *The Puritan Earl* (1966)

A. Davies, *Dictionary of British Portraiture*, Vol. 1, to 1700 (1979)

J. Dent, *The Quest for Nonsuch* (1962)

Dictionary of National Biography [*DNB*] (1908-9)

S. Doran, *Monarchy and Matrimony: The Courtships of Elizabeth I* (1996)

K. Downes, *Sir John Vanbrugh* (1987)

F. Edwards *The Dangerous Queen* (1964)

F. Edwards, *The Marvellous Chance* (1968)

F. Emmison, *Tudor Secretary* (1961)

J. Evans, *A History of the Society of Antiquaries* (1956)

E.H. Fellowes, *William Byrd* (1947)

A. Fletcher & D. MacCulloch, *Tudor Rebellions* (1997)

G. Fletcher & E. Walker, *Historical Portraits 1400-1600* (1909)

H. Foley, *Records of the English Province of the Society of Jesus* (8 vols. 1877-83)

W. Fordyce, *History and Antiquities of the County Palatine of Durham* (1857)

A. Fraser, *Mary, Queen of Scots* (1969)

L. Gent (Ed.) *Albion's Classicism: The Visual Arts in Britain 1550-1660* (1995)

J. Gillow, *Bibliographical Dictionary of the English Catholics* (4 vols. 1884-1902)

M.A.R. Graves, *The House of Lords in the Parliaments of Edward VI and Mary I* (1981)

R.L. Greaves, *Society and Religion in Elizabethan England* (1981)

P. Ganz, *The Paintings of Hans Holbein* (1956)

[GEC] *V. Gibbs et al* (Eds.) *The Complete Peerage* (1910-40)

M. Graves, *The House of Lords in the Parliaments of Edward VI and Mary I* (1981)

G.W. Gross (Ed.) *The Diary of Baron Waldstein* (1981)

B. Grosvenor, *Philip Mould Fine Paintings: Catalogue* (2008)

J. Hale, *England and the Italian Renaissance* (1954)

J. Harley, *William Byrd: Gentleman of the Chapel Royal* (1997)

K. Hearn (Ed.), *Dynasties: Painting in Tudor and Jacobean England 1530-1630* (1995)

M. Hervey, *The Life, Correspondence and Collections of Thomas Howard, Earl of Arundel, 'Father of Vertu in England'* (1921)

D. Howarth, *Lord Arundel and His Circle* (1985)

W. Howitt, *Visits to Remarkable Places* vol. II (1856)

R.W. Hoyle, *The Pilgrimage of Grace and the Politics of the 1530s* (2001)

R. Hugill, *The Castles and Towers of the County of Durham* (1979)

W. Hutchinson, *The History and Antiquities of the County Palatine of Durham* vol. II (1787)

M. James, *Family, Lineage and Civil Society* (1974)

M.E. James, *Society, Politics and Culture* (1986)

S. Jayne & F.R. Johnson, *The Lumley Library* (1956)

J.A. Jungmann, *The Mass of the Roman Rite* vol. 1 (1950)

J. Kerman, *The Masses and Motets of William Byrd* (1981)

K.J. Kesselring, *The Northern Rebellion of 1569* (2007)

A.A. King, *Liturgies of the Past* (1959)

W.S. Lewis, W.H.Smith, G.L. Lam (Eds.), *Horace Walpole's Correspondence with Sir Horace Mann*, vol. 22 (1960)

A. J. Loomie, *The Spanish Elizabethans* (1963)

J.K. Lowers, *Mirrors for Rebels* (1953)

W. MacCaffery, *The Shaping of the Elizabethan Regime* (1969)

T.M. McCoog, 'English and Welsh Jesuits 1555-1650', CRS Records vol. 74 (1994)

J. Macky (Ed. S. Macky), *Memoirs of the Secret Services of John Macky* (posth. 1733)

B. Magee, *The English Recusants* (1938)

R.B. Manning, *Religion and Society in Elizabethan Sussex* (1969)

D. Matthew, 'The Library at Naworth', E. Woodruff (Ed.), *For Hilaire Belloc* (1942)

D. Matthew, *The Jacobean Age* (1938)

D. Matthew, *The Age of Charles I* (1951)

D. Matthew, *The Courtiers of Henry VIII* (1970)

C. Menmuir, *The Rising of the North* (1907)

M.M. Merrick, *Thomas Percy, Seventh Earl* (1949)

O. Millar, *The Tudor, Stuart and Early Georgian Pictures in the Collection of Her Majesty the Queen* (2 vols., 1963)

H. Miller, *Henry VIII and the English Nobility* (1986)

E. Milner (ed. E. Benham), *Records of the Lumleys of Lumley Castle* (1904)

W.C. Mitchell, *History of Sunderland* (1919, repr. 1972)

A. Morey, *The Catholic Subjects of Elizabeth I* (1978)

S. Morison & N. Barker, *The Likeness of Thomas More* (1963)

J.E. Neale, *The Elizabethan House of Commons* (1967)

G. Neasham, *North-Country Sketches* (1893)

J. Nef, *The Rise of the British Coal Industry* vol. I (1923)

J.G. Nichols, *Literary Remains of King Edward the Sixth* (1857)

[*ODNB*] H. Matthew & B Harrison, (Eds.) *Oxford Dictionary of National Biography* (60 vols., 2004) [superseding *DNB*]

G. Parry, *The Golden Age Restor'd: The Culture of the Stuart Court 1603-1642* (1981)

L.P. Peck, *Northampton* (1982)

T. Pennant, *A Tour in Scotland in 1769* (1774); *ditto in 1772* (1776)

N. Pevsner, *The Buildings of England:*

County Durham (1953, rev. 1983 & 1985)
Surrey (2nd ed. 1971)

D. Piper, *Petre Family Portraits* (1956)

A. Plowden, *Marriage with my Kingdom* (1977)

J.H. Pollen, *The English Catholics in the Reign of Queen Elizabeth* (1920)

D.C. Price, *Patrons and Musicians of the English Renaissance* (1981)

A. Procktor & R. Taylor, *The A to Z of Elizabethan London* (1979)

J. Raine, *History and Antiquities of North Durham* (1852)

E.E. Reynolds, *Campion & Parsons* (1980)

J. M Robinson, *The Dukes of Norfolk* (1982)

A.L. Rowse, 'Nicholas Roscarrock and his Lives of the Saints', J.H. Plumb (Ed.), *Studies in Social History* (1955)

W.B. Rye, *England as seen by Foreigners in the Days of Elizabeth and James I* (1865)

J. Sears & F.R. Johnson, *The Lumley Library: The Catalogue of 1609* (1956)

D.G. Selwyn, *The Library of Thomas Cranmer* (1996)

C. Sharp, *History of Hartlepool* (1816, repub. 1851)

W.A. Shaw (Ed.), *Three Inventories of the years 1542, 1547 & 1549-50 of Pictures in the Collections of Henry VIII and Edward VI. (1937)*

L.B. Smith, *A Tudor Tragedy: The life and times of Catherine Howard* (1961)

L. Stone, *The Crisis of the Aristocracy 1558-1641* (1965)

L. Stone, *The Family, Sex and Marriage in England, 1500-1800* (1977)

R. Strong, *The English Icon: Elizabethan & Jacobean Portraiture* (1969)

J. Stowe, *Survey of London* (1603, repr. 1908)

R. Strong, *Tudor & Jacobean Portraits,* vol. 1, Text; vol. 2 Plates (1969)

R. Strong, *The Elizabethan Image* (Tate Gallery exhibition catalogue 1969)

R. Strong, *The Cult of Elizabeth: Elizabethan Portraiture and Pageantry* (1977)

R. Strong, *Henry Prince of Wales and England's Lost Renaissance* (1986)

J. Strype, *Annals of the Reformation* Vol. I Pt II (1824)

R. Surtees, *The History and Antiquities of the County Palatine of Durham,* vol. I (1816) vol. II (1820)

J. Sykes, *Local Records* (1833)

M.A. Tierney, *History of Arundel,* vol. II (1834)

D.W. Tough, *The Last Years of a Frontier* (1928)

P. Toynbee, (Ed.) 'Horace Walpole's Journals of Visits to Country Seats &c.' *Walpole Society* vol. 16 (1928)

J. Turner (Ed.) *The Dictionary of Art* (1996)

Victoria County History: [*VCH*]:

East Riding (1923)
Durham III (1928)
North Riding II, (1914)
Sussex III (1935), IV (1953)

R. Warner, *A Tour through the Northern Counties of England and the Borders of Scotland,* vol. 1 (1802)

A. Weir, *Children of England* (1996)

M. Weiss, *Illustrious Company: An Exhibition and Catalogue of Early Portraits 1545-1720* (Weiss Gallery, London 1998)

R. Welford, *History of Newcastle and Gateshead in 16th Century,* vol. II (1885)

R. Wendorf, *The Elements of Life* (1990)

M. Whinney, *Sculpture in Britain 1530-1830* (1964)

H. Willaert, *History of an Old Catholic Mission: Cowdray-Easeburne-Midhurst* (1928)

C. Williams (Ed.), *Thomas Platter's Travels in England 1599* (1937)

N. Williams, *Thomas Howard Fourth Duke of Norfolk* (1964)

N. Williams, *All the King's Men* (1972)

J. Wolfson, *Padua and the Tudors: English Students in Italy 1485-1603* (1998)

C. Wright, *Old Master Paintings in Britain* (Sotheby Parke Bernet Publications, London 1976)

Secondary Sources: Journal Articles

Anon., 'John, Baron Lumley, 1534?-1609', *Notes & Queries* 16 Aug 1941.

M. Biddle, 'The Vanished Gardens of Nonsuch', *Country Life,* October 26, 1961.

J. Blezzard, 'The Lumley Books: A Collection of Tudor Church Music', *Musical Times* vol. 112, 1971

A. Boyle, 'Hans Eworth's Portrait of the Earl of Arundel and the Politics of 1549-50', *English Historical Review*, cxvii, 470, 2002.

F.D. Crane, 'Euripides, Erasmus and Lady Lumley', *Classical Journal,* vol. 39, 1943-4.

C. Cross, 'Berwick on Tweed and the neighbouring parts of Northumberland on the eve of the Armada', *AA* (4) vol. 41, 1963

L. Cust, 'Notes on the Collection formed by Thomas Howard, Earl of Arundel and Surrey, K.G.', *BM* xix, 1911.

L. Cust, 'The Lumley Inventories', *Archaeologia* vol. 68, 1917

H. Dunk, 'The Lumley Monuments in the Ancient Church of St. Dunstan, Cheam, Surrey', *Ancient Monuments Society's Transactions*, NS2, 1954.

I. Dunlop, 'Nonsuch Palace', *Connoisseur,* vol. 128, 1951.

C.H. Firth, 'The Ballad History of the Reigns of the Later Tudors', *TRHS* (3) iii, 1909.

S. Foister, 'Paintings and other works of art in sixteenth-century English inventories', *BM* vol. cxxiii, No. 938, May 1981.

A. Forster, 'Bishop Tunstall's Priests', *Recusant History* vol. 9, no.4, 1968.

D. Greene, 'Lady Lumley and Greek Tragedy' *Classical Journal* vol. 36, 1940-1

E. Goldring, 'An Important Early Picture Collection', *BM* (March 2002).

M. Hervey, 'A Lumley Inventory of 1609', *Walpole Society* vi (1917-8).

M. Hislop, 'Lumley Castle, its antecedents and its architect', *AA* (5) vol. xxiv, 1996.

W. E. Houghton, 'The English Virtuoso in the Seventeenth Century', *Journal of the History of Ideas* iii, 1942.

'[W] Humberston's Survey', *YAJ* vol. 17, 1903.

W. I'Anson, 'Mediaeval military effigies of Yorkshire', *YAJ* vol. 28, 1926.

W. I'Anson, 'Kilton Castle', *YAJ* vol. 22, 1913

G. Jackson Stops, 'Riches of a Renaissance Courtier: The Lumley Inventory', *Country Life* June 5 1986.

M.E. James, 'The Concept of Order in the Northern Rising of 1569', *Past and Present* 60, 1973

C.L. Kingsford, 'Bath Inn or Arundel House', *Archaeologia* vol. 72, 1921-2.

H.B. McCall, 'The Rising of the North', *YAJ* vol. 18, 1904-5.

E. McCutcheon, 'Sir Nicholas Bacon's Great House Sententiae', *English Literary Renaissance Supplements* No 3, 1977

J.G. Nichols, 'Life of Fitzalan', *Gentleman's Magazine*, vol. 133, pt. ii, 1833.

D. Piper, 'The 1590 Lumley Inventory: Hilliard, Segar and the Earl of Essex', *BM* xcix, July/August 1957.

R.L. Poole, 'The Portraits of Richard II', *The Antiquaries Journal* vol. 11, 1931.

R. Reid, 'The Rebellion of the Earls', *TRHS* (2) vol. 20, 1906.

F.W. Steer, 'Lord Lumley's Benefaction to the College of Physicians' *Medical History* ii, No. 4, 1958.

D. Stevens, 'A songe of fortie partes, made by Mr Tallys', *Early Music,* April 1982.

R. Strong, 'Hans Eworth Reconsidered', *BM cvii,* 1966.

R. Strong, 'Some early portraits at Arundel Castle', *Connoisseur* March 1978.

C. Warren, 'Music at Nonesuch', *Musical Quarterly* vol. 54, 1968.

Theses

K. Barron, 'Classicism and Antiquarianism in Elizabethan Patronage: The Case of John, Lord Lumley' (M.Litt., Oxford 1996)

K. Hearn, 'Lucy Harington, Countess of Bedford, as Art Patron and Collector' (MA, Courtauld Institute, 1990)

S.M. Keeling, 'The Church and Religion in the Anglo-Scottish Border Counties, 1534 to 1572' (PhD, Durham, 1975)

T.M. McCoog, 'The Society of Jesus in England 1623-1688: An Institutional

Study' (PhD, Warwick, 1984)

M.J. Tillbrook, 'Aspects of the Government and Society of County Durham 1558-1642' (PhD, Liverpool 1981)

Index

Items listed in the Inventory are indexed under subject and indicated by page numbers in bold. Italic page numbers indicate pictures.

U

V

W

Z